Contents

Abstracts & keywords

A review of hospitality research in the Asia Pacific region 1989-1996: a thematic perspective
Nerilee Hing

Keywords Asia Pacific, Hospitality industry, Investment, Planning, Service quality, Travel

Identifies themes in the hospitality and tourism literature arising from articles published in Asia Pacific-based journals from 1989 to 1996 inclusive. The journals are the *Australian Journal of Hospitality Management*, the *Journal of Tourism Studies*, *Tourism Recreation Research* and the *Asia Pacific Journal of Tourism Research*. The themes are: attracting Asian outbound travel markets; stakeholder roles in service quality; workplace relations; investment, planning and development in the accommodation sector; and education and training.

Contemporary tourism issues in Asia Pacific journals 1989-1996: a thematic perspective
Nerilee Hing and Kay Dimmock

Keywords Asia Pacific, Development, Marketing, Tourism

Reviews articles published in three Asia Pacific-based tourism journals: the *Journal of Tourism Studies*, *Tourism Recreation Research* and the *Asia Pacific Journal of Tourism Research*. Identifies five tourism themes relating to articles published over an eight year period from 1989-1996. These are: tourist markets, tourist flows, tourism development, sustainable tourism development and social, economic and cultural impacts of tourism.

Hotel market trends in the UK
Trevor Ward

Keywords Competitive reaction, Hotels, Marketing, Structure

Assesses changes occurring in the UK hotel market during 1997 and relates these to current and predicted future developments. Identifies the key issues affecting supply and demand, competitive success and likely impacts and influences on the UK market during 1998.

Assessing information needs and external change
Richard Teare and John T. Bowen

Keywords Environmental scanning, Hospitality industry, Industry, Organizational learning, Organizational politics

The managerial activity of learning about events and trends in the organization's environment is known as environmental scanning. This process differs from industry or competitor analysis in two main respects: it is broad in scope and future-directed. Assesses the extent to which information needs are currently met by scanning activities and profiles the "top 30" hospitality industry issues as reflected by UK-based and North American hospitality management journals. Concludes with a priority ranking of the "top 30" issues assigned by UK hotel general managers and summary comments from this group on the implications for organizational learning.

Trends in hospitality: academic and industry perceptions
Jorge Costa, Gavin Eccles and Richard Teare

Keywords Environmental scanning, Europe, Human resource management, Industry, Research, Strategy

Reviews articles published during 1996 in the *International Journal of Contemporary Hospitality Management*, *International Journal of Hospitality Management*, *Tourism Management* and *Travel & Tourism Analyst*. Compares the central themes arising with those identified by a sample of hotel managers working in the UK and in Portugal, with particular reference to aspects of organizational performance. Compares and contrasts themes identified by academics and practitioners with reference to environmental scanning as a supportive process for trends identification and for strategy and decision-making purposes.

Performance management: processes, quality and teamworking
Hadyn Ingram

Keywords Europe, Hospitality industries, Performance measurement, Process efficiency, Teamworking

Reviews journal articles and worldwide hospitality and tourism trends research entries relating to three themes: business performance and performance measurement, process and quality improvement and teamworking. Draws on generic and industry-specific material to identify "best practice" approaches adopted in other industries that might be applied in the context of hospitality and tourism settings.

Supporting managerial learning in the workplace
Richard Teare

Keywords Action learning, Coaching, Competences, Learning, Management studies, Mentoring

Suggests that more and more organizations are attempting to establish a culture of learning that values the knowledge that employees have derived from learning how to perform effectively in the workplace. Reviews recent contributions to the literature on aspects of managerial learning and addresses the question "how do managers learn best in the workplace?" Draws from articles published between 1994-1996 in eight journals: *Executive Development*; *Journal of Management Development*; *Journal of Organizational Change Management*; *Leadership & Organization Development Journal*; *Management Development Review*; *Team Performance Management*; *The Journal of Workplace Learning*; *The Learning Organization*. Focuses on four themes: managerial learning and work; coaching, mentoring and team development; competences, managerial learning and the curriculum; work-based action learning. Concludes with a summary of the implications for managerial learning.

Enabling organizational learning
Richard Teare

Keywords Leadership, Organizational change, Organizational learning

It is clear from studies of organizations and a considerable body of anecdotal evidence that organizational life is strongly influenced by organizational leaders. In particular, the vision, style of leadership and motivation that enables them to "make things happen" and inspire others to follow their direction. Reviews recent contributions to the literature on aspects of organizational learning and considers how organizational processes might encompass effective learning support for individuals and groups of learners. Draws from articles published between 1994-1996 in seven journals: *Executive Development*; *Journal of Organizational Change Management*; *Journal of Management Development*; *Leadership & Organization Development Journal*; *Management Development Review*; *The Journal of Workplace Learning*; *The Learning Organization*. Concentrates on three areas: organizational vision; leadership and motivation; organizational change and performance. Concludes with a summary of the implications for organizational learning.

Empowerment and organizational change
Margaret Erstad

Keywords Employee participation, Empowerment, Europe, Organizational change, Organizational culture, Training

Among the many fashionable management terms, empowerment refers to a change strategy with the objective of improving both the individual's and the organization's ability to act. Reviews the various themes of empowerment with particular reference to articles published between 1994-1996 in the journal *Empowerment in Organizations*. The main themes are: creating an empowerment culture; empowerment as a management strategy; training and development for empowered employees; empowered teams and implementation techniques and empowerment and organizational change in the hospitality industry.

A market-driven approach to business development and service improvement in the hospitality industry
John T. Bowen

Keywords Brands, Business development, Marketing, North America, Segmentation, Service,

Reviews hospitality research relating to the themes of business development and service improvement. Relates this to five sub-theme areas: market sensitivity and competitiveness; segmentation; branding and service customization; service quality and customer retention; product design and internal marketing.

Responsive communication: the key to business development and service improvement
John T. Bowen

Keywords Business development, Decision making, Management information, Marketing, North America, Planning

In conducting marketing analysis, planning, implementation and control, managers need information at almost every point in the cycle. One marketing executive put it this way: "...to manage a business well is to manage its future and to manage the future is to manage information". Discusses the communication flows needed to manage business development activities effectively and relates them to practical illustrations and examples.

Current concerns: a thematic analysis of recent hospitality industry issues
Shane C. Blum

Keywords Customers, Human resources, Literature, North America, Organizational behaviour, Service quality

Reviews articles published during 1996 in the *Hospitality Research Journal*, *Cornell Hotel and Restaurant Administration Quarterly* and *Florida International University Review*. Identifies recent contributions to the literature in these North American-based journals with reference to: people and organizations; service quality and customers; strategy and operations; food service; education; and ecotourism and legal issues.

Editorial

Third annual review of worldwide hospitality and tourism trends

Welcome to the "Third annual review of hospitality and tourism trends" which reflects the recent hospitality and tourism literature published in selected academic journals on three continents. Our aim is to provide a concise overview and commentary on the themes portrayed in the literature, academic research and by industry reports as a resource for academics, managers, students, planners and writers. Beyond this, our ambition for the coming year is to provide an interactive service so that other might join us in discerning and interpreting the events that influence developments in our industry throughout the world. We have established two Internet web sites for this purpose. The HCIMA's worldwide hospitality and tourism trends (WHATT) databases will shortly be available to current and new subscribers at the Worldwide Hospitality and Tourism Trends Forum (at http://www.mcb.co.uk/htgf/whatt/) and we should like to receive contributors in the form of abstracts and contact details from analysts and researchers here too. Coupled with this, we shall be providing a facilitated electronic conferencing service in conjunction with the Hospitality and Tourism Global Forum (at http://www.mcb.co.uk/htg/) so that anyone interested in participating might do so. Our aim is to "capture" viewpoints from managers, key questions and aspects of academic debate so that we can embed a broad spectrum of opinion in the annual review itself and seek direction from industry about key themes that we should be exploring, debating and reporting on. During 1997 we took our first step towards wider participation by presenting key themes from the second annual review at two seminars held in London, and the views and priorities of a panel of hotel general managers have influenced the structure and content of this year's review. We shall also be establishing a fourth centre in Portugal during 1998. Directed by Jorge Costa (Fernando Pessoa University) he will be seeking to gather *Research Register* entries in Portuguese and Spanish languages (and provide a shortened English translation) from Spain, Portugal and South America.

This year's review begins with an overview of the hospitality and tourism literature published in selected Asia Pacific-based journals over an eight year period from 1989-1996 inclusive. Nerilee Hing discusses hospitality research in relation to five themes: attracting Asian outbound travel markets; stakeholder roles in service quality; workplace relations; investment, planning and development in the

Worldwide Hospitality & Tourism Trends: an HCIMA project with research centres in Europe, North America and Australia. The Annual Review is published by MCB University Press and Cassell plc (London & Hendon, VA) with sponsor support. Participation is encouraged via the Worldwide Hospitality and Tourism Trends Forum @ http://www.mcb.co.uk/htfg/whatt/ (for subscription details, our full text article service and contributions in the form of abstracts and contact details from analysts and researchers) and the Hospitality and Tourism Global Forum @ http://www.mcb.co.uk/htg/ (for facilitated electronic conferencing on key issues and questions, viewpoints, global networking and debate.

accommodation sector and education and training. Following this, Nerilee and Kay Dimmock consider some of the contemporary tourism issues with reference to tourist markets; tourist flows; tourism development; sustainable tourism development and social, economic and cultural impacts of tourism.

Trevor Ward from sponsors BDO Hospitality Consulting, assesses changes occurring in the UK hotel market during 1997 and relates these to current and predicted future market developments. This is followed by a piece entitled "Assessing information needs and external change" that profiles the "top 30" issues and reports on the priority rankings assigned by 25 UK hotel general managers during the 1997 business seminar series. Hosted by sponsors Forte Hotels and the HCIMA and presented by WHATT researchers from Europe and North America in conjunction with BDO, the "hot" topics as seen by managers are well represented in this year's review. Our "top 30" presentation reflected UK and US-based journal literature and was structured around six broad categories: business performance improvement; personal and organizational development; service improvement and competitiveness (UK) and marketing; human resource management and wider organizational issues (USA). To ensure that we "balance" the agenda and reflect the needs and concerns of industry as well as academia, we have taken as our starting point this year the key issues, priorities and concerns raised by the sample group of general managers. The remainder of the review therefore reflects an analysis of their priorities as well as other developments reported in the literature during 1996.

A number of topic areas not widely reported in the hospitality management literature were rated as "important" by the sample group of managers and so we have incorporated a review of the generic literature relating to empowerment, quality improvement, teamworking and workplace and organizational learning. We hope that by focusing on topics of interest to managers and continuing with our wide-ranging review of the hospitality and tourism literature, readers will find the third annual review a little different. We aim to provide a comprehensive resource of latest thinking and practice, so do please contact us or participate in our interactive forums on the Internet.

We would like to thank our sponsors and publishers and the HCIMA for their collective support and encouragement.

Richard Teare, John T. Bowen and Nerilee Hing
Guest Editors

A review of hospitality research in the Asia Pacific region 1989-1996: a thematic perspective

Nerilee Hing
Research Director (Asia Pacific) Worldwide Hospitality and Tourism Trends

Identifies themes in the hospitality and tourism literature arising from articles published in Asia Pacific-based journals from 1989 to 1996 inclusive. The journals are the *Australian Journal of Hospitality Management*, the *Journal of Tourism Studies*, *Tourism Recreation Research* and the *Asia Pacific Journal of Tourism Research*. The themes are: attracting Asian outbound travel markets; stakeholder roles in service quality; workplace relations; investment, planning and development in the accommodation sector; and education and training.

Introduction

To survive and prosper, organizations must carefully assess the changes and conditions in their given environment. With numerous and diverse forces shaping the future of the hospitality industry (Olsen, 1996, p. 7), environmental scanning is an effective means of analysing salient trends and patterns relating to the business environment in which hospitality organizations operate. Many of these forces for change are reflected in scholarly publications which draw on current research and thinking in the field. Thus, the purpose of this article is to review, from a thematic perspective, material published in major hospitality-related journals in the Asia Pacific region from 1989 to 1996 inclusive. These journals are the *Australian Journal of Hospitality Management*, the *Journal of Tourism Studies*, *Tourism Recreation Research* and the *Asia Pacific Journal of Tourism Research*.

Five themes reflect the major strands of research and thinking during the review period. These are attracting Asian outbound travel markets, stakeholder roles in service quality, workplace relations, investment, planning and development in the accommodation sector, and education and training. Publications relating to each theme are summarized in tabular form, while a linking thematic diagram is presented in Figure 1.

Theme 1: Attracting Asian outbound travel markets

In the Asia Pacific region, Japan has dominated as the major growth market for outbound travel. In their quest to attract Japanese tourists, many destinations in the Pacific Rim have altered their marketing strategies to accommodate particular needs and priorities of this market. However, with more recent emergence of other Asian outbound travel markets, it is a dangerous fallacy to assume that they display the same expectations and behaviour as the Japanese (Olsen, 1996, p. 53). The articles reviewed here (Table I) recognize that different national outbound markets, and segments within these markets,

have particular characteristics and that these will impose new challenges on hospitality managers.

Opperman (1996) provides useful insights into the four "Tiger" markets: Hong Kong, Singapore, South Korea and Taiwan. He discussed their importance as tourist generators for Pacific Rim countries, examined recent changes in tourist arrivals and outbound generation, compared tourist arrivals from the four countries with those of Japan, and analysed growth patterns in the context of life cycle theory. He concluded that, while several Pacific Rim countries have developed into the maturity stage in Japanese outbound tourism, the same countries are only in the development stage in the Asian Tigers' outbound tourism. Changing composition of international tourist arrivals constitutes one of the major challenges to the hospitality industry, which will need to accommodate the different expectations of these newer markets in the Pacific Rim. However, these changes offer excellent opportunities for innovative entrepreneurs who can anticipate them.

China is set to become one of the region's largest tourist markets. Li *et al.* (1996) reviewed current literature to reveal trends and characteristics of Chinese outbound travel. They noted the recent growth of total departures from China, relatively low use of air transport and preference for travel to Pacific Asian countries, particularly Hong Kong, Macau, Australia and Singapore. However, potential growth is currently curbed by government controls on travel documents, procedures for joining group tours and the amount of money that can be taken out. The authors (1996) concluded that China's economic reforms and open-door policy will continue to encourage growing demand for travel abroad. If current regulations are relaxed, Chinese tourism will likely increase to non-Asian destinations and Chinese travellers will become more sophisticated. Removal of barriers in destination countries and adaptation of products and services to meet the needs of Chinese tourists are necessary to capitalize on the enormous potential of Chinese outbound travel.

Mok, Armstrong and Go have variously contributed to three articles which focus on characteristics of outbound travellers from Hong Kong and Taiwan. In their 1996 study (Mok and Armstrong, 1996) they identified the two information sources most used by outbound travellers from both countries as friends and relatives and travel agents, meaning that tourist satisfaction through the provision of high quality hospitality/tourism services is particularly important. They also noted a significant relationship between sources of information and travel mode. Since the majority of tourists from both countries preferred all-inclusive package tours organized through travel agencies, effective communication between tour suppliers and potential tourists is essential. Mok *et al.* (1995) identified 13 attributes that Taiwanese travellers use in selecting leisure destinations. "Safety" and "scenic beauty" were the key attributes, with the former reflected in the high proportion of travellers who use all-inclusive package tours. Their study into the perceptions held by Hong Kong and Taiwanese travellers of Australia as a holiday destination (Mok and Armstrong, 1994) found that even those who had not visited had formed favourable organic images about Australia relating to its beautiful scenery, pleasant climate, friendly local people, good recreational and sports facilities, and safety. However, Hong Kong travellers perceived Australia as expensive and lacking night life

Figure 1
The service profit chain revisited

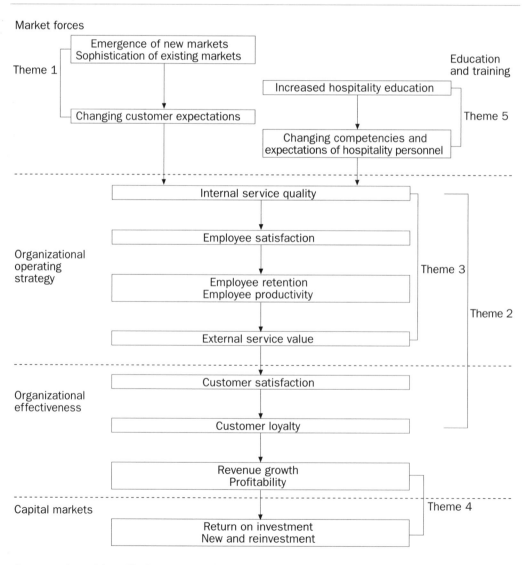

Source: adapted from Heskett *et al.* (1994, p. 166)

Table I
Attracting Asian outbound travel markets

Authors	Focus	Sub-theme
Opperman (1996)	Focuses on the development of outbound tourism from the four Asian "Tigers": Hong Kong, Singapore, South Korea and Taiwan	Emerging outbound "Tiger" markets
Li, Bai and McCleary (1996)	Describes current size, apparent trends, market characteristics and future prospects of outbound travel from China	Chinese outbound travel
Mok and Armstrong (1996)	Examines and compares the sources of information used by Hong Kong and Taiwanese leisure travellers and relates them to mode of travel	Hong Kong and Taiwanese tourist behaviour
Mok, Armstrong and Go (1995)	Uses survey research to identify 13 attributes which Taiwanese travellers appear to use in selecting leisure destinations	Taiwanese travel market
Mok and Armstrong (1994)	Reports on Hong Kong and Taiwanese tourists' perceptions of Australia as a holiday destination to show this is generally positive, but that perceptions of the two groups differ	Destination image of Australia
Cho (1996)	Examines perceptions of Korean youth visitors to Australia regarding the importance and performance of destination attractiveness and tourism activity attributes	Korean youth travel market
Wada, Waryszak and Bauer (1994)	Investigates characteristics of the Japanese student travel market and its potential for the Australian hospitality industry	Japanese student market
Prideaux and Dunn (1995)	Compares the incidence of crime on Australia's Gold Coast to the state average and explores measures to improve overall tourist safety	Tourism and crime

entertainment. Significant differences between the perceptions of these two markets underpins the need to avoid sweeping generalizations about Asian outbound travel markets.

Two additional articles examined the perceptions of Australia as a holiday destination by certain Asian markets. Cho (1996) surveyed Korean youth visitors to identify the importance of, and satisfaction with, various attributes of Australia in terms of destination attractiveness and tourist activity. In recommending appropriate promotion strategies for younger Korean travellers, Cho noted that Australia needs to deliver more information about cultural activities and nature-based ecotourism opportunities and to make these activities more available and accessible. Further research into the outbound Korean university student market to Australia was also recommended owing to this market's relative affluence and desire to travel.

Wada *et al.* (1994) also recognized the potential of the university student market to Australian tourism, but in the context of Japan. Unlike most Japanese tourists, the Japanese student market preferred more flexible travel arrangements, budget accommodation, and longer travel periods. To attain a fine balance between flexibility and convenience, the authors recommended packaging tours including only return flights and accommodation and promotion of such packages to Japanese tour operators and travel agents. Their findings also challenged the common

perception that providing service in the Japanese language is vital in attracting Japanese tourists as this may well repulse the more adventurous student market.

Given the value of outbound Asian markets to the Australian tourism industry and the importance placed by many Asian travellers on safety and security, Prideaux and Dunn's (1995) article on the relationship between tourism and crime is important. Their study focused on the Gold Coast, a premier tourist destination enjoying large numbers of Japanese tourists and increasing visitation from other Asian countries. While Australia generally enjoys a reputation as a safe tourist destination, the image of the Gold Coast based on sun, surf, sand, sex and romance is a significant factor in its high crime rate. The authors recommended strategies which can be taken by local businesses, governments and the destination to reduce crime. To ignore these, they warned, will mean visitors will eventually substitute safer destinations.

Theme 2: Stakeholder roles in service quality

In profiling a quality management programme designed for the Australian hospitality industry, Dwan (1994, p. 55) comments that quality management requires a "market focus to business strategy, an organized approach to planning and managing customers' service experiences, customer-centred and

[9]

Nerilee Hing
A review of hospitality research in the Asia Pacific region 1989-1996: a thematic perspective

enthusiastic staff and a solid underlying management system". Dwan's comments are instructive as they highlight the involvement of three key stakeholders in effective quality management: customers, management and employees. The importance of these stakeholders is reflected in the various articles reviewed here (Table II).

The construct of quality has traditionally been viewed from the customer's perspective and is often defined as meeting or exceeding customer expectations (Gronroos, 1984). However, while leading researchers in the field, Parasuraman *et al.*, maintain that there are universally valid and applicable determinants of service quality (1985), criticisms of this assumption (Carman, 1990) have led to methodologies to assess service quality in specific industry settings.

For example, Walker (1996) used focus groups of clients of five accommodation categories in Tasmania, Australia, to generate a set of attributes germane to measuring service quality within the specific industry context. These formed the basis of two survey instruments, the first administered at check-in to assess perceived customer importance of these attributes and the second at check-out to assess customer perceptions of these attributes' standards. Walker concluded that the locus of service quality is individually and contextually grounded, such that service quality is defined in different ways by different people with reference to different contexts and considerations.

Kivela (1996) also took a customer perspective in formulating a model of the restaurant choice process. Like Walker (1996), Kivela recognized that attributes important to restaurant patrons are industry specific and determined both by individual factors (such as age, gender, income, education, life cycle and reasons for eating out) and external factors (such as the customer's experience at the restaurant, media and merchandising efforts and communications with others). The model can also be used to predict return patronage intentions which depend on customer satisfaction with the dining experience.

Lyons (1996) also focused on customer satisfaction in restaurants. More specifically, she used qualitative methods to study restaurant complaint behaviour in Queensland, Australia. She concluded that factors influencing

Table II

Stakeholder roles in service quality

Authors	Focus	Sub-theme
Dwan (1994)	Profiles a quality management programme designed specifically for the Australian hospitality industry	Quality management programme
Walker (1996)	Explores how visitors to Tasmania, Australia define and assess service quality in the context of commercially provided accommodation	Definition and assessment of service quality
Kivela (1996)	Proposes a model for identifying determinant choice variables in restaurant selection and their impact on return patronage	Restaurant choice attributes
Lyons (1996)	Reviews literature and reports on a study of complaint attitudes and behaviour of restaurant patrons	Restaurant complaint behaviour
King (1994a)	Explores the concept of authenticity and its application in tourism activity in Australia, with particular reference to the hospitality sector	Historical integrity of Australian hospitality
Reisenger and Waryszak (1994)	Investigates Japanese tourists' expectations and perceptions of service provided in Australian hotels	Japanese assessed service quality in Australian hotels
Ross (1993)	Investigates service quality elements judged by hospitality industry employees to be important to hospitality industry management	Employee defined service quality
Huyton, Sutton and Xiu-Cheng (1994)	Investigates whether idealogical perceptions of wealth influence service attitudes and abilities of hotel employees in the Peoples Republic of China	Service quality in Chinese hotels
Yourston (1995)	Discusses whether the AS 3900 is poised to be an essential quality assurance tool for the Australian hospitality industry	Quality assurance techniques
Wilson and McPhail (1995)	Examines service culture, and investigates relationships between market orientation, organizational innovativeness and business performance	Service culture and business performance

complaint behaviour were the intensity of customer dissatisfaction and a host of personal and situational variables. Importantly, complaint behaviour in restaurants differed from that in other industries owing to social factors and the intangible causes of dissatisfaction.

Just as the preceding articles have emphasized that customer expectations, satisfaction and assessment of quality are individually and contextually specific, implicit in other publications is the notion that cultural factors are also important. For example, in their study of Japanese tourists' expectations and perceptions of service provided in Australian hotels, Reisenger and Waryszak (1994) found that the tourists perceived hotel employees to be less professional, friendly, informative, helpful, concerned about customers and able to speak Japanese than they had expected. Provision of more information, more Japanese speaking staff, staff training in Japanese language and culture, and welcome and farewell gifts, were recommended. Also adopting a customer perspective, King (1994a) explored the question of whether international tourists to Australia expect authentically Australian hospitality experiences. He proposed numerous ways in which authentic hospitality product development can be incorporated into physical items (e.g. food and drink), sensual benefits (e.g. service and atmosphere) and psychological benefits (e.g. comfort and status) so that tourist satisfaction levels can be improved.

Two articles in the review period studied service quality from the perspective of employees. Ross (1993) examined the perceptions of hospitality staff regarding management's service quality expectations, concluding that politeness, hard work and efficiency were the major perceived management service quality elements. Furthermore, being hard working and efficient was associated with higher levels of need for achievement, while politeness was inversely related to need for autonomy. Providing an Asian perspective, Huyton *et al.* (1994) investigated whether the extreme disparity between the perceived wealth of hotel visitors and the personal environment, lifestyle and existence of hotel employees in China would influence the latter's service attitudes and abilities. However, their interviews revealed this assumption to be incorrect and that Western materialism was seen by many employees as something worth striving for.

Providing a management perspective, Yourston (1995) emphasised increasing importance of quality management to hospitality managers, and discussed the potential of the Australian quality assurance standard

AS 3900 to improve the competitive edge of the Australian hospitality industry in a global market. Positive elements are that the standard has been developed specifically for service industries and its inclusion of a small business module is appropriate to the structure of the Australian hospitality industry.

In their empirical investigation of the relationships between market orientation, organizational innovation and business performance, Wilson and McPhail (1995) also reinforced that success in hospitality firms depends not only on service excellence when providing current services, but also on market intelligence to identify opportunities which add value to existing service offerings. They concluded that within hospitality firms, superior business performance is, to a large extent, dependent on the organization's ability to engender a service culture.

Theme 3: Workplace relations

Olsen (1996, p. 7) notes that some forces shaping the future hospitality industry are limited labour markets and downsizing, coupled with increasing customer demand for an excellent price/value ratio. Demands on organizations to increase productivity, while simultaneously maintaining or improving customer satisfaction, have been met with a variety of responses (Table III).

In Australia, hospitality enterprise agreements have been examined by Timo (1994) who argued that the labour characteristics, product composition and cyclic patterns of industry demand lend themselves to enterprise-based arrangements. He examined a small number of such arrangements to conclude that enterprise agreements can lead to productivity improvements, greater workplace harmony and significant progress in staff development.

Employee empowerment is considered another mechanism to deliver excellent customer service with fewer employees in flatter organizational structures. Arising in the 1980s from Edward Deming's concept of total quality management to increase customer satisfaction through greater employee involvement, employee empowerment has become one of the buzzwords of the 1990s. However, as Harrell (1996) revealed in his study of employee empowerment in the hotel industry, significant disparities existed between managers' and non-managers' understanding of the concept. He recommended that individual hotels needed to examine their empowerment programmes to ensure that "correct" employee empowerment messages were being sent to all employees. Doing so

Table III

Workplace relations

Authors	Focus	Sub-theme
Timo (1994)	Examines moves to a decentralized industrial relations system in Australia, characteristics of the hospitality labour market and impacts of an enterprise agreement at an Australian resort	Labour markets and enterprise agreements
Harrell (1996)	Investigates and measures the disparity in perceptions and applications of empowerment between hotel management and line/staff employees in hotels	Employee empowerment
Mallinson (1996)	Discusses the role, functions and status of executive housekeepers in Australian four and five star hotels	Executive housekeepers
You (1996)	Builds a working model of employment turnover theory and applies it to the Korean hospitality industry	Employee turnover
Qu and Tse (1996)	Explores Hong Kong hotel employee expectations, satisfaction and intentions to leave in relation to job satisfaction and demographics	Hotel employee satisfaction and turnover
Ross (1991)	Reports on preferences of Australian school leavers for tourism/hospitality industry work, potential work satisfaction, motivation and perceived employer estimation	Perceptions of work
Wilks and Atherton (1995)	Examines employment practices and their legal implications for workers in recreational scuba diving in Queensland, Australia	Employment practices in adventure tourism
Iverson (1995)	Develops and evaluates a variety of simple models to predict hotel employment levels for the island of Guam	Forecasting hotel employment
Yu and Pine (1995)	Reviews job and hotel characteristics which favour the use of local or expatriate hotel managers in Hong Kong	Local versus expatriate management
Francis (1996)	Identifies personal characteristics, education, allocation of time and importance to ten managerial roles, source of industry information and career intentions of New England hotel managers	Characteristics of hotel managers

may clarify existing misunderstandings over whether everyone was equal when it came to taking ownership and solving guests' problems and whether management was really capable of abandoning traditional management philosophy to increase guest satisfaction. He concluded that employee empowerment programmes can only be as effective as management allows them to become.

The delivery of high quality services which result in customer satisfaction is, to some extent, dependent on employee satisfaction. Mallinson (1996) conducted a study of one group of hospitality employees which has been largely ignored in the literature: executive housekeepers. While officially performing a managerial role in today's large hotels, the status of executive housekeepers continues to suffer from its historical performance by the hotelier's wife, mother or daughter when hotels were much smaller, and the traditional view of their work as prescriptive, low skill, boring and monotonous. Mallinson concluded that unless their image is improved in Australia, the industry may well have to import the next generation of executive housekeepers.

Two studies in the review period have been concerned with the relationship between employee satisfaction and labour turnover. You (1996) examined this relationship in the Korean hospitality industry. An integrated employee turnover model was developed by reviewing extensive turnover studies conducted in the USA, and validated in the context of Korean hotel employees. Qu and Tse (1996) also explored this relationship in the Hong Kong hotel industry. They examined the gaps between employees' expectations and satisfaction levels, and the relationship between employee satisfaction, their demographics and their intention to leave the organization. They concluded that, in general, Hong Kong hotel employees are dissatisfied with their job and organizational and working environment, which were rated significantly below their expectations and contributed to their intentions to leave. With the labour-intensive nature of the industry and its reliance on employee performance for success, employers need to take action to remedy employee dissatisfaction.

To maximize employee satisfaction, realistic expectations about job attributes would seem essential. Ross (1991) surveyed over 500 Australian school leavers to gather their perceptions of work life in the hospitality/tourism industry. Major sources of potential satisfaction were advancement, job interest, sense of achievement and working conditions and high importance was placed on recognition, sense of achievement and co-workers. A follow-up study would be useful in evaluating how realistic these perceptions proved to be.

Wilks and Atherton (1995) also explored why people seek employment in the hospitality/tourism industry. Specifically, they examined employment practices in the Queensland recreational scuba diving industry and concluded that the apparent willingness of some staff to forgo legal entitlements, such as holiday pay loading and overtime, reflect the lifestyle factor in their chosen field of employment. They identified flexibility to pursue a much-loved hobby and be paid at the same time as a clear characteristic of Australian adventure tourism workers. They advocated greater recognition of this lifestyle factor in designing and structuring optimum human resource arrangements for small business in the adventure tourism industry.

Iverson (1995) makes the point that, while service quality depends on training, reward structure and other factors, one fundamental requirement is an adequate supply of well-trained labour. He used quantitative modelling to predict hotel employment levels for the island of Guam. A variety of models were tested to determine which was most effective at predicting hotel employment needs in a dynamic tourism-based economy. Hotel managers, government officials, educators and customers can all benefit from accurate forecasts of this nature.

Cultural similarities between management, staff and customers may also impact on customer and employee satisfaction. Yu and Pine (1995) examined increased localisation in hotel management in Hong Kong, brought about by the handover of Hong Kong to Chinese rule in 1997 and increasing Chinese tourists. They noted that these factors have encouraged the adoption of localization policies by many Hong Kong hotels which gradually replace expatriate managers with locals. Their study found higher proportions of expatriate hotel managers in higher job levels of larger and more deluxe hotels which tended to be managed by multinational hotel companies based outside Hong Kong. Cultural capacities of the managers, background of hotel companies and employment cost were often key considerations in employing local or expatriate managers. The authors concluded that localization of hotel managers in Hong Kong will increase, and more

attention should be devoted to managing this transition in developing hotel industries.

Francis (1996) also focused on hotel managers with some interesting international comparisons. She provided a comprehensive profile of the average New Zealand hotel manager who typically manages an inner city or resort location under management contract, is 40 years old, male, has been employed in the hospitality industry for more than 16 years, has held his current position for one or two years and holds university entrance qualifications or a college diploma. In terms of Mintzberg's ten managerial roles (1975), he most frequently assumes the roles of leader, monitor, resource allocator and entrepreneur. As Francis notes, general managers are "the linchpin between employees, customers and owners", influencing employee productivity, customer satisfaction and return on assets. It is therefore an important finding that the New Zealand profile differs from that in other countries. It appears that more work could be done in exploring how differing backgrounds of hotel managers impact on both employees and customers of hospitality organizations.

Theme 4: Investment, planning and development in the accommodation sector

The articles which are discussed under this theme are notable for their diversity. Some have focused on long-term trends in sector development, some on property investment, and others on more specific managerial and operational concerns in specific properties (Table IV).

Two articles are concerned with historical trends in various sectors of the accommodation industry. McCulloch (1992) traced the origins of the contemporary Youth Hostel Association (YHA) movement, from the wandering scholars and travelling apprentices of earlier centuries, to its development in reaction to harsh conditions of urban life in industrial nineteenth century Europe, to the current liberalisation of YHA policies to accommodate budget and backpacker markets in Australia and other destinations. However, despite the importance of the backpacker market, this sector has attracted relatively little research. Such a comment could also be made about the caravan park industry, the focus of Kelly's (1994) article. He reviewed historical development of the industry in Australia and drew on a survey of users, as well as park usage data from Britain and the USA, to identify important future issues for the Australian sector. These included the potential for conflict in parks

Nerilee Hing
*A review of hospitality
research in the Asia Pacific
region 1989-1996: a thematic
perspective*

Table IV

Investment, planning and development in the accommodation sector

Authors	Focus	Sub-theme
McCulloch (1992)	Traces the origins of and historical influences on the Youth Hostel Association movement and its response in Australia to the backpacker phenomenon	Hostel development
Kelly (1994)	Examines recent performance of the Australian caravan park sector, its market segments, park facilities, shortcomings, management and future developments	Management and marketing of caravan parks
King and Whitelaw (1992)	Investigates key characteristics of resorts in Australia with particular reference to size, location and star rating, identifying inconsistency in the use of the term	Characteristics of resorts
Short (1996)	Examines recent developments in the New Zealand hotel sector, its major hotel companies, and growth and development of accommodation stock	Hotel development in New Zealand
Daly, Jenkins and and Stimson (1996)	Investigates the perceptions of financiers towards tourism investment in Australia in the mid-1990s	Tourism investment
Dwyer and Forsyth (1994)	Clarifies issues relevant to assessing leakages overseas from tourist expenditure owing to foreign ownership of tourism facilities in Australia	Foreign ownership and tourist expenditure leakages
Stanton and Aislabie (1992)	Illustrates how local government regulation can be used to encourage resort development and discusses problems which can be created by its use	Local governments and resort development
Saville (1994)	Examines two stages in developing hotel projects so that hotel operators obtain value for money in capital expenditure and energy conservation	Hotel development
Weenink (1994)	Discusses excess hotel energy usage despite the importance of environmental care in future planning and existence of good examples of energy control	Energy conservation in hotels
Burton (1995)	Examines various energy and control strategies used by the recreation building industry to save on costs and energy	Energy management in recreation facilities
A'Vard (1996)	Discusses environmental policies at an Australian resort which may have practical applications for resorts generally	Environmental resort policies

catering for both tourists and long-term residents, the need for the sector to market its product more effectively, and the value of a national rating system.

King and Whitelaw (1992) take a somewhat different line in examining the resort sector in Australia. Their concern lay in defining the term "resort" in view of the characteristics of properties advertised as such. They noted the inconsistent use of the term, displaying a mismatch between consumer understanding and the way the term is used for both classification purposes by motoring associations and marketing purposes by tour operators and the properties themselves. They postulated that this ad hoc use of the term is a "recipe for confusion".

Moving to New Zealand, Short (1996) clarified some issues relevant to future growth and development of the hotel sector. He concluded that if current trends continue, visitor arrivals will continue to climb, maintaining high interest in hotel investment and development, particularly from international hotel chains. However, he warned that, with industry exposure to economic vagaries, hotel managers need to think strategically to encourage customer loyalty and repeat business, to maintain profitability within their captured market share.

Daly *et al.* (1996) also focused on hotel investment by investigating the perceptions of financiers towards tourism investment in Australia. In explaining Australia's continued reliance on foreign investors, especially for large projects in luxury markets, they identified lack of expertise in assessing such high risk investments with variable cash flows, reluctance by Australian investors to invest heavily or in the long-term in the tourism industry, the growth in publicly listed companies, which make them more accessible to foreign investment, and the "hands-off" approach to tourism policy and investment taken by the Australian government. Daly *et al.* likened tourism investment

Nerilee Hing
A review of hospitality research in the Asia Pacific region 1989-1996: a thematic perspective

to a gambling game, "being high risk, understood by few and with no referee".

Foreign ownership of tourism facilities was also the central topic of Dwyer and Forsyth's (1994) article. They argued that the size of leakages overseas from tourist expenditure depends on how foreign owned facilities source their inputs compared to domestic owned facilities. They analysed the disbursement of prepaid and optional expenditure on a package tour to Australia to reveal that additional outflows owing to foreign ownership are quite low. A framework is provided whereby the income generating effects of foreign and domestic owned tourism facilities, in both their development and operational stages, can be determined in any country.

In addition to the effects of hotel ownership structure, two articles have focused on the role of local government in hotel development. Stanton and Aislabie (1992) discussed the functions of local government regulation in encouraging resort development. They pointed to a potential conflict, as local government is responsible not only for ensuring development is consistent with land use guidelines and does not burden the local community, but also for encouraging and promoting local economic development. Similarly, Saville (1994) identified the town planning role of local authorities in specifying land use, height, size, site cover, parking and vehicular access of developments as important influences on hotel design. Saville also examined the engineer's role in ensuring hotel operators' design standards are achieved and in offering valuable advice for the maintenance and serviceability of systems, particularly those which promote efficient energy use.

Energy efficiency is a theme taken up by the remaining articles reviewed in this section. Weenink (1994) argued that improperly managed energy use in the hotel sector is both unacceptable and costly and that there are many sources of helpful information and direction. Government agencies provide professional advice and energy logging, advising on energy per room compared with similar hotels, providing more friendly and accessible electrical demand metering, and ways of reducing this demand. Hotel associations provide a centralised databank of practical information for use by hotel designers, builders, operators and owners. Burton's (1995) article is also instructive in providing many practical ideas that can be implemented to reduce energy usage in tourist and recreational facilities.

Energy conservation was also addressed by A'Vard (1996) in her case study of environmental policies at an Australian island resort. The resort was designed to be self-sufficient and to minimise impacts on one of the most delicate ecosystems on earth. A'Vard's account of environmentally friendly practices in all resort areas, including landscaping, power and water usage, noise pollution, housekeeping, front office, guest relations, concierge, marina and administration, may have practical applications for resorts generally.

Theme 5: Education and training

McIntosh (1992) has pointed out that tertiary level hospitality and tourism education is a relatively recent phenomenon, originating with the 1920s US extension programmes to assist those interested in planning and managing their own hospitality businesses (Table V). In contrast, hospitality/tourism degrees in Pacific Rim countries developed much later, but are currently flourishing with expanding numbers of specific programmes and majors, and adjustments to course content to reflect global and local trends (Wells, 1996). However, Wells contends that a fundamental question is the contribution such education makes to delivering an effective workforce. Similar concerns were expressed by Morrison (1994) who argued that expansion in the number of hospitality degree places has been driven by student, rather than industry, demand. The vast majority of employment opportunities in the industry do not require the intellectual capabilities of competent graduates and the match between type of employment and expectations of graduates is often incongruous. Morrison contended that if a relatively small number of quality, skilled operational managers are required by industry, then that is what should be produced. The finding that 54 per cent of first-year hospitality students from four Australian universities expected to start work in trainee/junior management/ supervisory positions also lends weight to Morrison's concerns (Davidson, 1996).

Perhaps the solution to this dilemma is more involvement of relevant stakeholders in hospitality/tourism curriculum design. Shepherd and Cooper (1995) identified these stakeholders as students, tourists, educational institutions, government, media and the tourist industry. They noted that the implicit nature of tourism as a diverse and complex activity among such stakeholders necessitates taking account of their views, actions and influences on education and training. The importance of stakeholder

Table V
Education and training

Authors	Focus	Sub-theme
McIntosh (1992)	Reviews early tourism education in the USA and argues that tourism's success is partly due to efforts of visionary educators	Role of educators in tourism
Wells (1996)	Analyses curriculum trends in Australian tourism/hospitality degree programmes and offers suggestions for curriculum developers	Longitudinal curriculum trends
Morrison (1994)	Argues that expanding the number of Australian hospitality degree places has been driven by student, not industry, demand	Expansion of hospitality courses
Davidson (1996)	Establishes the demographic profile of hospitality and hotel management students and their expectations of study in four Australian universities	Hospitality student profiles
Shepherd and Cooper (1995)	Analyses relevant stakeholders, examines their specific influence on tourism/hospitality education and examines responses by educators and trainers	Stakeholder involvement in education
Ritchie (1995)	Presents a framework on which to base the design and development of tourism/hospitality management programmes	Curriculum design
King (1994b)	Evaluates the development of Australian co-operative education by comparing one Australian travel and tourism course to overseas experience	Co-operative education
King (1994c)	Discusses the level of Australian course-related materials used in hospitality and tourism education in Australia	Course material
Go and Mok (1995)	Explores hotel and tourism management education in Hong Kong, examines key industry issues and outlines the Chinese cultural context for education	Education programmes in Hong Kong
Echtner (1995)	Highlights challenges facing developing nations in designing tourism/hospitality education programmes and advocates a three-pronged approach	Education programmes in developing nations
Sindiga (1994)	Examines the level and magnitude of tourism employment in Kenya and assesses the relationship between training and employment in tourism	Employment and training in Kenya
Dowell (1995)	Discusses the role of training, training expenditure and training evaluation in the Australian hospitality industry	Evaluation of training
Robson (1995)	Discusses the role of the National Employment and Training Taskforce to stimulate and fulfil demand for traineeships in tourism industries	Traineeships
Peacock (1995)	Outlines challenges and opportunities arising for Australian training providers from the rapidly growing tourism industry in the Asia Pacific	Training provision in the Asia Pacific

groups in hospitality/tourism curricula is also implicit in a framework developed by Ritchie (1995) for designing and developing tourism/hospitality management programmes. Criteria emphasised include sensitivity to industry needs, balance between economic development and environmental protection, building on and developing skills of faculty members, location where tourism is a significant component of the local economy, and a balance of conceptual material and practical experience.

The importance of integrating "hands-on" experience into a more formal educational framework (Shepherd and Cooper, 1995) is also advocated by King (1994b) who reviewed the development of hospitality/tourism co-operative education, defined as a pedagogical process involving a relationship between educators, industry employers and students. The espoused benefits of this approach are that students are introduced to the working environment of their chosen industry, develop awareness of supervision, management, motivation, and decision making, apply academic knowledge in employment situations, and learn to accept individual responsibility by working as part of a team. King concluded that the sound philosophical principles of co-operative education are essential for hospitality/tourism education and that urgent action is needed in Australia to protect earlier advances made.

In addition to incorporating stakeholder needs, cultural factors are also important in curricula design. King (1994c, p. 38) contends that "no body of knowledge can be right for all places and all seasons because knowledge

Nerilee Hing
*A review of hospitality
research in the Asia Pacific
region 1989-1996: a thematic
perspective*

alters as the society it supports changes". He criticised lack of acknowledgement shown for social, cultural, biological and physical landscapes in which tourism operates and argued it is imperative to provide professional education in a national context. Go and Mok (1995) demonstrated the importance of cultural factors in examining hotel and tourism management education in Hong Kong and the influence of the Chinese cultural context in which such education takes place; while Echtner (1995) examined the challenges facing developing nations when designing tourism education programmes. She concluded by advocating a three-pronged approach: professional education, vocational training and entrepreneurial development. In the context of Kenya, Sindiga (1994) also called for further training and extension services so that increased indigenization can proceed in a country where high levels of foreign ownership and control have resulted in foreign domination of hospitality/tourism management positions.

As Sindiga (1994, p. 45) points out, "training is the transition between formal education and the needs of occupation and employment". Dowell (1995) discussed the role of training in the Australian hospitality industry and concluded that the link between productivity and training investment is at the enterprise level. Studies of effective Australian service sector enterprises show they devote more attention to training and deliberately attempt to recruit more highly skilled and qualified workers than their less effective counterparts. Also in the Australian context, Robson (1995) echoed Dowell's support for training. He described the work of the National Employment and Training Taskforce in encouraging demand for trainees and delivering simple access for employers to traineeships. Peacock (1995) also recognized recent advancements made in Australian training systems which provide significant opportunities for expansion into hospitality/tourism training in the Asia Pacific region. He argued that rapid economic growth of Pacific Asian countries has increased demand for education and training which they cannot meet. The challenge will be a commitment to quality, and creative and flexible delivery of these services.

Concluding observations

The five themes discussed in this review reflect some emerging issues of importance to the hospitality industry and allow identification of the following opportunities and challenges.

- Our understanding of the characteristics of emerging Asian outbound tourist markets is relatively limited. Further research is needed for hospitality establishments to capitalise on the potential offered by these markets by adapting products and services according to their specific needs, expectations and behaviour (theme 1).
- Further attention should be devoted to defining quality expectations of specific market segments in specific industry contexts. Assuming that customer expectations of quality are homogeneous is misleading. Management will need to nurture employees and implement appropriate systems so that service excellence, as defined by their customers, is delivered (theme 2).
- Further organizational efforts to promote job satisfaction of employees, which in turn can translate into service excellence, will help meet the challenge of simultaneous improvement in employee productivity and customer satisfaction. Case research into exemplary firms and benchmarking of successful systems may prove more beneficial than a trial and error approach (theme 3).
- Reliance on foreign investment in tourist facilities in many Pacific Asian countries seems unlikely to wane, at least in the shorter term. This presents significant challenges, not only in attracting such capital investment in an increasingly global and competitive environment, but also in maximizing the benefits of tourism in such destinations while minimizing associated costs (theme 4).
- Meeting both industry and student expectations of hospitality/tourism education is an ongoing challenge which may best be met by further stakeholder involvement in the design and improvement of course curricula. In addition, hospitality/tourism education needs in the Asia Pacific region provide both challenges and opportunities for education and training providers (theme 5).

References

A'Vard, M. (1996), "Preserving a paradise", *Australian Journal of Hospitality Management*, Vol. 3 No. 1, pp. 63-6.

Burton, S. (1995), "Building energy conservation and demand control", *Australian Journal of Hospitality Management*, Vol. 2 No. 2, pp. 41-8.

Carman, J.M. (1990), "Consumer perceptions of service quality: an assessment of the SERVQUAL dimensions", *Journal of Retailing*, Vol. 66 No. 1, pp. 33-55.

Cho, B.H. (1996), "An analysis of the Korean youth tourist market in Australia", *Australian*

[**17**]

Journal of Hospitality Management, Vol. 3 No. 2, pp. 15-26.

Daly, M., Jenkins, O. and Stimson, R. (1996), "Investing in the tourism game", *Australian Journal of Hospitality Management*, Vol. 3 No. 2, pp. 41-52.

Davidson, M. (1996), "Demographic profile and curriculum expectations of first year hospitality management degree students", *Australian Journal of Hospitality Management*, Vol. 3 No. 2, pp. 69-74.

Dowell, R. (1995), "Training evaluation for profit: the challenge of evaluation", *Australian Journal of Hospitality Management*, Vol. 2 No. 1, pp. 51-5.

Dwan, T. (1994), "'Excellence in hospitality': quality management for the hospitality industry", *Australian Journal of Hospitality Management*, Vol. 1 No. 2, pp. 55-7.

Dwyer, L. and Forsyth, P. (1994), "Foreign ownership and leakages from tourist expenditure: a framework for analysis", *Australian Journal of Hospitality Management*, Vol. 1 No. 2, pp. 1-10.

Echtner, C.M. (1995), "Tourism education in developing nations: a three pronged approach", *Tourism Recreation Research*, Vol. 20 No. 2, pp. 32-41.

Francis, S. (1996), "A profile of general managers of international hotels in New Zealand", *Australian Journal of Hospitality Management*, Vol. 3 No. 2, pp. 53-8.

Go, F. and Mok, C. (1995), "Hotel and tourism education: building a center of excellence in Hong Kong", *Tourism Recreation Research*, Vol. 20 No. 2, pp. 46-57.

Gronroos, C. (1984), "A service quality model and its marketing implications", *European Journal of Marketing*, Vol. 18 No. 4, pp. 36-44.

Harrell, H. (1996), "Differences in perception of employee empowerment between managers and non-managers in the hotel industry", *Tourism Recreation Research*, Vol. 21 No. 2, pp. 69-75.

Heskett, J.L., Jones, T.O., Loveman, G.W., Sasser, W.E. Jr and Schlesinger, L.A. (1994), "Putting the service profit chain to work", *Harvard Business Review*, March-April, pp. 164-74.

Huyton, J., Sutton, J. and Xiu-Cheng, B. (1994), "A cultural clash – revolution or reform: a snapshot of the hotel industry in the Peoples Republic of China", *Australian Journal of Hospitality Management*, Vol. 1 No. 2, pp. 29-36.

Iverson, T.J. (1995), "Forecasting hotel employment with simple time series models", *Tourism Recreation Research*, Vol. 20 No. 2, pp. 58-62.

Kelly, I. (1994), "Caravan parks: the Cinderella subsector", *Australian Journal of Hospitality Management*, Vol. 1 No. 2, pp. 37-46.

King, B. (1994a), "How Australian is hospitality and tourism education in Australia?", *Australian Journal of Hospitality Management*, Vol. 1 No. 1, pp. 37-8.

King, B. (1994b), "Hospitality and tourism co-operative education: its development and prospects", *Australian Journal of Hospitality Management*, Vol. 1 No. 2, pp. 17-24.

King, B. (1994c), "Bringing out the authentic in Australian hospitality products for the international tourist: a service management approach", *Australian Journal of Hospitality Management*, Vol. 1 No. 1, pp. 1-8.

King, B. and Whitelaw, P. (1992), "Resorts in Australian tourism: a recipe for confusion?", *Journal of Tourism Studies*, Vol. 3 No. 2, pp. 41-8.

Kivela, J (1996), "Marketing in the restaurant business", *Australian Journal of Hospitality Management*, Vol. 3 No. 1, pp. 1-12.

Li, L., Bai, B. and McCleary, K. (1996), "The giant awakens: Chinese outbound travel", *Australian Journal of Hospitality Management*, Vol. 3 No. 2, pp. 59-68.

Lyons, J. (1996), "Getting customers to complain: a study of restaurant patrons", *Australian Journal of Hospitality Management*, Vol. 3 No. 1, pp. 37-50.

McCulloch, J. (1992), "The Youth Hostels Association: precursors and contemporary achievements", *Journal of Tourism Studies*, Vol. 3 No. 1, pp. 22-7.

McIntosh, R.W. (1992), "Early tourism education in the United States", *Journal of Tourism Studies*, Vol. 3 No. 1, pp. 2-7.

Mallinson, H. (1996), "Executive housekeeper: the Cinderella profession", *Australian Journal of Hospitality Management*, Vol. 3 No. 1, pp. 56-8.

Mintzberg, H. (1975), "The manager's job: folklore and fact", in Mintzberg, H. and Quinn, J. (Eds) (1990), *The Strategy Process: Concepts, Contexts and Cases*, 3rd edition, Prentice-Hall, NJ, pp. 19-34.

Mok, C. and Armstrong, R.W. (1994), "Perception of Australia as a holiday destination: a case of Hong Kong and Taiwanese tourists", *Australian Journal of Hospitality Management*, Vol. 1 No. 2, pp. 25-8.

Mok, C. and Armstrong, R.W. (1996), "Sources of information used by Hong Kong and Taiwanese leisure travellers", *Australian Journal of Hospitality Management*, Vol. 3 No. 1, pp. 31-8.

Mok, C., Armstrong, R.W. and Go, F.M. (1995), "Taiwanese travellers' perception of leisure destination attributes", *Australian Journal of Hospitality Management*, Vol. 2 No. 1, pp. 17-22.

Morrison, P. (1994), "Degrees in hospitality management: quality or quantity?", *Australian Journal of Hospitality Management*, Vol. 1 No. 1, pp. 38-9.

Olsen, M.D. (1996), "Events shaping the future and their impact on the multinational hotel industry", *Tourism Recreation Research*, Vol. 21 No. 2, pp. 7-14.

Opperman, M. (1996), "The changing market place in Asian outbound tourism: implications for hospitality marketing and management", *Tourism Recreation Research*, Vol. 21 No. 2, pp. 53-62.

Parasuraman, A., Zeithaml, V.A. and Berry, L.L. (1985), "A conceptual model of service quality and its implications for future research", *Journal of Marketing*, Vol. 49, Fall, pp. 41-50.

Peacock, R. (1995), "International tourism and hospitality training – expanding the expertise", *Australian Journal of Hospitality Management*, Vol. 2 No. 1, pp. 55-9.

Prideaux, B. and Dunn, A. (1995), "Tourism and crime – how can the tourism industry respond?", *Australian Journal of Hospitality Management*, Vol. 2 No. 1, pp. 7-16.

Qu, H. and Tse, S.C.S. (1996), "An analysis of employees' expectations, satisfaction levels and turnover in the Hong Kong hotel industry", *Tourism Recreation Research*, Vol. 21 No. 2, pp. 15-23.

Reisenger Y. and Waryszak, R.Z. (1994), "Assessment of service quality for international tourists in hotels: an exploratory study of Japanese tourists in Australia", *Australian Journal of Hospitality Management*, Vol. 1 No. 2, pp. 11-16.

Ritchie, J.R.B. (1995), "Design and development of the tourism/hospitality management curriculum", *Tourism Recreation Research*, Vol. 20 No. 2, pp. 7-13.

Robson, D. (1995), "Nettforce and training – the challenge begins", *Australian Journal of Hospitality Management*, Vol. 2 No. 1, pp. 49-51.

Ross, G. (1991), "School-leavers and their perceptions of employment in the tourism/hospitality industry", *Journal of Tourism Studies*, Vol. 2 No. 2, pp. 28-35.

Ross, G.F. (1993), "Service quality and management: the perceptions of hospitality employees", *Journal of Tourism Studies*, Vol. 4 No. 2, pp. 12-32.

Saville, B. (1994), "The development of new hotel projects", *Australian Journal of Hospitality Management*, Vol. 1 No. 1, pp. 27-30.

Shepherd, R. and Cooper, C. (1995), "Innovations in tourism education and training", *Tourism Recreation Research*, Vol. 20 No. 2, pp. 14-24.

Short, D.G.T. (1996), "The New Zealand hotel sector", *Australian Journal of Hospitality Management*, Vol. 3 No. 1, pp. 51-6.

Sindiga, I. (1994), "Employment and training in tourism in Kenya", *Journal of Tourism Studies*, Vol. 5 No. 2, pp. 45-52.

Stanton, C. and Aislabie, C. (1992), "Local government regulation and the economics of tourist resort development: an Australian case study", *Journal of Tourism Studies*, Vol. 3 No. 2, pp. 20-31.

Timo, N. (1994), "Enterprise bargaining in the Australian hospitality industry", *Australian Journal of Hospitality Management*, Vol. 1 No. 1, pp. 31-8.

Wada, A., Waryszak, R. and Bauer, T. (1994), "Intentions to use hospitality services in Australia by Japanese tertiary students", *Australian Journal of Hospitality Management*, Vol. 1 No. 1, pp. 17-22.

Walker, R.H. (1996), "Towards identifying how visitors to Tasmania define and assess service quality in the hospitality industry", *Australian Journal of Hospitality Management*, Vol. 3 No. 2, pp. 27-40.

Weenick, N.J. (1994), "The hospitality industry and energy management", *Australian Journal of Hospitality Management*, Vol. 1 No. 1, pp. 9-12.

Wells, J. (1996), "The tourism curriculum in higher education in Australia: 1989-1995", *Journal of Tourism Studies*, Vol. 7 No. 1, pp. 20-30.

Wilks, J. and Atherton, T. (1995), "The lifestyle factor: employment practices in the Queensland recreational diving industry", *Australian Journal of Hospitality Management*, Vol. 2 No. 1, pp. 23-30.

Wilson, I. and McPhail, J. (1995), "Strategic implications of market orientation and organizational innovativeness on the business performance of hospitality service firms in Australia", *Australian Journal of Hospitality Management*, Vol. 2 No. 2, pp. 1-12.

You, Y.J. (1996), "An empirical test of turnover theory: in the case of Korean hotel employees", *Asia Pacific Journal of Tourism Research*, Vol. 1 No. 1, pp. 50-60.

Yourston, D. (1995), "The Australian hospitality industry's application of quality assurance AS 3900", *Australian Journal of Hospitality Management*, Vol. 2 No. 2, pp. 65-8.

Yu, R. and Pine, R. (1995), "Use of local and expatriate hotel managers in Hong Kong", *Australian Journal of Hospitality Management*, Vol. 2 No. 2, pp. 25-34.

Contemporary tourism issues in Asia Pacific journals 1989-1996: a thematic perspective

Nerilee Hing
Research Director (Asia Pacific) Worldwide Hospitality and Tourism Trends
Kay Dimmock
Research Manager (Asia Pacific) Worldwide Hospitality and Tourism Trends

Reviews articles published in three Asia Pacific-based tourism journals: the *Journal of Tourism Studies, Tourism Recreation Research* and the *Asia Pacific Journal of Tourism Research*. Identifies five tourism themes relating to articles published over an eight year period from 1989-1996. These are: tourist markets, tourist flows, tourism development, sustainable tourism development and social, economic and cultural impacts of tourism.

Introduction

This paper reviews articles published in the three major tourism journals in the Asia Pacific region: the *Journal of Tourism Studies, Tourism Recreation Research* and the *Asia Pacific Journal of Tourism Research*. The review period covers eight years, from 1989 to 1996 inclusive. Articles reviewed are summarized in tabular form and grouped into five main themes: tourist markets, tourist flows, tourism development, sustainable tourism development, and social, economic and cultural impacts of tourism. A linking thematic diagram is included as Figure 1.

Theme 1: Tourist markets

While diverse in focus, the articles concerned with tourist markets reflect growing recognition of the value of VFR and domestic tourism markets, the emergence of particular niche markets and the importance of understanding tourist behaviour (Table I).

The significance of VFR markets was raised by Jackson (1990), who noted that VFR travel constitutes a major proportion of world tourism but is readily underestimated unless available data are carefully examined. He contended that further work in explaining VFR flows is warranted and that changing patterns of migration will create ongoing changes in VFR tourism. Similarly, Yuan *et al.* (1995) supported the sizeable economic contribution made by international VFR markets to local communities in their comparison of travel patterns of Dutch long-haul VFR and non-VFR travellers to the USA and Canada.

A number of scholars have also recognised the importance of VFR travel to repeat visitation. Opperman (1996) pointed out that, while it is less expensive to reattract previous visitors than acquire new ones, few tourism destinations actively pursue current visitors. In comparing repeat and first-time visitors to Rotorua, New Zealand, he found significant differences regarding trip characteristics and attractions frequented. Meis *et al.* (1995) also noted the cumulative revenue from repeat visitors and the importance of VFR travellers within this segment.

An aspect of the VFR market which is often understated is its use of tourist facilities and services. In their study of inbound tourism to the East North Central region of the USA, Braunlich and Nadkarni (1995) found that VFR travel comprises over half of all pleasure travel and that over one-fifth of VFR travellers use hotels. VFR travel constituted nearly 9 percent of all trips in which a hotel room was purchased, with VFR hotel users having longer stays, but lower per night expenditures than pleasure travellers. Morrison *et al.* (1995) also demonstrated that VFR travellers to Queensland Australia use the same tourism facilities and attractions as other pleasure travellers.

Disaggregation of the VFR market was proposed by Seaton and Tagg (1995) who suggested segmenting this supposedly homogeneous group into visiting friends (VF), visiting relatives (VR) and visiting both friends and relatives (VFR). Morrison *et al.* (1995) also challenged the assumption that VFR travel represents one homogeneous market. They suggested segmenting the VFR market by holiday activity participation to help explain past, and predict future, holiday behaviour in order to guide tourist destination marketing (Morrison *et al.*, 1994). They showed that sub-groups of Australian domestic VFR travellers differed on many key characteristics.

While the value of the VFR market is often underestimated, so too is the economic contribution of domestic tourism. Helleiner (1990) noted that within developing countries, the value of domestic tourism may not directly attract foreign exchange, but still has substantial economic impact through employment and the development of infrastructure that can attract international tourists. In his case example of Nigeria, Helleiner found that, while many conventional tourist attractions are of little interest to domestic tourists, facets of modern technology and cities are sufficiently interesting to generate domestic trips.

Other articles reviewed here have focused on the value of particular niche markets. For example, Weiler and Kalinowski (1990) analysed potential versus actual participation in educational travel programs, revealing significant opportunities for product development and diversification. Murray and Sproats

Nerilee Hing and
Kay Dimmock
*Contemporary tourism issues
in Asia Pacific journals 1989-
1996: a thematic perspective*

Figure 1
Contemporary influences on the tourism system

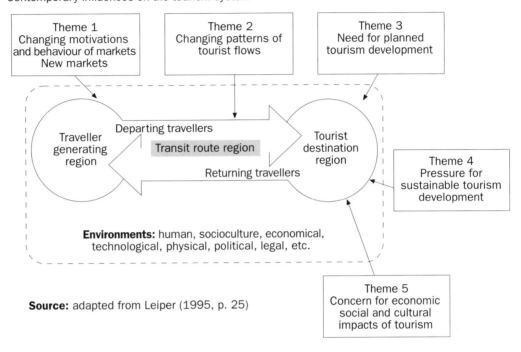

Source: adapted from Leiper (1995, p. 25)

Table I
Tourist markets

Authors	Focus	Sub-theme
Jackson (1990)	Discusses international tourism which involves visits to friends and relatives and examines in detail the phenomenon in Australia	VFR travel
Yuan, Fridgen, Hsieh and O'Leary (1995)	Explores the role of VFR travellers in the international market, concluding that the VFR traveller represents a sizeable segment of the market travelling to the USA and Canada	VFR travel
Opperman (1996)	Analyses international repeat and first-time visitors to Rotorua, New Zealand, to gain insights into their respective visitation of tourist attractions, trip and expenditure patterns	First-time vs. repeat visitors
Meis, Joyal and Trites (1995)	Determines how past experience visiting a Canadian destination affects US travellers' perceptions of Canada, their trip planning, buyer behaviour and future travel plans to Canada	Repeat visitation
Braunlich and Nadkarni (1995	Investigates VFR, pleasure and business travel to the East North Central region of the USA, comparing demographics, travel habits and hotel expenditures of hotel users from each group	VFR travel
Morrison, Hsieh and O'Leary (1995)	Challenges the assumption that the VFR market is one homogeneous market by dividing VFR travellers to Queensland, Australia into six distinct segments by past holiday activity participation	VFR market segmentation
Seaton and Tagg (1995)	Based on international tourist data, explores hypotheses proposed about potential value of disaggregating the VFR market to provide separate accounting of its component elements	VFR market segmentation
Morrison, Hsieh and O"Leary (1994)	Identifies six market segments of Australian domestic travellers with unique sets of activity participation and other characteristics to argue that activity-based segmentation is a viable approach to segmenting travel markets	Activity-based market segmentation
Helleiner (1990)	Describes research in Nigeria to determine the demand for tourism as perceived by Nigerians themselves in order to recommend promotional efforts to increase domestic tourism	Domestic tourism in Nigeria

(Continued)

Nerilee Hing and
Kay Dimmock
*Contemporary tourism issues
in Asia Pacific journals 1989-
1996: a thematic perspective*

Table I

Authors	Focus	Sub-theme
Weiler and Kalinowski (1990)	A case study of educational travel programmes, describing potential and actual participants in terms of their values, demographics, activities and resources to assess the propensity for participating in educational travel	Educational travel
Murray and Sproats (1990)	Discusses the potential market value of providing facilities accessible to the disabled community and results of a survey of disabled facilities in North Queensland and disabled tourists and their families	Disabled travellers
Carlsen (1995)	Reviews meetings and conventions research in Australia, Asia, USA and Europe, discusses specific problems in conducting this research and identifies issues requiring further investigation	Meetings and conventions research
Zeppel and Hall (1991)	Provides an overview of cultural and heritage tourism by considering visitor motivations and market characteristics for the cultural tourism sector, strategies for marketing cultural tourism and a discussion of key management issues relating to cultural tourism	Cultural and heritage tourism
Moscardo (1992)	Takes a knowledge-based approach to understanding differences between international and domestic tourists and resident visitors in four Australian interpretive settings	Differentiating tourist and resident visitors
Heath (1990)	Compares local and foreign visitors to major resort areas of Zimbabwe and assesses whether they are seeking similar facilities and experiences and whether the Zimbabwe tourist industry should cater to two different markets	Distinguishing local and foreign tourists
Pearce (1996)	Reviews research projects in tourist behaviours by an Australian research team and specifies the value of four integrating concepts linking this research – the travel career ladder, cognitive steps, mindfulness and social situations	Tourist behaviour
Crompton (1996)	Focuses on four research programme endeavours into tourist decision making – choice sets, trip patterns, motivations and positioning	Tourist decision making
Hsieh, O'Leary, Morrison and Chang (1993)	Presents a choice model of package tours by Australian outbound travellers using socio-demographics, travel characteristics and psychographic attributes to predict the probability of choosing package tours	Tourist decision making
Kim, Pearce, Morrison and O'Leary (1996)	Attempts to reveal comprehensive information on the travel motivations of Korean tourists with regard to overseas trips by employing concepts in the travel career ladder (Pearce, 1991)	Tourist motivations
McGehee, Loker-Murphy and Uysal (1996)	Examines female Australian leisure travellers and their motivations from a gendered perspective to examine differences in push and pull motivational factors	Tourist motivations
Pyo (1996)	Segments the Far East Asia tourist market by using push attributes to identify six clusters with unique characteristics and delineates related implications	Tourist motivations
Fielding, Pearce and Hughes (1992)	Examines how different motivations influence the experience of climbing Ayers Rock, Australia, exploring the effect of intrinsic versus achievement motivation on task enjoyment and time perception of the climbers	Tourist motivations

(1990) commented that the value of providing facilities and services to accommodate needs of disabled travellers has been underestimated and that market size warrants increased community awareness of opportunities for disabled travellers and effective marketing strategies by tourism operators. Carlsen (1995) noted that the meetings and conventions sector has the highest economic yield of all visitor types, necessitating a database to monitor overall sector growth and its economic, technological and cultural benefits for a destination. Meanwhile, Zeppel and Hall (1991) identified increasing value placed on cultural and heritage tourism. They argued for effective management strategies to ensure a sustainable approach to resources. Within museums and other interpretive settings, Moscardo (1992) contended that visitation differences between residents and tourists should be recognized as part of a management strategy to enhance visitor satisfaction. Similar conclusions were

Nerilee Hing and
Kay Dimmock
*Contemporary tourism issues
in Asia Pacific journals 1989-
1996: a thematic perspective*

drawn by Heath (1990) in his study of the differences between domestic and international visitors to attractions in Zimbabwe.

The remaining articles reviewed here have focused on aspects of tourist behaviour. Pearce (1996) highlighted four concepts which link research in this area: the travel career ladder which is an approach to tourist motivation, cognitive steps and mindfulness which are conceptual organizers of how people think and process information, and social situations which provide an integrative view of key factors in describing social behaviour. Crompton (1996) provided an alternative framework for understanding tourist behaviour. He explained that tourism decisions are made through a complex process of evaluating and eliminating various choices. While there are numerous choice sets a tourist may select from, the initial consideration set and the late consideration set often provide conflicting marketing implications. However, by defining market segments according to choice set patterns, this conflict can be overcome. Hsieh *et al.* (1993) also adopted the concept of choice sets in designing a model of Australian outbound travellers to predict the choice of package tours. They found that package purchasers are likely to be older, travel with larger party sizes and seek a "being and seeing" benefit.

Kim *et al.* (1996) note that, while motivation is fundamental to explaining tourist behaviour, it has received only moderate research attention. Empirically, they utilised the travel career ladder (Pearce, 1996) to explain tourist motivation for Korean outbound travel. Conversely, McGehee *et al.* (1996) used the concept of "push" and "pull" motivations to examine the motivations of female Australian leisure travellers. As women are generally accepted as primary holiday planners, it is important to identify what motivates women to select travel destinations. "Push" factors were also utilized by Pyo (1996) to segment the potential tourist market to Far East Asia. He identified six segments differing in destination, country of origin and "push" attributes. Meanwhile, Fielding *et al.* (1992) examined how individual differences in motivation affect visitor experiences. From their study of climbers to Ayers Rock, Australia, they concluded that intrinsic motivation, rather than achievement motivation, led to greater enjoyment of the experience.

Theme 2: Tourist flows

Discussion of tourist flows in the review period has taken two distinct streams: theoretical and descriptive (Table II).

From a theoretical perspective, Morley (1990) drew on various models of tourism to build a more general and inclusive framework based on two dimensions: tourist-tour-others and demand-supply-impacts. An alternative model, the travel dispersal index (TDI), was used by Opperman (1992a) to analyse intranational travel flows of international tourists in destination countries. Drawing on data from Malaysia, he demonstrated that the TDI has utility in developing tourist typologies and as a market segmentation tool. Morley (1993) was also concerned with tourist flows and specifically in methodologies for forecasting these. He argued that extrapolative time series models are an appropriate alternative to multiple regression which has shortcomings of heteroscedasticity, multicollinearity and autocorrelation. Crouch (1993) evaluated the impact of exchange rates on the pattern of international tourism demand using meta-analysis. His findings highlighted that changes in currency exchange rates can impact on international tourism demand.

Recent changes in the world political map have been dramatic with the partitioning of many single states. Ramifications for business and family ties are numerous. Butler and Mao (1996) suggest that newly partitioned states experience several stages in building a new identity, with travel and tourism being significant to this process. The notion of counter-trade techniques was discussed by Wilson and Wang (1996) as useful in facilitating international tourism flows. A case study of counter-trade in tourism between Moscow and Shanghai suggested that barter in tourism might be worthwhile to promote tourism flows in areas where none previously existed.

From a more descriptive perspective, a number of scholars have examined domestic tourist flows in Muslim countries. While the accepted view is that recreational styles in Muslim and Western countries are distinctly different, Ritter (1989) argued that this may be due to an evolutionary time lag. He confirmed that domestic tourism in many Muslim countries has started to boom with a preference for spending leisure time in public spaces open to recreational use, such as beaches and deserts. He suggested that similar reasons may have lured English lower middle classes to resorts 120 years ago. Kopp (1989) also recognised evolutionary differences in tourism to Muslim countries. In his study of international tourism to the Yemen-Arab Republic, he noted that many centuries of restricted visitor access provide opportunities to study the juxtaposition of traditional native recreation with the effects of a recent influx of Western tourists.

Recent changes in domestic tourist flows in North African countries have also been the focus of other studies. For example, Hoehfeld (1989) noted the emerging preference for

Nerilee Hing and
Kay Dimmock
*Contemporary tourism issues
in Asia Pacific journals 1989-
1996: a thematic perspective*

Table II
Tourist flows

Authors	Focus	Sub-theme
Morley (1990)	Draws on various tourism models to build a more general and inclusive model, based on two dimensions: Tourist-Tour-Other and Demand-Supply-Impacts	Modelling tourism flows
Opperman (1992a)	Proposes the traversal dispersal index to analyse intra-national travel behaviour of international tourists in the designation country, as a differentiating variable for a tourist typology and as a market segmentation tool	Intra-national tourism flows
Morley (1993)	Investigates the use of extrapolative time series methods in forecasting tourist demand, with application to Australian tourism data	Forecasting tourism flows
Crouch (1993)	Provides a meta-analysis of empirical studies which have evaluated the impact of exchange rates on the pattern of international tourism demand	Exchange rates
Butler and Mao (1996)	Discusses separation of single states, stages partitioned countries goes through to build new identities and trust and the role of tourism in the reconciliation process between the partitioned states	Partitioned states
Wilson and Wang (1996)	Examines countertrade techniques in facilitating international tourism flows, particularly between foreign currency-starved Third World countries, drawing on countertrade in tourism between Moscow and Shanghai	Countertrade
Ritter (1989)	Discusses recreational tourism trends of Muslim tourists, identifies clear preferences for deserts and beaches and compares these trends to English lower middle class tourism a century earlier	Domestic Muslim tourism
Kopp (1989)	Juxtaposes recreation and native recreational travelling in Yemen with effects of an influx of Western sightseeing tourism	Domestic Muslim tourism
Hoehfeld (1989)	Discusses the recent development of seaside holidays by the native population in Turkey, which is replacing the age-old tradition of holidays in the mountains	Domestic Muslim tourism
Berriane (1989)	Presents results of a survey into recreational activities of the Moroccan population, modifying the notion that Third World countries do not have their own tourism	Domestic Morrocan tourism
Standl (1989)	Discusses rapid tourism development in Egypt due to increased awareness by Egyptians of the recreational potential of their own country, favourably influenced by government sponsored sightseeing programmes	Domestic Egyptian tourism
Barham (1989)	Measures the flow of excursionists to the Dead Sea region and explains motives behind such trips	Domestic tourism in Jordan
Al Moosa (1989)	Discusses domestic tourism trends in Kuwait, with new facilities available in the metropolitan areas and the proliferation of private coastal bungalows	Domestic tourism in Kuwait
Schliephake (1989)	Discusses domestic tourism trends in Saudi-Arabia, characterized by an "American" emphasis on motor cars and outdoor activities, but also development of recreational and accommodation facilities	Domestic tourism in Saudi-Arabia

seaside holidays by domestic tourists in Turkey, simulating development of coastal strips near larger cities, with simple wooden huts built as holiday homes. Moroccan nationals are also holidaying at seaside villages and towns, with large family groups preferring camping facilities and privately rented rooms to hotels (Berriane, 1989). Egypt has also witnessed recent growth in domestic tourism, with historic sites and coastal regions being primary destinations (Standl, 1989). This has encouraged private investment in small hotels and holiday residences. In Jordan, climatic differences between cooler upland cities and the milder Dead Sea valley are one reason for the increase in domestic excursions to the valley area (Barham, 1989). While all strata of society are represented among these excursionists, the emphasis is on the better educated and

Nerilee Hing and
Kay Dimmock
*Contemporary tourism issues
in Asia Pacific journals 1989-
1996: a thematic perspective*

salaried groups. Al Moosa (1989) has studied leisure and recreation in Kuwait. Its growing importance among the resident population has encouraged new facilities in metropolitan centres and private bungalows in coastal regions. However, residents of Kuwait are still to be convinced of the quality of services offered in their country. Saudi Arabians, however, are increasingly fond of domestic travel owing to their increased mobility and urbanization (Schliephake, 1989). Schliephake notes that travelling for pleasure here is characterised by an almost "American" emphasis on using the motor car and outdoor activities. However, in some parts of the country, investments in recreational facilities and accommodation have also become important.

Theme 3: Tourism development

Development of tourist destinations, especially in developing countries, has been the focus of numerous articles in the review period (Table III).

Butler's tourist destination lifecycle has formed the basis for some studies in the review period. For example, Barr (1990) examined trends in tourist development in the Whitsundays, Australia, to show that, while many principles of the model still applied, the region experienced atypical patterns of facility growth, particularly regarding the transition from locally to externally funded expansion. These differences were attributed to indifferent community attitudes to tourism enterprise which stimulated the early influence of non-local entrepreneurs. Williams (1993) presented an expanded version of Butler's model to incorporate aspects of dependency and external control theories of tourism development. In the context of Minorca, Spain, he demonstrated that, despite high levels of industrialization before the arrival of tourism, it experienced similar developmental problems to less industrialised destinations, such as decline in indigenous economic sectors and external control of tourism development.

External control, as well as other challenges to tourism development, has concerned a number of scholars writing about developing nations. For example, Hall (1994a) concluded that, while Vanuatu has welcomed foreign investment in tourism development, it has attempted to maximise the benefits of tourism, through developing secondary transport activities and retaining local culture and heritage. Similarly in Fiji, Hall (1994b) noted that, although several aspects of the industry are dominated by foreign interests, the development of secondary tourism opportunities

and the absence of a single source of foreign tourism investment provides the Fijian government with greater bargaining power in international relations. Conversely, Adu-Febiri (1994) argued that Ghana's failure to develop a viable tourism industry based on its vast tourism resources is not due to foreign ownership and control, but rather to the wholesale adoption of conventional mass tourism which does not fit with the country's low capital accumulation capacity, unskilled tourism personnel and traditional entrepreneurial and management styles.

Also focusing on countries where tourism is rapidly developing, Dieke (1993) identified general planning and policy principles by examining tourism development in Kenya and Gambia. He highlighted the need for forward and flexible planning and considerable caution in monitoring and reviewing the effects of tourism to serve national development goals. Similarly, Chon and Oppermann (1996) reviewed progress of tourism development in the Philippines. After significant growth during the 1970s, political turmoil, natural disasters and bad publicity of sex tourism have severely impacted on its international image. The authors reviewed the potential impact of the new tourism master plan on the future of tourism in the area.

Opperman (1992b) makes the point that understanding the spatial distribution of tourists and tourism development is essential for successfully implementing tourism projects in developing nations. He analysed the spatial distribution of tourism in Peninsular Malaysia, concluding that variation existed both among regional areas, and between domestic and foreign tourists. Similarly, Zhang (1996) identified the spatial disparities in the location of tourism resources in China with the development of resorts in prominent tourism provinces and the designation of many attractions as scenic wonders and historic sites. Opperman *et al.* (1996) noted that in developing countries, national capitals have developed as gateway cities containing the largest proportion of hotel capacity. They examined Kuala Lumpur as an example of the importance of tourism to central business districts of developing countries.

With tourism development often concentrated in major cities (Timothy and Wall, 1995), urban tourism planning has attracted much attention. For example, Singh (1992) expressed concern at the deteriorating urban environment in India and noted that, while tourism can contribute to the problem, it can also encourage urban revival and revitalization. Similarly, Bhattacharya (1992) noted that the tourist attraction of Indian cities, such as Darjeeling and Sikkim, has created problems

Nerilee Hing and
Kay Dimmock
*Contemporary tourism issues
in Asia Pacific journals 1989-
1996: a thematic perspective*

of amenity. To overcome such problems, Haywood (1992) called for urban development which both satisfies tourists and enhances residents' quality of life. Similarly, Dredge and Moore (1992) recommended a methodology to plan proactively for tourism development. They noted that the integration of town planning is important in tourism development, influencing the efficiency and functioning of a destination, its image and character, and ultimately the host-guest relationship. However, this integration has been limited by town planners' lack of understanding of the nature and workings of tourism.

The promotion of heritage is one avenue for attracting tourists to urban centres. Black (1990) argued that a method for preserving heritage buildings is to adapt them to alternative, economically viable uses. External changes to facades are acceptable if the impact of change is overridden by basic authenticity and uniqueness of the heritage building. In the context of Malaysia, Cartier (1996) described how political and financial support has been provided to preserve historic buildings and attract tourists. Alabi (1994) also identified the potential for the promotion of heritage tourism in Nigeria, as a strategy for development.

In addition to the impact of tourism on urban development, other scholars have focused on the linkage between tourism development and the rural sector. Bowen *et al.* (1991) presented a conceptual model of linkages between the agricultural and tourism

Table III

Tourism development

Authors	Focus	Sub-theme
Barr (1990)	Examines the Whitsundays in Australia to reveal developmental trends similar to models of tourism development, but dissimilarities due to community attitudes and strategies of key entrepreneurs	Destination lifecycle
Williams (1993)	Presents expanded version of Butler's lifecycle model by incorporating aspects of dependency and external control theories belonging to tourism development, with emphasis on tourism development in Minorca	Destination lifecycle
Hall (1994a)	Provides a case study of tourism industry development, the effects of tourism and the role of government policy in Vanuatu	Tourism development in Vanuatu
Hall (1994b)	Examines the proposition that international tourism in the South Pacific has the characteristics of a new plantation economy, with reference to tourism development in Fiji	Tourism development in Fiji
Adu-Febiri (1994)	Discusses tourism industry development in Ghana, attributing its failure to development which has favoured wholesale adoption of conventional, mass tourism	Tourism development in Ghana
Dieke (1993)	Examines tourism development in Kenya and The Gambia to identify general planning and policy principles appropriate for where tourism is developing rapidly	Tourism development in Kenya and Gambia
Chon and Opperman (1996)	Analyses current tourism development and planning in the Philippines, discusses its competitive position, scrutinises regional effects of tourism and reviews the new tourism plan	Tourism development in the Philippines
Opperman (1992b)	Analyses spatial variation of tourism in Peninsular Malaysia to identify considerable differences between regions	Tourism development in Malaysia
Zhang (1996)	Reviews tourism growth in China, emphasizing resource planning, development, regional patterns, impacts of tourism, current problems and future prospects	Tourism development in China
Opperman, Din and Amri (1996)	Analyses the evolution of hotel locations in Kuala Lumpur, identifying five stages and revealing insights into urban tourism development patterns in a developing country	Tourism development in Malaysia
Timothy and Wall (1995)	Focuses on urban tourism, specifically tourist-historic cities to apply models of urban tourism to Yogyakarta, Indonesia	Urban tourism
Singh (1989)	Advocates image restoration of Lucknow, India, necessary owing to haphazard urban development and non-sustainable development policy which is adversely affecting the environment	Urban tourism

(Continued)

Nerilee Hing and
Kay Dimmock
*Contemporary tourism issues
in Asia Pacific journals 1989-
1996: a thematic perspective*

Table III

Authors	Focus	Sub-theme
Singh (1992)	Examines, within the framework or urban tourism, some problems associated with urban development and urban tourism with reference to Lucknow in India	Urban tourism
Bhattacharya (1992)	Examines the phenomenon of urban tourism in Darjeling and Sikkam in India	Urban tourism
Haywood (1992)	Discusses aspects of urban tourism, advocating development with emphasis not simply on tourism development, but overall urban development	Urban tourism
Dredge and Moore (1992)	Describes a methodology for town planners to meet challenges of significant growth expected in the tourism industry and to plan proactively for its development	Town planning
Black (1990)	Examines appropriateness of alternate futures for heritage buildings and explores what changes and what degree of change in heritage buildings appear acceptable	Heritage tourism
Cartier (1996)	Uses heritage tourism studies to compare the evolution of historic conservation based tourism in Malaysia	Heritage tourism
Alabi (1994)	Describes the tourism potential of Nigeria's traditional heritage and suggests alternative product-market development strategies for promoting heritage tourism	Heritage tourism
Bowen, Cox and Fox (1991)	Models linkages between agricultural and tourism sectors of a destination's economy, arguing that unique agricultural products, government policy and resources are key determinants of the linkage's character	Agricultural tourism
Cox and Fox (1991)	Presents a classification scheme and definition for agriculturally based leisure attractions	Agricultural tourism
Long and Nuckolls (1994)	Reviews development of local authority tourism strategies to appraise critically the approaches adopted and their underlying rationale	Regional tourism strategies

sectors, arguing that such linkages can benefit both sectors and enhance greater co-operation while contributing to industry growth. By providing services to support agriculturally-based leisure attractions, profit can be enjoyed by farmers and others in rural economies (Cox and Fox, 1991). For rural communities to benefit from tourism requires leadership, planning and technical assistance in the early stages of tourism development to address critical elements that lead to sustainable development (Long and Nuckolls, 1994).

Theme 4: Sustainable tourism development

Many factors are driving the call for more sustainable forms of tourism. These include increased environmental concern, greater interest in protecting remaining vestiges of natural ecosystems, empowerment of indigenous people in developing countries, and a significant rise in nature-based travel (McCool, 1994, p. 51). Pigram (1990) noted that the past decade has witnessed growing

endorsement of the concept of sustainability as the logical approach to matching both conservation and development requirements. He called for greater public involvement in decision making and continuing education of all tourism interest groups to achieve greater tourism-environment compatibility.

Ecotourism has been described as a potentially sustainable form of visitor demand and resource supply, requiring the operationalisation of ethics-based principles (Wight, 1993, p. 54). A number of articles have focused on the expectations and behaviour of ecotourists. Weiler and Richins (1995) described the "true" ecotourist as not just satisfied with a natural experience, but as wanting to be environmentally responsible, expecting to interact and engage with the natural environment, and prepared to be physically and intellectually challenged in doing so. They investigated characteristics of Earthwatch participants as a group of "extreme" ecotourists. However, they noted that not all ecotourists share these characteristics but that most may simply be seeking enjoyment of some relatively undisturbed phenomenon of nature.

[27]

Nerilee Hing and
Kay Dimmock
*Contemporary tourism issues
in Asia Pacific journals 1989-
1996: a thematic perspective*

Table IV
Sustainable tourism development

Authors	Focus	Sub-theme
McCool (1994)	Discusses how changes in the nature of tourism and its relationship with the natural environment require new paradigms to manage tourism development	Limits of acceptable change model
Pigram (1990)	Discusses principles of sustainable resource management and the gap between policy endorsement and policy implementation in tourism development, necessitating continuing education of all interest groups	Stakeholder consultation
Wight (1993; 1995)	Views ecotourism as having a spectrum of demanded and supplied products, considers constraints of ecotourism and indicates relationships among adventure, nature-based and cultural tourism	Ecotourism
Weiler and Richins (1995)	Presents a case study of Earthwatch participants, concluding that they are "extreme" ecotourists, wanting not only to be environmentally responsible, but to enhance the environment visit	"Extreme" ecotourists
Finucane and Dowling (1995)	Discusses survey of Western Australian ecotourism operators, concluding that ecotourism has the potential for sustainable, low impact tourism, but can also destroy the natural base on which it depends	Ecotourism operators
Weiler (1993)	Examines nature-based tour operators in Australia to determine the extent to which they promote themselves as environmentally friendly, their perceptions of their environmental friendliness and ways in which they can contribute to an environmentally friendly industry	Nature-based tour operators
Fennell and Smale (1992)	Examines the concept of ecotourism, presents case examples that exemplify special concerns for the natural resource base of host nations and discusses implications of ecotourism for host nations and ecotourists	Ecotourism
Buckley and Pannell (1990)	Discusses environmental impacts of tourism and recreation in national parks and conservation reserves, strategies to minimise associated environmental degradation and provision of incentives to encourage low-impact and discourage high-impact recreation	Protected area management
Henning (1993)	Discusses potential socio-economic benefits to rural populations and the national economy of nature-based tourism in tropical forests, arguing that ecotourism can help protect and preserve national parks and reserves	Protected area management
Hvenegaard (1994)	Applies an integrated conceptual framework to ecotourism that identifies main actors, relationships, possible progressions over time and a suitable mode of thinking	Modelling ecotourism
Russell (1994)	Discusses whether present legislation and protection codes do enough to protect New Zealand's natural heritage beauty and systems	Environmental protection
Ding and Pigram (1995)	Discusses how environmental auditing can assist in environmental management of tourism, by providing feedback about environmental performance, specific problem areas and corrective actions	Environmental auditing
Hall (1993)	Examines implications of ecotourism for the sub-Antarctic islands of Australia and New Zealand, outlines the nature of sub-Antarctic tourism, its impacts and management, and discusses implications of sub-Antarctic ecotourism for notions of sustainable tourism	Sustainable Antarctic tourism
Smith (1993)	Discusses visitor guidelines of ship tour operators made available to all visitors travelling with them to Antartica to protect and preserve the continent	Sustainable Antarctic tourism
Stettner (1993)	Defines concepts of sustainable development, growth, community, commodity and carrying capacity and discusses ethics, environment and economics as criteria for sustainable tourism development in mountain resorts	Sustainable mountain tourism
Singh (1991)	Discusses opportunities and challenges of mountain tourism, noting that policy considerations warrant economically productive, socially responsible and ecologically sound development strategies	Sustainable mountain tourism
McIntyre and Boag (1995)	Provides insights into the effects of high user density on a variety of crowding variables within Uluru National Park, Australia	User density
Markwell (1995)	Explores ways in which attractions are used by ecotourists and non-ecotourists, and tensions between the ecotourist's demands for authentic experiences and resource management imperatives of the natural area management authorities	Ecotourists vs. non-ecotourists

Nerilee Hing and
Kay Dimmock
*Contemporary tourism issues
in Asia Pacific journals 1989-
1996: a thematic perspective*

However, this enjoyment may not be free from environmental impacts. In their study of ecotourism operators in Western Australia, Finucane and Dowling (1995) identified some of these impacts as damage to vegetation, disturbance of wildlife, soil erosion and compaction, water pollution and noise. They concluded that although ecotourism has potential for sustainable, low impact tourism, it can also destroy the natural base on which it depends. They called for a code of practice to guide future ecotourism developers and operators. Similarly, Weiler (1993) studied nature-based tour operators in Australia to determine the extent to which they promoted themselves as environmentally friendly, their perceptions of themselves as environmentally friendly operators, and ways in which they can contribute to an environmentally friendly industry. She then developed a framework for analysing environmental friendliness in future research. Fennell and Smale (1992) also recognised the need to protect the resource base of a tourist destination while simultaneously providing the types of visitor experiences expected by ecotourists. They called for management strategies in host nations to facilitate economic benefits from ecotourism while conserving natural attributes.

Other articles have focused on potential conflict between conservation and recreation objectives of protected areas. In examining environmental impacts of tourism and recreation in national parks and conservation reserves, Buckley and Pannell (1990) contended that to minimize environmental degradation requires appropriate land use zoning, regulation and surveillance of access and activities, direct physical protection of particular areas, on and off site education, incentives for contemplative, naturalist and wilderness travel activities, and discouragement of high impact pursuits. Henning (1993) went further to argue that ecotourism can be a powerful force for protecting and promoting national parks and reserves, while increasing sustainable rural and national development. In the context of developing countries, he noted that the ecotourism attraction of tropical forests presents opportunities for their protection, in contrast to current deforestation and degradation patterns. He noted, however, that this requires cooperation by public and private sectors, as well as adequate funding, planning and training.

McCool (1994) also argued that tourism planning systems need a systematic and cohesive context to achieve the broadly stated philosophies of sustainability, environmental integrity and quality in recreational opportunities. He proposed a framework, the limits of acceptable change, which provides planners with ways of thinking about acceptable levels of visitor impacts and how to manage them. He argued that this is a superior approach to the carrying capacity model which suffers conceptual and practical weaknesses. An alternative approach has been proposed by Hvenegaard (1994), who developed a model of ecotourism that identifies the main actors, relationships involved, possible progressions over time and a suitable mode of thinking.

Other writers have called for a more regulated approach to environmental protection from tourism. For example, Russell (1994) questioned whether current legislation and protection codes are sufficient to protect New Zealand's natural heritage beauty. He examined possible systems to ensure New Zealand has a sustainable tourism industry. Ding and Pigram (1995) proposed environmental audits as an alternative control mechanism. They contended that while environmental impact assessment prior to approving new tourism developments is necessary, post-development auditing could also assist by providing feedback about overall environmental performance, specific problem areas and corrective actions.

Given that Antarctica is the world's last pristine environment, it is appropriate that some scholars have been concerned with its protection in the face of increasing human presence. For example, Hall (1993) noted that tourists now exceed the number of government personnel in the Australian and New Zealand sub-Antarctic islands. He outlined the nature of sub-Antarctic tourism, its impacts, management and implications for sustainable tourism. Smith (1993) also noted the stress placed on the region by increasing human visitation. She described visitor guidelines to protect and preserve the environment made available by US cruise operators to all passengers travelling with them to the Antarctic.

Fragile mountain landscapes have also attracted research interest in sustainability. Stettner (1993) identified ethical differences between environmental and business interests towards developing mountain resorts. He discussed the role of ethics, environment and economics in achieving sustainable development. Singh (1991) noted that, while examples of sustainable tourism development in mountain regions are rare, the mountain environment provides both opportunities and challenges for wholesome tourism development. He advocated research-based, medium sized, integrated and controlled tourism involving local participation as the only hope of benign tourism which enriches both hosts and guests.

Growth in ecotourism also poses potential conflicts between ecotourists and other tourists. McIntyre and Boag (1995) examined the relationship between visitor density and

Nerilee Hing and
Kay Dimmock
*Contemporary tourism issues
in Asia Pacific journals 1989-
1996: a thematic perspective*

perceptions of crowding at Uluru National Park and the effect such perceptions had on visitor satisfaction. They highlighted growing concern about the effect that high visitor numbers may have on quality of the tourism experience. Similarly, Markwell (1995) explored different ways in which attractions may be used by ecotourists and non-ecotourists and tensions between the former's demands for authentic experiences and the resource management imperatives of the natural area management authorities. He drew on examples from East Malaysia to illustrate his arguments.

Theme 5: Social, economic and cultural impacts of tourism

Mings and Chulikpongse (1994) have noted tourism's role as an agent of change, bringing myriad impacts on regional economic conditions, social institutions and environmental quality. While articles reviewed in the preceding section reflect concern with environmental impacts of tourism, the articles reviewed here emphasise ongoing interest in economic and social consequences of tourism (Table V).

At a general level, Preister (1989) reviewed research on effects of tourism development, and proposed a modified dependency theory to account for many observed impacts. At the national level, Lee (1996) favoured the use of an input-output model to study economic effects of the tourism industry in South Korea. He concluded that tourism performed better than most industries in generating employment and tax revenues and performed moderately well in distributing income among household income classes. Pearce (1990) examined tourism development in New Zealand, noting that increasing visitor arrivals and a changing market mix have meant the economic impacts of tourism have not been uniformly spread throughout the country. However, while international tourism has concentrated growth in major metropolitan gateways and resort areas, domestic tourism has had some redistributive effect, with metropolitan centres being prime generators of domestic travel.

Altman's (1996) interest in economic impacts of tourism has been at a community level, specifically the Torres Strait Islander community of Seisia where nearly 15,000 tourists per annum visit an area inhabited by only 100 people. He assessed the current economic impact of tourism on the community and examined some wider economic development and policy issues to evaluate the potential of tourism as the leading sector of economic development for Seisia.

Other articles in the review period have focused on particular types of economic impacts, rather than a holistic approach. For example, Cukier-Snow and Wall (1994) examined tourism employment growth in Bali, noting its association with increasing imbalances in regional development, migration to southern resorts, and increased employment of women. With tourism employment set to exceed traditional agricultural employment, significant challenges are evident for maintaining a vibrant culture and landscape historically rooted in agriculture. The impact of tourism on the traditional economic base of local residents has also been examined by Sindiga in Kenya (1995). With much of Kenya's tourism being wildlife based, about 8 percent of the country has been set aside for wildlife protection. However, this has denied access to invaluable herding and agricultural resources by local communities, who also suffer destruction of life and property from wildlife. While revenue sharing schemes have been initiated, questions have been raised whether local governments, communities or individual landowners should be compensated.

A different economic focus is taken by Din (1992) who, in a case study of the Penang Langkawi region of Malaysia, examined whether there is a definitive relationship between tourism and local entrepreneurship. He argued that, while most introductory tourism texts devote a small section to this issue, there are very few specific works which address this relationship.

Two studies have examined the economic impacts of special events. McCann and Thompson (1992) conducted a cost-benefit analysis of the first State Masters Games in Albany, Western Australia, while Jeong *et al.* (1990) surveyed Korean tourism professionals, academics and media editors to assess the expected impacts of the 1988 Seoul Olympic Games. Primary expectations for hosting the Olympics were increased international awareness of Korea as a tourist destination, modification of Korea's image, and strengthening of Korean cultural values.

Other articles have examined cultural impacts of tourism. Teye (1991) argued that tourism can contribute to greater understanding between North and South Africa through developing genuine cultural tourism which promotes host-guest experiences, rather than superficial encounters. Similarly, Ahmed *et al.* (1994) described ethical problems within the tourism industry in developing countries and proposed that interaction problems between ethnocentric tourists and resentful hosts could be alleviated by introducing people-to-people programmes to reduce misunderstanding.

"Ethnic tourism" has been coined to describe authentic, traditional culture as a tourist attraction (Sofield, 1991). Singh (1989) pointed

Nerilee Hing and
Kay Dimmock
*Contemporary tourism issues
in Asia Pacific journals 1989-
1996: a thematic perspective*

Table V
Social, economic and cultural impacts of tourism

Authors	Focus	Sub-theme
Mings and Chlikpongse (1994)	Provides insights into tourism as an agent of local and regional change, with particular focus on southern Thailand	Regional impacts
Preister (1989)	Evaluates tourism development effects, suggests a modified dependency theory and outlines a philosophy of management consistent with both theory and experience	Dependency theory
Lee (1996)	Estimates the economic effects of the tourism industry in South Korea by using the input-output model	National economic impacts
Pearce (1990)	Focuses on regional implications to changing market mix of visitors to New Zealand in the context of recent reorganization of tourism within restructuring of the New Zealand economy	Regional economic impacts
Altman (1996)	Assesses economic impact of tourism on the Seisia (Torres Strait Islander) community and examines a range of wider economic development and policy issues	Community economic impacts
Cuckier-Snow and Wall (1994)	Examines tourism employment in Bali, associated with growing imbalances in regional development, migration to southern resorts, increased female employment and challenges to local culture and landscapes	Employment impacts
Sindiga (1995)	Examines government revenue-sharing policies for rural people who support wildlife conservation in national parks using the examples from Kenya	Regional economic impacts
Din (1992)	Uses a case study of Penang Langkawi region of Malaysia to establish whether there is a definitive relationship between tourism and entrepreneurship	Tourism and entrepreneurship
McCann and Thompson (1992)	Presents benefit-cost analysis of the first State Masters Games in Western Australia and describes procedures for undertaking similar analyses of other sporting events	Impacts of special events
Jeong, Jafari and Gartner (1990)	Presents a survey of Korean tourism professionals, members of the acedemic community and mass media editors to assess impacts of the 1988 Seoul Olympics	Impacts of special events
Teye (1991)	Discusses obstacles and potential for developing the kind of tourism which could foster greater understanding between north and south cultures in Africa	Cultural impacts
Ahmed, Krohn and Heller (1994)	Describes ethical problems of tourism in third world countries and offers recommendations to improve host-guest relations	Ethical issues
Sofield (1991)	Examines case from Vanuatu to draw out general principles of ethnic tourism and to define a model organization for sustainable ethnic tourism in the South Pacific	Ethnic tourism
Singh (1989)	Comments on contributions made by the Nawab Wazirs to Lucknow's cultural milieu, a precious tourist product which needs to be conserved, protected and preserved against eroding forces of modernization	Cultural impacts
Jain (1990)	Presents findings of a survey on the socio-economics impacts on the local people of the tourist attraction attraction of the Khajuraho temples in India	Socio-economic impacts
Altman and Finlayson (1993)	Reviews research on the impacts of tourism on Aboriginal communities and discusses policy alternatives to achieve an ecologically sustainable tourism industry for Aboriginal communities	Ethnic tourism
Swain (1989)	Discusses ethnic tourism in Yunnan and uses a model of indigenous tourism to promote ethnic group maintenance through indigenous control of resources	Ethnic tourism
Crotts (1996)	Uses hot spot theory and routine activity theory, to explore how communities expose tourists to risks of crime and what can be done about it	Tourism and crime
Kelly (1993)	Examines annual crime statistics in Queensland, Australia to ascertain whether popular tourist destinations differ from the state average in frequency and types of offences	Tourism and crime
Smith (1990)	Examines social and environmental impacts of "drifter" tourism to places such as Ceylon, Pattaya, Mombasa and Borocay	Social impacts
Long (1989)	Provides a case study of a social impact mitigation programme, with a community survey finding the response to be mixed, but largely negative	Social impact mitigation

Nerilee Hing and
Kay Dimmock
*Contemporary tourism issues
in Asia Pacific journals 1989-
1996: a thematic perspective*

out that cultural aspects of host regions act as tourist attractors, but are simultaneously vulnerable to acculturation. She commented on contributions made by the Nawab Wazirs to Lucknow's culture, a precious tourism product that needs protection and preservation among eroding forces of modernisation. Similarly, Sofield (1991) presented a case study from Vanuatu, to identify general principles of ethnic tourism and define a model organization for ethnic tourism in the South Pacific. He commented that, while much attention has been given to environmentally sustainable tourism, little has been devoted to sustaining traditional cultures which can be just as fragile as the physical environment. However, a case study by Jain (1990) of the impacts of tourism on the Khajuraho temples in India provides an example of how tourism can bring economic relief and prosperity to local populations, with minimal socio-cultural costs.

Altman and Finlayson (1993) examined the impacts of tourism on Australian aboriginal communities. They outlined characteristics of an ecologically sustainable tourism industry and noted that interest in aboriginal involvement in tourism has increased with a national tourism strategy that makes specific reference to indigenous Australians. Swain (1989) also advocated indigenous involvement in tourism, focusing on Yunnan province in China. She used a model of indigenous tourism to explore articulation of state political economy, tourism capitalism and local ethnic group economy as ways of promoting maintenance of ethnic groups and indigenous control of resources. She noted that, worldwide, ethnic minorities involved in tourism face a paradoxical push for change from tourist trade based on expectations that they will stay quaintly "ethnic".

Another social impact of tourism which continues to attract research attention is crime. Crotts (1996) noted that there are few tourist destinations immune to this problem. He used hot spot and routine activity theory to explore how communities expose tourists to risks of being criminally victimised. By placing the location and incidence of such crimes into a theoretical framework, Crotts provided insights into how communities can understand and manage their particular crime-related problems. Kelly (1993) examined the incidence of crime in Cairns and the Gold Coast, Australia, to compare their crime rates to the state average. He concluded that most criminal offences are overrepresented in these two areas, but that the predominant types of offences differ between the two destinations.

He proposed explanations for these differences and strategies for crime reduction.

More holistic assessments of the social impacts of tourism have been made. For example, Smith (1990) examined the "socially disruptive trail" left by "drifter" tourists, beginning with overland travels to Nepal by the 1960s drug cult "hippies". She noted that during the 1980s, a more affluent itinerant young population from industrialised countries moved from one tropical beach to the next, leaving a wake of social problems such as prostitution, alcoholism, juvenile crime and narcotics. Environmental impacts also followed. Long's (1989) interest in the social impacts of tourism were directed more at the success of social mitigation programmes, designed to alleviate negative effects. She presented a case study of a social impact mitigation programme in a desert beach destination in Mexico.

Conclusion

While diverse in their focus, it is possible to draw some general conclusions from the articles reviewed here.

- Better understanding of the motivations and behaviour of particular market segments, and of very specialized and/or emerging market segments, is gaining increased importance for tourism operators (theme 1).
- Changes in the world political map and increased affluence and mobility of residents in some developing countries will continue to change patterns of tourism flows, with accompanying implications for tourism destinations and operators (theme 2).
- Development of tourist destinations and their associated facilities and services are increasingly requiring planned strategies for success, especially in developing countries where particular opportunities and challenges are apparent in safeguarding the quality of life of resident populations while enjoying the economic benefits of tourism (theme 3).
- Demands for more sustainable forms of tourism have helped to stimulate the development of ecotourism and nature-based travel. However, even these forms of tourism are not free from environmental impacts and the management of such impacts will remain a major challenge for the future (theme 4).
- While the economic and social impacts of tourism have attracted substantial research interest in the past, there is increasing concern for the cultural consequences of tourism and ways to promote greater indigenous participation in, and control of, tourism resources (theme 5).

Nerilee Hing and
Kay Dimmock
*Contemporary tourism issues
in Asia Pacific journals 1989-
1996: a thematic perspective*

References

Abu-Febiri, F. (1994), "Developing a viable tourist industry in Ghana", *Tourism Recreation Research*, Vol. 19 No. 1, pp. 5-11.

Ahmed, Z.U., Krohn, F.B. and Heller, V.L. (1994), "International tourism ethics as a way to world understanding", *Journal of Tourism Studies*, Vol. 5 No. 2, pp. 36-44.

Alabi, S. (1994), "Nigerian tradition, culture and environment: opportunities for heritage tourism development", *Tourism Recreation Research*, Vol. 19 No. 2, pp. 69-77.

Al Moosa, A.R. (1989), "Recreation: the Kuwait model", *Tourism Recreation Research*, Vol. 14 No. 2, pp. 49-56.

Altman, J. and Finlayson, J. (1993), "Aborigines, tourism and sustainable development", *Journal of Tourism Studies*, Vol. 4 No. 1, pp. 38-50.

Altman, J.C. (1996), "Coping with locational advantage: tourism and economic development at Seisia community, Cape York Peninsula", *Journal of Tourism Studies*, Vol. 7 No. 1, pp. 58-71.

Barham, N. (1989), "Winter recreation in the Jordan Rift Valley", *Tourism Recreation Research*, Vol. 14 No. 2, pp. 33-9.

Barr, T. (1990), "From quirky islanders to entrepreneurial magnates: the transition of the Whitsundays", *Journal of Tourism Studies*, Vol. 1 No. 2, pp. 26-32.

Berriane, M. (1989), "Holiday migrations of Moroccan nationals", *Tourism Recreation Research*, Vol. 14 No. 2, pp. 23-6.

Bhattacharya, B. (1992), "Urban tourism in the Himalayas in the context of Darjeeling and Sikkim", *Tourism Recreation Research*, Vol. 17 No. 2, pp. 79-83.

Black, N.L. (1990), "A model and methodology to assess changes to heritage buildings", *Journal of Tourism Studies*, Vol. 1 No. 1, pp. 15-23.

Bowen, R.L., Cox, L.J. and Fox, M. (1991), "The interface between tourism and agriculture", *Journal of Tourism Studies*, Vol. 2 No. 2, pp. 43-54.

Braunlich, C.G. and Nadkarni, N. (1995), "The importance of the VFR market to the hotel industry", *Journal of Tourism Studies*, Vol. 6 No. 1, pp. 38-47.

Buckley, R. and Pannell, J. (1990), "Environmental impacts of tourism and recreation in national parks and conservation reserves", *Journal of Tourism Studies*, Vol. 1 No. 1, pp. 24-32.

Butler, R.W. and Mao, B. (1996), "Conceptual and theoretical implications of tourism between partitioned states", *Asia Pacific Journal of Tourism Research*, Vol. 1 No. 1, pp. 25-34.

Carlsen, J. (1995), "Gathering information: meetings and conventions sector research in Australia", *Journal of Tourism Studies*, Vol. 6 No. 2, pp. 21-9.

Cartier, C.L. (1996), "Conserving the built environment and generating heritage tourism in Peninsular Malaysia", *Tourism Recreation Research*, Vol. 21 No. 1, pp. 45-53.

Chon, K. and Oppermann, M. (1996), "Tourism development and planning in Philippines", *Tourism Recreation Research*, Vol. 21 No. 1, pp. 35-43.

Cox, L.J., and Fox, M (1991), "Agriculturally based leisure attractions", *Journal of Tourism Studies*, Vol. 2 No. 2, pp. 18-27.

Crompton, J.L. (1996), "Priorities in tourists' decision making research in the 1990s and beyond: from a North American perspective", *Asia Pacific Journal of Tourism Research*, Vol. 1 No. 1, pp. 18-24.

Crotts, J.C. (1996), "Theoretical perspectives on tourist criminal victimisation", *Journal of Tourism Studies*, Vol. 7 No. 1, pp. 2-9.

Crouch, G.I. (1993), "Currency exchange rates and the demand for international tourism", *Journal of Tourism Studies*, Vol. 4 No. 2, pp. 45-53.

Cukier-Snow, J. and Wall, G. (1994), "Tourism employment in Bali, Indonesia", *Tourism Recreation Research*, Vol. 19 No. 1, pp. 32-40.

Dieke, P.U.C. (1993), "Cross-national comparison of tourism development: lessons from Kenya and The Gambia", *Journal of Tourism Studies*, Vol. 4 No. 1, pp. 2-18.

Din, K.H. (1992), "The 'involvement stage' in the evolution of a tourist destination", *Tourism Recreation Research*, Vol. 17 No. 1, pp. 10-20.

Ding, P. and Pigram, J. (1995), "Environmental audits: an emerging concept in sustainable tourism development", *Journal of Tourism Studies*, Vol. 6 No. 2, pp. 2-10.

Dredge, D. and Moore, S. (1992), "A methodology for the integration of tourism in town planning", *Journal of Tourism Studies*, Vol. 3 No. 1, pp. 8-21.

Fennell, D.A. and Smale, B.J.A. (1992), "Ecotourism and natural resource protection: implications of an alternative form of tourism for host nations", *Tourism Recreation Research*, Vol. 17 No. 2, pp. 21-32.

Fielding, K., Pearce, P.L. and Hughes, K. (1992), "Climbing Ayers Rock: relating visitor motivation, time perception and enjoyment", *Journal of Tourism Studies*, Vol. 3 No. 2, pp. 49-57.

Finucane, S.J. and Dowling, R.K. (1995), "The perceptions of ecotourism operators in Western Australia", *Tourism Recreation Research*, Vol. 20 No. 1, pp. 14-21.

Hall, C.M. (1993), "Ecotourism in the Australian and New Zealand sub-Antarctic islands", *Tourism Recreation Research*, Vol. 18 No. 2, pp. 13-22.

Hall, C.M. (1994a), "Tourism in Pacific Island microstates: a case study of Vanuatu", *Tourism Recreation Research*, Vol. 19 No. 1, pp. 59-63.

Hall, C.M. (1994b), "Is tourism still the plantation economy of the South Pacific: the case of Fiji", *Tourism Recreation Research*, Vol. 19 No. 1, pp. 41-8.

Haywood, K.M. (1992), "Identifying and responding to challenges posed by urban tourism", *Tourism Recreation Research*, Vol. 17 No. 2, pp. 9-23.

Heath, R. (1990), "The relationship between domestic and international tourism in Zimbabwe: a case study of the Victoria Falls and Hwange National Parks and Lake Kariba", *Tourism Recreation Research*, Vol. 15 No. 1, pp. 7-17.

Nerilee Hing and
Kay Dimmock
*Contemporary tourism issues
in Asia Pacific journals 1989-
1996: a thematic perspective*

Helleiner, F.M. (1990), "Domestic and international tourism in third world nations", *Tourism Recreation Research*, Vol. 15 No. 1,pp. 18-25.

Henning, D. (1993), "Nature-based tourism can help conserve tropical forests", T*ourism Recreation Research*, Vol. 18 No. 2, pp. 45-50.

Hoehfeld, V.V. (1989), "Beach holidays – an innovation in Turkish tourism", *Tourism Recreation Research*, Vol. 14 No. 2, pp. 17-21.

Hsieh, S., O'Leary, J.T., Morrison, A.M. and Chang, P.S. (1993), "Modelling the travel mode choice of Australian outbound travellers", *Journal of Tourism Studies*, Vol. 4 No. 1 pp. 51-61.

Hvenegaard, G.T. (1994), "Ecotourism: a status report and conceptual framework", *Journal of Tourism Studies*, Vol. 5 No. 2, pp. 24-36.

Jackson, R.T. (1990), "VFR tourism: is it underestimated?", *Journal of Tourism Studies*, Vol. 1 No. 2, pp. 10-17.

Jain, D.K. (1990), "Impact of tourism on Khajuraho, India: a preliminary survey", *Tourism Recreation Research*, Vol. 15 No. 1, pp. 43-4.

Jeong, G.H., Jafari, J. and Gartner, W.C. (1990), "Expectations of the 1988 Seoul Olympics: a Korean perspective", *Tourism Recreation Research*, Vol. 15 No. 1, pp. 26-33.

Kelly, I. (1993), "Tourist destination crime rates: an examination of Cairns and the Gold Coast, Australia", *Journal of Tourism Studies*, Vol. 4 No. 2, pp. 2-11.

Kim, Y.J. Pearce, P.L. Morrison, A.M. and O'Leary, J.T. (1996), "Mature vs. youth travellers: the Korean market", *Asia Pacific Journal of Tourism Research*, Vol. 1 No. 1, pp. 102-12.

Kopp, H. (1989), "Tourism and recreation in Northern Yemen", *Tourism Recreation Research*, Vol. 14 No. 2, pp. 11-15.

Lee, C. (1996), "Input-output analysis and income distribution patterns of the tourism industry in South Korea", *Asia Pacific Journal of Tourism Research*, Vol. 1 No. 1, pp. 35-49.

Leiper, N. (1995), *Tourism Management*, TAFE Publications, Melbourne.

Long, P.T. and Nuckolls, J.S (1994), "Organising resources for rural tourism development: the importance of leadership, planning and technical assistance", *Tourism Recreation Research*, Vol. 19 No. 2, pp. 19-34.

Long, V.H. (1989), "Social mitigation of tourism development impacts: Bahias De Huatulco, Oaxaca, Mexico", *Tourism Recreation Research*, Vol. 14 No. 1, pp. 5-14.

McCann, C. and Thompson, G. (1992), "An economic analysis of the first Western Australian State Masters Games", *Journal of Tourism Studies*, Vol. 3 No. 1, pp. 28-34.

McCool, S.F. (1994), "Planning for sustainable nature dependent tourism development; limits of acceptable change system", *Tourism Recreation Research*, Vol. 19 No. 2, pp. 51-5.

McGehee, N.G., Loker-Murphy, L. and Uysal, M. (1996), "The Australian international pleasure travel market: motivations from a gendered perspective", *Journal of Tourism Studies*, Vol. 7 No. 1, pp. 45-57.

McIntyre, N. and Boag, A. (1995), "The measurement of crowing in nature-based tourism

venues: Uluru National Park", *Tourism Recreation Research*, Vol. 20 No. 1, pp. 37-42.

Markwell, K.W. (1995), "Ecotourist attraction systems: case studies from East Malaysia", *Tourism Recreation Research*, Vol. 20 No. 1, pp. 43-50.

Meis, S., Joyal, S. and Trites, A. (1995), "The US repeat and VFR visitor to Canada", *Journal of Tourism Studies*, Vol. 6 No. 1, pp. 27-37.

Mings, R.C. and Chulikpongse, S. (1994), "Tourism in far southern Thailand: a geographical perspective", *Tourism Recreation Research*, Vol. 19 No. 1, pp. 25-31.

Morley, C.L. (1990), "What is tourism?", *Journal of Tourism Studies*, Vol. 1 No. 1, pp. 3-8.

Morley, C.L. (1993), "Forecasting tourism demand using extrapolative time series methods", *Journal of Tourism Studies*, Vol. 4 No. 1, pp. 19-25.

Morrison, A.M., Hsieh, S. and O'Leary, J.T. (1994), "Segmenting the Australian domestic travel market by holiday activity participation", *Journal of Tourism Studies*, Vol. 5 No. 1, pp. 39-56.

Morrison, A.M., Hsieh, S. and O'Leary, J.T. (1995), "Segmenting the visiting friends and relatives market by holiday activity participation", *Journal of Tourism Studies*, Vol. 6 No. 1, pp. 48-62.

Moscardo, G. (1992), "The tourist-resident distinction: implications for the management of museums and other interpretive settings", *Journal of Tourism Studies*, Vol. 3 No. 2, pp. 2-18.

Murray, M. and Sproats, J. (1990), "The disabled traveller: tourism and disability in Australia", *Journal of Tourism Studies*, Vol. 1 No. 1, pp. 9-14.

Oppermann, M. (1992a), "Travel dispersal index", *Journal of Tourism Studies*, Vol. 3 No. 1, pp. 44-9.

Oppermann, M. (1992b), "Spatial structure of tourism in peninsular Malaysia: a preliminary study", *Tourism Recreation Research*, Vol. 17 No. 1, pp. 54-9.

Oppermann, M. (1996), "Visitation of tourism attractions and tourist expenditure patterns – repeat versus first-time visitors", *Asia Pacific Journal of Tourism Research*, Vol. 1, Issue 1, pp. 61-8.

Oppermann, M., Din, K.H. and Amri, S.Z. (1996), "Urban hotel location and evolution in a developing country: the case of Kuala Lumpur Malaysia", *Tourism Recreation Research*, Vol. 21 No. 1, pp. 55-63.

Pearce, D.G. (1990), "Tourism, the regions and restructuring in New Zealand", *Journal of Tourism Studies*, Vol. 1 No. 2, pp. 33-42.

Pearce, P.L. (1996), "Recent research in tourist behaviour", *Asia Pacific Journal of Tourism Research*, Vol. 1, Issue. 1, pp. 7-17.

Pigram, J.J. (1990), "Sustainable tourism – policy considerations", *Journal of Tourism Studies*, Vol. 1 No. 2, pp. 2-9.

Preister, K. (1989), "The theory and management of tourism impacts", *Tourism Recreation Research*, Vol. 14 No. 1, pp. 15-22.

Ritter, W. (1989), "On deserts and beaches: recreational tourism in the Muslim world", *Tourism Recreation Research*, Vol. 14 No. 2, pp. 3-9.

Nerilee Hing and
Kay Dimmock
*Contemporary tourism issues
in Asia Pacific journals 1989-
1996: a thematic perspective*

Russell, G. (1994), "On the New Zealand natural heritage trail", *Tourism Recreation Research*, Vol. 19 No. 2, pp. 65-8.

Schliephake, K. (1989), "Saudi-Arabians on the Move", *Tourism Recreation Research*, Vol. 14 No. 2, pp. 57-63.

Seaton, A.V. and Tagg, S. (1995), "Disaggregating friends and relatives in VFR tourism research: the Northern Ireland evidence 1991-1993", *Journal of Tourism Studies*, Vol. 6 No. 1, pp. 6-18.

Sindiga, I. (1995), "Wildlife-based tourism in Kenya: land use conflicts and government compensation policies over protected areas", *Journal of Tourism Studies*, Vol. 6 No. 2, pp. 45-55.

Singh, S. (1989), "Lucknow: a study in cultural expressions of Nawabs of Avadh", *Tourism Recreation Research*, Vol. 14 No. 2, pp. 75-80.

Singh, S. (1992), "Urban development and tourism: case of Lucknow, India", *Tourism Recreation Research*, Vol. 17 No. 2, pp. 71-8.

Singh, T.V. (1991). "The development of tourism in the mountain environment", *Tourism Recreation Research*, Vol. 26 No. 2, pp. 3-12.

Smith, V.L. (1990), "Geographical implications of 'drifter' tourism Borocay, Philippines", *Tourism Recreation Research*, Vol. 15 No. 1, pp. 34-42.

Smith, V.L. (1993), "Safeguarding the Antarctic environment from tourism", *Tourism Recreation Research*, Vol. 18 No. 2, pp. 51-4.

Sofield, T.H.B. (1991), "Sustainable ethnic tourism in the South Pacific: some principles", *Journal of Tourism Studies*, Vol. 2 No. 1, pp. 56-72.

Standl, H. (1989), "Recent development of tourism in Egypt", *Tourism Recreation Research*, Vol. 14 No. 2, pp. 27-31.

Stettner, A.C. (1993), "Commodity or community? Sustainable development in mountain resorts", *Tourism Recreation Research*, Vol. 18 No. 1, pp. 3-10.

Swain, M.B. (1989), "Developing ethnic tourism in Yunnan, China: Shilin Sani", *Tourism Recreation Research*, Vol. 14 No. 1, pp. 33-40.

Teye, V.B. (1991), "Bridging the north-south divide through tourism", *Tourism Recreation Research*, Vol. 16 No. 2, pp. 13-22.

Timothy, D.J. and Wall, G. (1995), "Tourist accommodation in an Asian historic city", *Journal of Tourism Studies*, Vol. 6 No. 2, pp. 63-73.

Weiler, B. (1993), "Nature-based tour operators: are they environmentally friendly or are they faking it?", *Tourism Recreation Research*, Vol. 18 No. 1, pp. 55-60.

Weiler, B. and Kalinowski, K.M. (1990), "Participants of educational travel: a Canadian case study", *Journal of Tourism Studies*, Vol. 1 No. 2, pp. 43-50.

Weiler, B. and Richins, H. (1995), "Extreme, extravagant and elite: a profile of ecotourists on Earthwatch expeditions", *Tourism Recreation Research*, Vol. 20 No. 1, pp. 29-36.

Wight, P.A. (1993), "Sustainable ecotourism: balancing economic and social goals within an ethical framework", *Journal of Tourism Studies*, Vol. 4 No. 2, pp. 54-66.

Wight, P.A. (1995), "Sustainable ecotourism: balancing economic, environmental and social goals within an ethical framework", *Tourism Recreation Research*, Vol. 20 No. 1, pp. 5-13.

Williams, M.T. (1993), "An expansion of the tourist site cycle model: the case of Minorca (Spain)", *Journal of Tourism Studies*, Vol. 4 No. 2, pp. 24-32.

Wilson, K. and Wang, W. (1996), "Countertrade and tourism development", *Journal of Tourism Studies*, Vol. 7 No. 1, pp. 31-44.

Yuan, T., Fridgen, J.D., Hsieh, S. and O'Leary, J.T. (1995), "Visiting friends and relatives travel market: the Dutch case", *Journal of Tourism Studies*, Vol. 6 No. 1, pp. 19-26.

Zeppel, H. and Hall, C.M. (1991), "Selling art and history: cultural heritage and tourism", *Journal of Tourism Studies*, Vol. 1 No. 1, pp. 29-45.

Zhang, Y. (1996), "Tourism resource development in China: an overview of the growth, prospects and problems", *Tourism Recreation Research*, Vol. 21 No. 1, pp. 19-27.

Hotel market trends in the UK

Trevor Ward
Joint Managing Director, BDO Hospitality Consulting, UK

Assesses changes occurring in the UK hotel market during 1997 and relates these to current and predicted future developments. Identifies the key issues affecting supply and demand, competitive success and likely impacts and influences on the UK market during 1998.

Many commentators and operators believe that history conclusively demonstrates the existence of an economic cycle in the UK hotel industry. Few involved in the profession believe that current growth rates are sustainable, and the question being asked is when will growth inevitably plateau, and when will the subsequent downturn in fortunes take place?

We all remember the disastrous years for the economy in the early 1980s and the late 1980s/early 1990s, and their affect on the hotel industry. During the first quarter of 1992, for example, average occupancy levels in England's hotels slumped to their lowest rate (37 per cent) since 1980, and were even lower than for the same quarter in 1991 (44 per cent) when the Gulf War was being waged. What these changes in the industry's fortunes had in common was that they, like previous hotel slumps, followed economic recessions. In each case there had been a brief delay between the onset of recession and a downturn in hotel demand; and equally, between recovery in the economy and in hotels.

This, of course, only confirms what operators already know. So, if the health of the hotel markets is allied to that of the economy, what is the current outlook?

Earlier this year, prior to the general election, *Barclays Economic Review* suggested that the overall economy was generally in good shape. GDP was forecast to continue growing, accompanied by the resulting good news for both unemployment and public sector borrowing requirements (PSBR). According to the *Sunday Times* Databank and latest government figures, following four-and-a-half months of Labour Government, GDP is up 3.4 per cent on last year; unemployment is down to just under 1.5 million (the lowest figure for 17 years); and the base rate has been fixed at 7 per cent with the Bank of England not envisaging any rate rise in the immediate future. The Treasury's latest compilation of independent forecasts, at the time of writing, suggest that economic growth will slow from 3.4 per cent to 2.5 per cent, leading to more sustainable growth and greater stability in the economy.

In addition, since New Labour came to power, there have been four 0.25 per cent interest rate rises, which have helped slow down an overheating economy and put it back on track. It is now expected that the underlying rate of inflation will reach the Government's target of 2.5 per cent soon. Given these factors, the overall prospects for the economy are still looking good, which will favour the hotel trade.

The only significant blip for the hotel industry this summer has been the strength of sterling, which may in the long-term affect inbound tourism by presenting the UK as an expensive destination. Over the past 12 months sterling has appreciated significantly against continental currencies. For example, as of September 1997, the exchange rates in the *Financial Times* for the deutschmark against sterling, and the French franc against sterling were 15 to 16 per cent up on the rates recorded in the *Financial Times* in October 1996. However, despite this factor, latest Government figures on overseas visitors are encouraging, showing that spending by overseas visitors to the UK increased by 2 per cent to £5.3b in the first six months of 1997. The good news, for the industry has been that the number of overseas visitors remained unchanged for that period at 11.5 million; and the number of US visitors rose by 15 per cent to 1.9 million. This is probably a reflection of the fact that the pound has been weaker against the US dollar.

So, all things considered, is the hotel industry guaranteed continued growth? All other things being equal, I believe the answer is yes. In fact, the preparations for the millennium celebrations, with their attendant spend on regeneration and development, should provide a handy boost to domestic trade and well as the hotel market.

However, it must be remembered that trading conditions are not affected solely by domestic economic movement. We know this to be true anecdotally and have witnessed it happening so many times before. It only takes an unexpected realignment of interest rate policy by the Bundesbank or a sharp loss of confidence in the Japanese stock market to have an immediate impact on world economies and, more crucially, in consumer confidence. The effects may often be contained and have only transitory impact.

However, global economies have one thing in common these days – nervousness.

Alternatively, current political instability is rife in the Middle East and the impact of renewed international terrorism is sudden and can be devastating to tourism confidence. Over recent months civil unrest in Kenya, for example, has led to the closure of a number of hotels in some of the country's key tourism areas. On the domestic front, the impact of the 1986 Libyan crisis on our tourism industry is still fresh in our minds, as indeed are IRA atrocities. These provide constant reminders of what can happen.

However, one thing is for certain – 1996 proved to be yet another record-breaking year for the UK hotel industry. Our 1997 *UK Hotel Industry (UKHI) Report*, published in June, revealed that UK hotel profits had risen 13 per cent in 1996 and annual room occupancies had exceeded the previous highest figure for ten years – 69.6 per cent in 1995 – by rising to 72.6 per cent.

London led the boom with the capital's hotel profits rising 24 per cent in 1996, and annual room occupancies exceeding the 1995 figure of 81.9 per cent by climbing 2 per cent to 83.8 per cent. North of the border, Scotland recorded the UK's highest increase in annual room occupancy – up 4.4 per cent from 68.4 per cent in 1995 to 72.8 per cent in 1996.

Given that 1996 was undoubtedly a resounding success for the hotel industry, is the boom set to continue? We believe it is, provided that the current strength of the pound does not significantly affect the number of overseas visitors to Britain and the business market in general in the latter half of 1997.

The continued potential of the UK hotel market was underlined by the recent high prices paid for premium central London hotels – such as the £86 million acquisition by the Mandarin Oriental Group of the 185-bedroom Hyde Park Hotel from Granada; and the £81 million purchase by Millennium & Copthome of the 318-bedroom Britannia from Inter-Continental Hotels & Resorts. However, it is vital for developers and funders to be taking decisions now if we are to have the infrastructure in place to ensure London and the UK have a prominent position in celebrating the millennium.

In BDO's 1997 UKHI report, we expect that the UK and London annual room occupancy levels will rise to 73 and 84 per cent respectively in 1997, and remain static in 1998. In addition we envisage that the UK average daily room rate will rise from £55 in 1996 to £59 in 1997, and climb to £62 in 1998. We forecast that London will experience the biggest rise in average daily room rates, increasing by 10 per cent from £98 in 1996 to £108 in 1997,

and by a further 4.5 per cent to £113 in 1998. These rises will be partly due to the current lack of bed-space in the capital. Except in the depths of the recession, demand for rooms in London has traditionally exceeded supply. With their hotel rooms in effect fully booked, the capital's operators have been able to concentrate on getting a higher price for every room sold.

However, we believe that the rise in London's average room rates will slow to 4.5 per cent in 1998, due in part to a forecast 1,400 new rooms entering the capital's hotel market by that date.

There can be little doubt from this evidence that the UK hotel industry is currently thriving – with further growth forecast for 1997 and 1998. This is further underlined by findings from our Summer Confidence Survey, comparing the first six months of 1997 with the corresponding period in 1996. It revealed that optimism was still high – 85.3 per cent of the 100 UK hoteliers surveyed nationwide, were either "very optimistic" or "optimistic" about the future of the industry, compared with 83.1 per cent when measured in January.

The survey showed that achieved room rates were increasing in the light of sustained buoyant demand.

Four out of five hoteliers were achieving increased average room rates. Compared with January to June 1996, the largest percentage of the hoteliers surveyed (45.3 per cent) were ahead for the same period this year by between £3 and £5. Though the long-term effects of the current strength of sterling on the marketplace are difficult to predict, nearly 50 per cent of hoteliers surveyed expect to raise their tariffs during the next three to six months. Less than one in five had "no plans at present". Of those implementing an increase, the majority (54.8 per cent) will apply an increase of between 0 and 5 per cent.

However, though the hotel industry continues to boom, there is no room for complacency. As the Labour Party have themselves pointed out, tourism still runs at a net deficit to the balance of payments owing to the enormous flows of outbound tourists. As a result our share of the world tourism markets has fallen from its position of the early 1980s to only 5 per cent of the total now.

Thus there is plenty to aim for in growing our tourism base. Evidence shows that European Union (EU) membership has been significantly beneficial in this respect – both in terms of overnight visitor and daytripper potential. Equally important to the industry is the strength of the North American market. However, there are major sources of inbound tourism which are now assuming more importance in volume terms than the

North American market. These are the Middle East, the Far East and Australasia.

The UK today is acknowledged in many sources as one of the world's most fashionable, historic and scenic destinations. Through the medium of film and subsequent Oscar successes – such as *Braveheart* and *Sense and Sensibility* – much has been done to boost Britain's image abroad, and attract overseas visitors to these shores. Popular television drama series, such as Yorkshire Television's *Heartbeat* – set in the North York Moors National Park – have also proved a boon in drawing tourists to Britain, and have promoted domestic tourism. London is now viewed by many as the culinary and fashion capital of the world. Ironically, it has just been given one of its biggest ever promotional boosts through the worldwide coverage of one of the nation's saddest occasions – the funeral of Diana, Princess of Wales.

All these factors have a strong but unquantifiable positive effect on tourism. However, we must guard against complacency. There are some emerging destinations competing fiercely for their share of world demand. These include China and South Africa. As a result, the traditional destinations are having to invest hard to sustain their share.

Clearly, how we market ourselves abroad is crucial to maintaining and growing our fashionable image. Equally important is the domestic economic health of our main markets.

Finally, another crucial factor is the quality of our transport infrastructure. Quality improvements such as the Channel Tunnel, as well as additional terminals and runways at our airports can only boost our tourism potential. The decay and mismanagement now endemic in our road and rail transport systems will only do the reverse.

As an industry, therefore, we need much support and action from the Government, and will have to lobby hard to ensure we do not come second in the race for scarce government resources.

In my role as an industry advisor to the Department of Culture, Media and Sport, I have experienced a highly positive and supportive attitude to our industry from Tourism Minister Tom Clarke and his team. They fully recognise its importance and contribution to the national economy as a major growth industry; and are determined to improve standards throughout the profession, as well as understand its particular needs. New Labour is committed to the Social Chapter and the introduction of a minimum wage, which will affect the industry. As yet the Government will not be drawn on the actual minimum wage rate, but it will undoubtedly be set at a level that will not be threatening to any responsible employer.

Away from politics, one of the most notable industry trends in recent years has been the significant growth in the budget lodge sector. While supply growth has been minimal in other sectors of the hotel industry, this sector shows no sign of abating. For example, Whitbread has been committed throughout the year to opening a new lodge every ten days, and now claims, through "Travel Inn", to operate the largest chain of branded lodges in the UK. As far as other sectors of the hotel industry are concerned, much of the present supply growth is based on the trend to add extensions to existing properties. A lot has been said about the new technologies enabling low cost additions to hotels and it is likely that this method of expansion will be utilised by many operators while they still have the space potential.

The other trend in new rooms development is the conversion of buildings from other uses. This has become particularly prevalent in London owing to the lack of opportunity for new builds. However, there is some new building taking place, but it is limited. Examples include hotels in London's Islington, as well as in Liverpool, Belfast, and Cardiff Bay.

Having looked at some of the present trends, what are the lessons to be learned from the UK hotel industry's recent experiences?

In the early 1990s, as an industry, we paid the price for much unrealistic expansion in the late 1980s. The severe downturn in market demand caused a major realignment of practice and product. We are now enjoying the gain after the pain – with buoyant markets and full hotels. The operational mentality is now one of maximisation rather than survival. If we see the next downturn as inevitable, then the survivors will be those who consistently invest in and maintain a high quality product, and who:

- do not lose sight of the probability of unexpected events having a great impact; and
- who have realistic contingency plans in place against this happening.

Having looked at the dynamic of the market, we must also consider the other side of the equation, namely, what is shaping management trends in the industry today, and what other external opportunities and challenges exist?

"Branding" has become undoubtedly a core management practice. Having said that, it can be argued that many brand propositions in the UK market today are little more than attempts to:

- ensure some recognisable commonality in style and standard; and
- put across a clear corporate identity, while still permitting much variance in core product.

There is great pressure from US brand operators, anxious to gain a foothold in the UK market. They include: Marriott, Carlson, and Choice which are already here. In addition, Doubletree, HFS and Westin are all seeking UK and European representation. The extent of their ultimate penetration will be of great importance to the development of branding in the UK. If they begin to change the nature of consumer expectation, then domestic brands will be forced into change. You only have to witness the impressive impact that Marriott has already had in the UK.

Information technology (IT) is intrinsically bound up in the branding argument, as in many cases it is one of the main vehicles for delivering the brand proposition. IT is developing and changing all the time and the scope of its usage for hoteliers is mind-boggling, as in the case of "data warehousing". In the case of the Internet, for example, the future is highly promising. The prospect of direct consumer booking, cutting out third party agents, has to be a prize worth fighting for.

One of the major challenges faced by hoteliers today is what to do with catering? This debate has raged for some time with little agreement on the eventual outcome. However, the issue is live and many operators are dipping toes in the water, piloting branded or franchised operations at selected sites to test the feasibility of a wider roll-out. The industry is watching the outcome with more than passing interest. At BDO Hospitality Consulting we believe that the suggestion – being mooted by some members of the industry – that it could prove in some cases to be more beneficial to replace existing hotel restaurants with extra bedrooms, has no credence. The restaurant is an integral part of the total hotel product, which customers expect and in most cases need. If a hotel restaurant is operated and marketed correctly, there is no reason why it should not prove a major revenue generator and marketing tool for attracting guests.

There are, of course, some more mundane management challenges that face hoteliers. The rising costs of labour are not a new phenomenon, but the acute growing shortage of skilled labour is an issue that is being urgently addressed by many, through industry recruitment and training initiatives, and the use of continuing professional development (CPD). In addition, there is an increasingly pressing need to bridge the gap even more effectively between industry and education. In this respect, the Hotel & Catering International Management Association (HCIMA) has created "The Corpus of Management Excellence" – a benchmark to be launched early in 1998, which recognises the breadth of the hospitality industry and the differing ways of acquiring the necessary knowledge and skills.

Another challenge for managers today is to decide whether it is more profitable to outsource key service functions both centrally and operationally. Certainly, in my view, more companies need to climb aboard the central purchasing bandwagon – with the emergence of third parties now performing central purchasing services on behalf of clients.

As we have seen of late, the development of hotel portfolios has been severely constrained – with banks proving cautious in funding proposals. The latest problem to be faced by hoteliers will be the severe cost inflation now endemic to the building industry. With costs predicted to rise at 8-10 per cent per annum, this should presage a continued spate of merger and acquisition activity.

Finally, one of the newer challenges to face hotel managements is dealing with the City. A higher level of involvement is demanded by the City that many in the industry have not been exposed to before. There is a big learning curve for any proposing to take that route. However, there is a silver lining since the results of greater City involvement should be good for the industry as a whole. To be more open to public scrutiny should assist us in keeping abreast of the best and most modern management practice, and help us move away rapidly from some of our old fashioned and inwardly focused management thinking.

Returning to the start of this article, there is one major continuing issue. However we may view our industry, the City still sees us as being highly capital intensive, riddled with outmoded cost structures, and short-term in its prospects. We still face the challenge of demonstrating that profitability can be a longterm feature of our industry, through the lean times as well as the good ones.

If we can meet all these challenges successfully, then there is no real reason why we cannot fulfil the enormous potential predicted for this industry in the millennium.

Assessing information needs and external change

Richard Teare
Research Director (Europe), Worldwide Hospitatlity and Tourism Trends
John T. Bowen
Research Director (North America) Worldwide Hospitality and Tourism Trends

The managerial activity of learning about events and trends in the organization's environment is known as environmental scanning. This process differs from industry or competitor analysis in two main respects: it is broad in scope and future-directed. Assesses the extent to which information needs are currently met by scanning activities and profiles the "top 30" hospitality industry issues as reflected by UK-based and North American hospitality management journals. Concludes with a priority ranking of the "top 30" issues assigned by UK hotel general managers and summary comments from this group on the implications for organizational learning.

Introduction

The managerial activity of learning about events and trends in the organization's environment is known as environmental scanning. This process differs from industry or competitor analysis in two main respects; it is broad in scope and future-directed. Looking back, the 1980s was a decade of turbulence for hotel companies. Inflation, terrorism, recession, war, political upheaval, global airline restructuring and the continued advancement of technology are but a few of the major events influencing performance. While some of these affected firms operating in other sectors of the hospitality industry, hotel firm leaders might reasonably be expected to learn from the past and think ahead so as to ensure that their companies are better equipped to face similar events as and when they re-occur. The purpose of this article is to assess the extent to which information needs are currently met by scanning activities and second, to profile the "top 30" hospitality industry issues as reflected by the UK-based and North American hospitality management journals. The chapter concludes with a priority ranking of the "top 30" issues assigned by UK hotel general managers and summary comments from this group on the implications for organizational learning.

Does environmental scanning assist strategic planning?

Most authors agree that the main functions of environmental scanning are: to learn about events and trends in the external environment; to establish relationships between them; to make sense of the data and to extract the main implications for decision making and strategy development. In the hospitality industry, most hotel chains are aware of the need to relate environmental information to long-range plans, but so far, the majority seem more concerned with gathering sufficient information to make short-term decisions. In fact, to derive the main benefits from environmental scanning, the activity should be linked to the formal planning process. A study of hotel chains in Portugal (Costa *et al.*, 1996) sought to explore these interrelationships and address three questions:

1   How do planning and non-planning chains differ in their approach to strategy making?
2   What external factors do planning and non-planning chains regard as affecting their performance?
3   What type of scanning process is followed by planning and non-planning chains?

The findings reveal that the differences between "planners" and "non-planners" in their approach to strategy making are not significant. Both groups show concern for the long term but non-planners are generally less proactive in their efforts to understand the behaviour of competitors. This is especially evident in relation to anticipating competitor behaviour and developing long-term competitive advantage. The non-planning approach to strategy making appears to be more participative than the planning approach, although a written strategy seems to be easier to communicate both internally and externally. In terms of decision making, both groups reported their decisions as being frequent, opportunistic and market oriented. This pattern would suit non-planners but for organizations with a formal planning approach, their plans have to be flexible to allow this type of behaviour. Overall, the scanning methods used by both groups are similar and the sources are the same, with a predominance of informal sources. The existence of a strategic plan does not seem to affect the scanning behaviour of firms. These findings suggest that the hotel firms sampled rely mainly on experience, intuition and informal, personal information gathering to construct their view of the future.

Is it possible to foresee the future?

Evidence suggests that executives who are able to scan their business environment will derive benefits for their business from doing so, especially if they are able to detect threats and opportunities and respond accordingly. Yet, many choose not to devote much energy to the scanning of their business environment because they are uncertain about the cause and effect relationships which exist between environmental events and firm performance. Second, executives are reluctant to engage in a significant scanning

Richard Teare and
John T. Bowen
*Assessing information needs
and external change*

activity if they have concerns about the quality of the sources of information available to them. A third concern relates to the difficulty of correctly assigning probabilities to the likelihood of events actually occurring in the environment and their impact on the firm. Thus, it is often easier to make decisions about more immediate threats and opportunities rather than long term trends. The first comprehensive survey of chief executive officers (CEOs) of multinational hotel chains sponsored by the International Hotel Association (IHA) sought to assess the environmental scanning practices of member hotel firms and to learn how their executives view the uncertainty of the global business environment (Olsen *et al.*, 1994). Additionally, the survey sought to determine the key issues that are driving the strategies of these firms and their view of patterns of change in the industry. Aspects of this study are re-visited in the following section.

Assessing information needs

Accurately perceiving the environment is a difficult task and to assist this effort, a classification of the environment is needed. A general category refers to broad-based arenas such as the economic, political, socio-cultural, technological and ecological domains. The forces and trends in this category represent the most difficulty for scanners when they try to identify threats and opportunities, as they are the most abstract and the timing of their development is more difficult to estimate. The task category (customers, suppliers, competitors, regulators) is usually easier to scan, the timing is more easily understood, and the impact is more predictable. The functional category (finance, human resources, operations, administration, marketing, research and development) narrows the scan to specializations within the firm (see Table I). By scanning these categories of the environment, the executive can then decide on the appropriate sources of information to use, both personal and non-personal.

How do executives scan?

The question most often posed by executives when developing strategic plans is: what are the most significant threats and opportunities we will face in the short and long term? The survey questionnaire with responses from 52 CEOs (or their designates), sought to address the following areas:
• Did respondents view various aspects of the environment of their operating domain as stable or volatile? (See Table II).

Table I
Categories of the business environment

General environment	Task environment	Functional environment
Political	Customers	Finance
Technological	Suppliers	Human resources
Economic	Competitors	Operations
Socio-cultural	Regulators	Administration
Socio-cultural	Regulators	Administration
Ecological		Marketing Research and Development

Source: Olsen *et al.* (1994)

• How frequently did they scan various categories of their environment?
• What level of interest did they have in scanning various events and trends occurring in their environment?
• Do they rely more on internal and personal sources than external and impersonal ones?
• Who is responsible for scanning activities in their firm?
• What types of decisions depend on the firm's scanning activities?
• What are the most important threats and opportunities for their firms in the next one and five-year periods?

Of the respondent firms, 60 per cent, were multinational in their scope of operations. As many as 85 per cent of these firms had less than 50 hotels each. It is these multinationals (as opposed to firms whose scope was strictly national) which indicated greater interest in scanning current/future conditions of the labour market, new legislation/regulations enacted or considered for enactment, acquisition of existing competitors by firms outside the industry, and current/future cost of real estate. Faced with a greater diversity of environmental conditions in the different countries they operate in, international firms seem to be more conscious of environmental scanning than are firms which are national in scope.

Environmental scanning and performance
The study produced enough evidence to show that better scanning of the environment leads to improved performance. For instance, the study indicates that:
• Firms with higher growth in sales show greater interest in customer-related issues.
• Firms with higher growth in income show greater interest in demographic changes in terms of product/service demands, competitor product/service offerings, and new

Richard Teare and
John T. Bowen
*Assessing information needs
and external change*

Table II
Operating domain variables used to asses the relative degree of stability-volatility

Category	Variables
Suppliers of food, beverage and operating supplies	Prices charged, product quality standards, product/service expectations, introduction of new products
Competitors' actions	Supply of rooms, rates charged, renovation and refurbishment, new services and facilities offered, attempts at differentiating the product
Customers' demand	For your services, for new facilities/services
Financial/capital markets	Interest rates: availability of capital, cost of capital other than debt
Labour markets	Wages and salary rates, availability of employees, union activities
Government regulations	Regarding rates you can charge, regarding room, food and beverage quality, regarding provision of your services, affecting personnel/labour decisions, affecting sales and marketing, affecting accounting/book-keeping, imposing new tax measures
Technological development	In the application of computers and communication technologies, in the application of expert systems/decision support systems, in reservation systems, in training and development

technological developments with industry applications.

· Firms with high growth in rooms show slightly more interest in customer needs/trends, demographic changes in terms of product/service demands, expansion plans of competitors, competitor pricing strategies, and new technological developments with industry applications.

Overall, there was a stronger short-term focus among respondents, characterized by a relatively consistent view of the key short-term issues. As might be expected, a broader range of opinions and priorities characterize the longer-term view (see Table III). The attention paid to short term issues appeared to be directed at the high impact concerns of the economy, financing and customer needs and expectations. While it is important to focus on these issues, it is also important for executives to keep track of events that are influencing change in the longer term.

The survey findings revealed a gap in both the provision and use of hospitality and tourism industry databases. The Hotel and Catering International Management Association (HCIMA) had also identified a need to provide an enhanced information service in the form of its Worldwide Hospitality and Tourism Trends (WHATT) CD-ROM product which was established in 1994 (Teare, 1995a). WHATT uses a classification scheme designed to provide an overview of the many types of industry-related information in the public domain (Cullis and Teare, 1996). The product, with its three key information sources, addresses hospitality and tourism research (*International Hospitality and Tourism Research Register* with four categories: academic, associations, government, industry);

industry trends (as reflected by academic journals in the *World Trends* database) and industry current awareness (contained in the HCIMA's *Current Awareness Bulletin*). The research teams responsible for maintaining the *Research Register* and *World Trends* databases in Europe, North America and Australia respectively, provide an on-going review and assessment of industry changes and this is disseminated by means of an annual publication. The following section profiles the structural changes that are occurring in the hospitality industry in the UK and North America and in response, lists the priorities assigned by a panel of general managers.

Assessing external change

The Annual Review of Hospitality and Tourism Trends, published in the *International Journal of Contemporary Hospitality Management*, draws on several thousand records contained in two of the three WHATT databases (*World Trends, Research Register*) to interpret and comment on the themes portrayed in the literature, by academic research and by the wide range of reports emanating from industry, analysts, consulting firms, trade and professional associations and government organanizations. The 1995 and 1996 publications provide a thematic analysis of the articles published in European and North American-based academic journals spanning a seven year period from 1989-1995. The aim here is to present the "top 30" issues emerging from the Annual Review so far, and to assess their implications for hospitality operations in the UK with reference to priority rankings made by a panel of 25 hotel general managers in the UK.

Richard Teare and
John T. Bowen
*Assessing information needs
and external change*

Table III

Short-term and long-term threats and opportunities

Environment category	One-year (early 1990s)	Five-year (late 1990s)
Economic	Recession, low inflation	Slow economic recovery, Pacific Rim explanation potential, low hotel real estate values
Political	Instability, shifting government policies, increasing taxation of the industry	Instability, shifting government policies, increasing taxation of the industry, regional trading blocks
Socio-cultural	Diversity and changing profile of customers, security issues	Diversity and changing profile of customers
Technological	Integrating new technology, cost of investment, improved MIS	Integrating new technology, cost of investment, distribution and capacity control
Ecological	Adapting current lodging/tourism products, education of costs and issues	Restrictions on property development
Finance	Availability of long-term financing	Availability of long-term financing, fluctuating cost of capital
Marketing	Pricing strategies, brand positioning	Protecting brand identities
Human resources	Skilled labour shortage	Skilled labour shortage
Operations	Skills upgrading	Better management systems (consistency and reliability)

Source: Olsen *et al.* (1994)

To facilitate the task of identifying key developments in the literature, a "top 15" is derived for each of the European and North American segments of the *World Trends* database, using different focal points (or themes) to avoid repetition. The themes are: business performance improvement; personal and organizational development; service improvement and competitiveness (UK) and marketing, human resource management and organizational issues (North America).

Patterns in management, service improvement and business performance (United Kingdom)

The following issues were identified from an analysis of articles in four UK-based hospitality and service industry journals: *International Journal of Contemporary Hospitality Management*; *International Journal of Hospitality Management*; *International Journal of Service Industry Management* and the *Service Industries Journal*. Each issue is discussed briefly and some examples are provided. The examples relate to the journals that were analysed – for example, Harris (23), refers to citation (23) in "Hospitality operations: patterns in management, service improvement and business performance" (Teare, 1996). The "top 15" also draws on the 1995 Review (see also Teare, 1995b).

The top 15 issues are clustered into three themes: business performance improvement; personal and organizational development;

service improvement and competitiveness, and the relationships are shown in Figure 1.

Business performance improvement

Top five: strategic systems; business performance measures; process and quality improvement; radical business structures and approaches; sustainable business development.

Strategic systems

Computer-based "strategic" systems – capable of delivering organization-wide benefits – embrace a range of initiatives, from external analysis (or environmental scanning) linked to business planning to systems for locational analysis of new units, yield management and facilities management. Information technology provides a feasible way of harnessing full operational capability and Donaghy *et al.* (5) review the application of yield management to profit maximization. The main challenge is to engage the full potential of information technology and Crichton and Edgar (6) foresee that as technology develops further, the concept of managing complexity as opposed to minimizing or adapting to it will be become more important.

Business performance measures

Managers depend on an array of tools to gauge workplace success and it has been argued that a balanced set of measurements is needed. Brander Brown and McDonnell (3) investigate whether "the balanced scorecard" performance measurement method

Richard Teare and
John T. Bowen
*Assessing information needs
and external change*

Figure 1
Patterns in management, service improvement and business performance

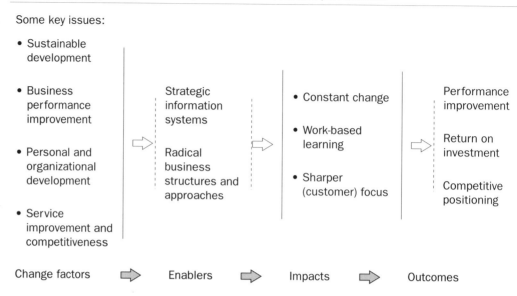

Some key issues:

- Sustainable development

- Business performance improvement

- Personal and organizational development

- Service improvement and competitiveness

Strategic information systems

Radical business structures and approaches

- Constant change

- Work-based learning

- Sharper (customer) focus

Performance improvement

Return on investment

Competitive positioning

Change factors ➪ Enablers ➪ Impacts ➪ Outcomes

provides a practical solution. They found that hotel general managers saw benefits in preparing a detailed score-card for each of the areas or departments controlled by senior managers within an individual hotel, providing the score-cards are reviewed and updated regularly. In this way, unit management teams can share the responsibility for achieving goals relating to a set of critical success factors for the unit as a whole.

Process and quality improvement
Yasin and Zimmerer (4) link the application of "benchmarking" to the hotel's ability to achieve its goals in the area of quality improvement. They present a practical framework for this which defines both the operating and service subsystems of the hotel and propose specific methods for quality improvement in each. Congram and Epelman (11) recommend the use of the structured analysis and design technique (SADT) to review service processes and achieve improvements. However, the concept and application of continuous quality improvement (CQI) has yet to make a significant impact on the international hospitality business, but it appears inevitable as organizations seek to establish a dynamic, quality-driven culture of process improvement.

Radical business structures and approaches
The notion of "business excellence" introduced by Peters and Waterman in the early 1980s was derived from a study of successful firms, some of whom were unable to sustain their achievements in the longer term. Caruana *et al.* (1) evaluate the concept of business excellence as it relates to a sample of large UK

service firms and Burgess *et al.* (30) examine the "success studies" in the context of multi-unit and multinational hotel groups and internationalization. The pace of change in the competitive arena and need to "re-invent" traditional methods (that impede responsiveness) calls for new ways and methods or organizing business activity.

Sustainable business development
While internal systems and procedures are important, Kim and Olsen (40) note that public concerns and greater external awareness are influencing trends in facilities management and design. Improvements in energy conservation and recycling mean that "green" marketing strategies will be more widely adopted in the future, especially as new design technologies enable hotels and resorts to use natural resources more efficiently (41).

Personal and organizational development
Top five: work-based learning; the adaptive manager; the adaptive organization; the responsive employee; teamworking.

Work-based learning
A number of studies have sought to identify career path competences for hotel managers (see for example, 17 and 18) and while there are core requirements, managerial effectiveness needs to be viewed in relation to a framework for continuous skills and knowledge updating, in keeping with the pace of change that is occurring (19-23). The workplace is increasingly seen as the learning environment of the future and organizations will need to encourage a personal commitment to learning.

Richard Teare and
John T. Bowen
*Assessing information needs
and external change*

The adaptive manager

It is evident that many managers are enjoying successful careers and are well suited to the nature of the work involved but there are signs that managerial roles are becoming more stressful. There are a number of key contributory factors including: the breadth of choice available to consumers in mature markets; the pressure to "do more with fewer people" to preserve or enhance profit margins; and the pace of change in business and commerce as a whole. In response, some organizations are seeking to build on the skills, talents and experience available to them by establishing a "learning organization" culture, climate and approach to business and human resource development.

The adaptive organization

Evidence suggests that hospitality firms are generally bound by traditional working methods and employment policy in comparison with other service industry firms. A more open-minded approach is needed to maximize the potential that exists in the industry's skilled and unskilled workforce. The concept of life-long learning and the mechanisms for supporting this are yet to be firmly established. The impact of new technology, maturing markets and other agents of change mean that managers, supervisors and operatives need to adapt and regularly update their skills and knowledge base. This calls for a closer "learning partnership" between industry and education and more flexible, work-based delivery mechanisms for education and training.

The responsive employee

In general terms, rates of innovation have been held back by traditional methods and practices. This is particularly the case in the human resources field where low pay, low esteem jobs have contributed to high rates of labour turnover. There are, however, signs that different approaches to managing and deploying human resources are being used. Several writers have reported encouraging results from studies of flexible working (45, 46) and Luckock concludes that job roles can be re-shaped in a more flexible way to suit both employees and employers. A more imaginative approach is needed though, and a good deal more could be done to make jobs more interesting, less stressful and less unsocial from the employee's viewpoint.

Teamworking

To compete successfully, organizations need to encourage innovation and a culture of continuous improvement in business processes, quality and service. The key implication here is that managers should seek to create an organizational climate that supports the change agenda and enhances the nature of communications between employees and employees and customers. To promote openness and involvement, traditional styles of management will need to be replaced by a teamworking structure and beyond this, self-managed work teams.

Service improvement and competitiveness

Top five: market sensitivity and competitiveness; service customization; customer orientation; measuring service quality; service excellence.

Market sensitivity and competitiveness

A growing body of evidence suggests that service firms are experimenting with a wide array of approaches and methods designed to narrow the gap between the provider and the consumer of services. Edvardsson (42) argues that it is not sufficient to focus on the encounter with the customer but that organizations should study all the critical incidents in the production chain so as to derive a deeper understanding of how weaknesses affect customer satisfaction with the end product. The alignment between groups of customers which constitute market segments, product specification and consistent service delivery reflects the product differentiation challenge. It seems likely that brands based on customized service packages will be needed in the future so that marketing strategy might emphasize service enhancement as well as socially and ecological responsible leisure and tourism experiences.

Service customization

The concept of mass customization has emerged, in part, from a decade of debate centred on the mass production of inexpensive, commodity-like products or services (the assembly line approach) on the one hand and premium-priced, individually-tailored and highly differentiated offerings on the other. Hart (7) observes that much of the power of mass customization, like total quality management before it, lies in its visionary and strategic implications. Its application should enable companies to produce affordable, high-quality goods and services, but with shorter cycle times and lower costs. The key dimensions of his diagnostic framework for assessing the potential for mass customization are: customer sensitivity, process amenability, competitive environment and organizational readiness. Taylor and Lyon (8) discuss the application of mass customization to food service operations and its likely adoption in a rapidly maturing marketplace.

Customer orientation

A compatible service customization step is for management to create an appropriate form of internal customer orientation and Stauss (9) notes that a deliberate and

Richard Teare and
John T. Bowen
*Assessing information needs
and external change*

sustained effort is needed to create a climate that promotes a customer's viewpoint of work activities, processes and non-standardized support services. Customer orientation also implies a readiness to measure and where necessary improve the quality of service and support in keeping with customer expectations.

Measuring service quality

Lee and Hing (10) assess the usefulness and application of the SERVQUAL technique in measuring service quality in the fine dining sector. They demonstrate how easily and inexpensively the technique can be used to identify the strengths and weaknesses of individual restaurants' service dimensions. The interpersonal aspects of service delivery are potentially the most difficult to audit and improve. A useful starting point is to undertake a programme of job analysis for service staff to identify the best fit between tasks, behaviours and personal attributes. Papadopoulou *et al.* (12) identify the dimensions of a higher customer contact with the food and beverage operative's job as perceived by managers, supervisors and operatives and examine within-source and between-source differences in perceptions. Their study confirms the versatility of job analysis as an organizational and diagnostic tool. Among other uses, it depicts the dimensions of a job, the related personal qualities and experience and the training implications. In most cases, it is also helpful to profile ideal combinations of age and experience for different service roles, especially as the industry relies heavily on younger workers (13).

Service excellence

Corporate level concern about service excellence has stimulated interest in employee empowerment. In theory, empowered employees will be more committed to ensuring that service encounters satisfy customers as they have the necessary discretion and autonomy to "delight the customer". Lashley (14) explores the implications of empowering employees and provides a framework for understanding managerial motives in selecting different forms of empowerment and their consequences for achieving improvements in customer service.

Managing change in the US hospitality industry: human resource, marketing and organizational trends (North America)

The following issues were identified from an analysis of articles in four hospitality journals published in North America during the period from 1989-1995 inclusive. Each issue is discussed briefly and some specific research examples from these journals are provided. Citations are related to the journals that were analysed: The *Cornell Hotel and Quarterly Restaurant Administration* (Prabhu, 1996), *Florida International University Hospitality Review* (Bowen, 1996), *Hospitality Research Journal* (Blum, 1996), and *The Journal of Travel and Tourism Marketing* (Hu, 1996).

The top fifteen issues are grouped into three themes: marketing, human resource management and organizational issues, and the relationships are shown in Figure 2.

Marketing

Top five: customer retention; internal marketing; segmentation; product design; promotion.

Internal marketing

Internal marketing is marketing aimed internally at the firm's employees. The objective is to ensure that employees are able and willing to deliver quality service. Internal marketing integrates human resource management with marketing and so the review spans these functional areas. Sternberg (Prabhu, 1996, p. 10) for example, reports on the benefits of empowerment to hospitality operations. One of the most important processes associated with internal marketing is the orientation of employees. Kennedy and Berger (Prabhu, 1996, p. 13) recommended ways to increase the effectiveness of orientation programmes. Dienhart and Gregoire (Blum, 1996, p. 11) provide evidence to suggest that a sense of increased job satisfaction and job security may improve an employee's customer focus. Rainero and Chon (Bowen, 1996, p. 4) suggested how marketing principles can be used to attract quality employees. Hotels in a given class offering similar services and superior customer service is one way to differentiate a product and gain competitive advantage and in this endeavour, internal marketing should be viewed as an integral part of the customer service programme.

Customer retention

A 1990 article in the *Harvard Business Review* reports that a 5 per cent increase in customer retention can add 25 to 85 per cent to the bottom line. This article initiated a research frenzy in the customer retention and customer loyalty area. Several studies published in the *Cornell Quarterly* (Prabhu, 1996, pp. 34-35) looked at frequent guest programmes and an on-going study at the University of Nevada

Richard Teare and
John T. Bowen
*Assessing information needs
and external change*

Figure 2
Environmental influences on US academic research

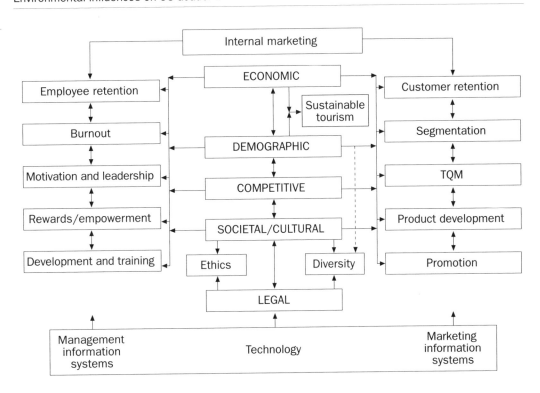

Las Vegas is currently investigating customer loyalty in luxury hotels.

Segmentation
A simple and concise definition of marketing strategy is: "selecting market segments and developing an effective marketing mix for those segments". As firms fine tune their marketing strategies and approaches to segmentation and explore emerging markets, the segmentation issue has become increasingly important to practitioners and, in turn, to academics interested in observing hospitality markets. For instance, the ageing baby boomers generation has been the subject of an array of academic research (see for example, Bowen, 1996, pp. 43-47).

Product design
A number of articles consider the importance of product attributes to the consumer and several studies reveal how managers might fine tune their products to create more value. For instance, Evans and Murman (Bowen, 1996, pp. 48) review the value added attraction of guest room personal hair care products and Kapoor (Bowen, 1996. p. 49) identifies the food attributes that are important to the young adult segment. Other researchers have investigated the product attributes that help to create value in a range of different market segments.

Promotion
Promotion is the perennial favourite of marketing researchers. Uysal and Schoenbachler (Hu, 1996, pp. 37, 39) examine the use of advertising in destination marketing. Other study clusters include: the use of marquees as promotional tools, the impact of publicity from restaurant reviews and advertising in the gaming sector.

Human resource management
Top five: employee retention; burnout; motivation and leadership; rewards and empowerment; development and training

Employee retention
Historically, the US hospitality industry has been plagued by labour shortages and triple-digit employee turnover rates. George (Bowen, 1996, p. 6) found employee turnover rates of 150 per cent with an average cost of $2,500 per incident to be common. Turnover, associated costs, and methods of reduction are some of the most frequently addressed topics in the field of hospitality research. The US Bureau of Labor Statistics predicts 165,000 job vacancies annually in the food service industry and the demand for workers will grow by 2 to 3 per cent annually (Bowen, 1996, p. 2). This and other figures have led some researchers to analyse the potential use of

Richard Teare and
John T. Bowen
*Assessing information needs
and external change*

non-traditional sources of labour. Older workers, working mothers, and the disabled are a few sources that may help to alleviate the predicted labour shortage.

Burnout

Another cause of turnover, particularly among middle-level managers (Prabhu, 1996, p. 16), is the phenomenon of burnout. The prevalence of burnout is higher in service industries where the job involves a high degree of interaction with clients. The Maslach Burnout Inventory has frequently been used to measure a person's level of burnout in relation to: personal accomplishment, emotional exhaustion, and de-personalization (Prabhu, 1996, p. 15).

Motivation and leadership

One way of attempting to decrease turnover and burnout is to increase employee levels of motivation to work. Although motivation is a personal and emotive issue, outside incentives can encourage employees to renew their personal commitment to the job they hold. If this approach is to work, managers must understand the needs of their employees. A survey of 278 hospitality workers revealed that the three things employees wanted most were: good wages, job security, and opportunities for advancement and development (Prabhu, 1996, p. 11).

Rewards and empowerment

The most obvious form of tangible reward is pay related, but much has been written about intangible incentives too. Sparrowe (Blum, 1996, p. 4) discovered that psychological benefits of empowerment seemed to increase perceived levels of job satisfaction and decrease job turnover intentions. Employee empowerment has also been found to improve operational efficiency and increase employee productivity and guest satisfaction (Prabhu, 1996, p. 10).

Development and training

All the above topics relate to the development and training of employees in the hospitality industry. Employee retention and motivation can be increased through empowerment, which must be accompanied by appropriate training. On the other hand, burnout and turnover may be reduced through employee empowerment and personal development programmes. Although many agree that training is important, few firms seem willing to pay for it. Conrade (Prabhu, 1996, p. 2) found that 77 per cent of the US lodging firms he surveyed spent less than 1 per cent of their payroll expenses on training. If, as previously mentioned, training affects so many other important areas, should not we "pay" more attention to it?

Organizational

Top five: sustainable tourism; ethics/social responsibility; employee diversity; use of technology; information systems.

Ethics/social responsibility

The value of trust is increasing and the growing number of alliances and partnerships in the industry means that firms must rely on and trust each other. Internally, there are signs that firms are paying more attention to ensuring that their employees are treated equitably and ethically (Prabhu, 1996, pp. 17-18). Additionally, more corporations are accepting a degree of social responsibility for community care in locations where they operate their businesses. For instance, Schmdigall (Bowen, 1996, p. 40) reports on the findings of a survey of hotel managers in which he seeks reactions to a number of ethical considerations and scenarios.

Sustainable tourism

Sustainable tourism involves two elements, preserving the environment and preserving the culture. In North America the research in this area has focused mainly on the environment. Ways of reducing solid waste in hotels have gained the attention of several researchers, Jaffe (Bowen, 1996, p. 41) and Shanklin (Blum, 1996, p. 63) and in tourism, Manning and Dougherty (Prabhu, 1996, p. 45) discuss the need to manage capacity of tourist destinations. Other focal points for research include: the development of environmental programmes in hotels, the impact of hospitality businesses in national parks and ecotourism.

Employee diversity

The Asian and Hispanic population in the USA is growing at a faster pace than the population in general. It is also interesting to note that women now hold more senior positions in corporations than ever before and this trend is accelerating. In the near future the white male will become a minority in the workforce and when this occurs the workforce will consist of an array of minority groups. Christenson (Blum, 1996, p. 7) stated that firms must identify how to benefit from a diverse employee group. He claims those that do not will be operating at a disadvantage. Other studies in this area include: the employees of workers with disabilities (Prabhu, 1996, p. 19), economically disadvantaged employees (Bowen, 1996, p. 3) and the use of older workers as a source of labour (Bowen, 1996, pp. 1-2).

Use of technology

The application of technology covers all areas of hospitality operations and there were many articles published during the review

Richard Teare and
John T. Bowen
*Assessing information needs
and external change*

period on the use of technology. Chevernak (Blum, 1996. p. 53) discusses the potential uses of fibre optic cable to transmit information both within the hotel and to link the hotel with organizations around the world. A number of articles in the *Journal of Travel and Tourism Marketing* discuss the application of technology to marketing (Hu, 1996, pp. 9, 45-58) and several articles in the *Cornell Quarterly* discuss the application of technology to training (Prabhu, 1996, p. 8-9). See for example, Kasavanva's work on the use of technology in food and beverage operations (Prabhu, 1996, pp. 30-31,).

Information systems
The increasing pace of change and employee involvement in information gathering means that most firms are interested in developing better ways to access, capture and process information. These issues are reflected in a number of articles published in *Florida International Review* (Bowen, 1996, pp, 108-111) concerned with information systems. For example, one article by Jenso (Bowen, 1996, p. 111) discusses the outsourcing of information systems.

What are the priorities?

A group of 25 hotel general managers participating in a seminar on market trends and industry issues held during Spring 1997 were asked to record their own responses to the "top 30" issues. After this, participants were asked to rank order their own "top 10" set of priorities from the list of 30 issues. An overall ranking was devised by allocating ten points for a 1st place ranking, nine points for a 2nd place and so on. The priority ranking is shown in Table IV.

Summary comments

Seminar discussion summary points reflect the participants' own "top 10" priority ranking and reveal a number of implications for organizational learning.

People
The problem of retaining high calibre employees is related to the industry's inability to attract the right people (managers claimed that entrants have unrealistic expectations regarding hours of work and wages). The highest level of turnover occurs if expectations are not met during the first few weeks of employment.

High turnover is also attributed to inadequate training and lack of on-going development for employees – a need exists for initial

Table IV
Priority issues for the UK hotel sector (ranked by a group 25 hotel general managers in the UK)

1. Customer retention (91 = 7.4 per cent)
2. Motivation and leadership (88 = 7.2 per cent)
3. Development and training (83 = 6.8 per cent)
4. Employee retention (66 = 5.4 per cent)
5. Radical business structures and approaches (60 = 4.9 per cent) (top 5 – 31.7 per cent)
6. Market sensitivity and competitiveness (58 = 4.7 per cent)
7. Teamwork (57 = 4.6 per cent)
8. Rewards and empowerment (56 = 4.6 per cent)
9. Strategic systems (55 = 4.5 per cent)
10. Process and quality improvement (52 = 4.2 per cent) (top 10 – 54.3 per cent)
11. The adaptive organization (51 = 4.2 per cent)
12. Measuring service quality (50 = 4.1 per cent)
13. Internal marketing (49 = 4.0 per cent)
14. Business performance measures (47 = 3.8 per cent)
15. Work-based learning (46 = 3.7 per cent) (top 15 – 74.1 per cent)
16. Service excellence (45 = 3.7 per cent)
17. The responsive employee (42 = 3.4 per cent)
18. Sustainable business development (39 = 3.2 per cent)
19. The adaptive manager (36 = 2.9 per cent)
20. Information systems (35 = 2.9 per cent)
21. Use of technology (34 = 2.8 per cent)
22. Customer orientation (30 = 2.4 per cent)
23. Service customization (22 = 1.8 per cent)
24. Employee diversity (12 = 1.0 per cent)
25. Promotion (8 = 0.7 per cent)
26. Product design (7 = 0.6 per cent)
27. Burnout (5 = 0.4 per cent)
28. Ethics and social responsibility (3 = 0.2 per cent)
29. Segmentation (1 = 0.1 per cent)
30. Sustainable tourism (0 = 0 per cent)

Note:
Total points = 1,228, scores rounded to nearest decimal place, total 100.2 per cent, $n = 25$

management training and continuous, self-directed learning for all. "Investors in People" is seen as a positive step (especially for managing front-line employees) but other areas are viewed as equally important, e.g. leadership training, "adaptive manager" techniques, information management skills and responding effectively to challenging financial targets (among many others). Maximizing "effectiveness" both individually and in team performance is seen as the prime means of delivering better results – financial, customers, employees, systems.

Business
Participants are keen to see industry-wide improvements in strategic systems,

Richard Teare and
John T. Bowen
*Assessing information needs
and external change*

especially relating to information and yield performance. In turn, this will help to focus more attention on organizational indicators that are harder to monitor and measure but are potentially important measures of success (e.g. effectiveness of communications, morale, "best practice breakthroughs").

Branding and brand awareness coupled with operational consistency and perceptions of quality are seen as key issues now and in the immediate future, especially in relation to the trends towards the "outsourcing" of hotel restaurants.

The top priorities (31 per cent of the total score)

Overall, the discussion groups felt that the most pressing priorities for the UK hotel sector are: customer retention and being customer-focused; motivating employees with a vision of the long term; and personal development so that employees are equipped with the skills necessary to "make things happen". Other key benefits will include improved retention rates among the pool of "good" managers and operatives and this is linked to development initiatives to lead, motivate, inspire, recognize and reward the workforce.

References

Blum, S. C. (1996), "Organizational trend analysis of the hospitality industry: preparing for change", *International Journal of Contemporary Hospitality Management*, Vol. 8 No. 7, pp 20-32.

Bowen, J.T. (1996), "Managing environmental change: insights from researchers and practitioners", *International Journal of Contemporary Hospitality Management*, Vol. 8 No. 7, pp 75-90.

Costa, J., Eccles, G. and Teare, R. (1996), "Environmental scanning and strategic planning activities by hospitality managers", in Kaye Chon, K.S. (Ed.), *Advances in Hospitality and Tourism Research*, Omnipress, Wisconsin, pp. 174-88.

Cullis, A. and Teare, R. (1996), "Information technology: its uses in strategic analysis", in Kotas, R., Teare, R., Logie, J., Jayawardena, C. and Bowen, J.T. (Eds), *The International Hospitality Business*, Cassell, London and New York, pp 77-87.

Hu, C. (1996), "Diverse developments in travel and tourism marketing: a thematic approach", *International Journal of Contemporary Hospitality Management*, Vol. 8 No. 7, pp. 33-43.

Olsen, M.D., Murthy, B. and Teare, R. (1994), "CEO perspectives on scanning the global hotel business environment", *International Journal of Contemporary Hospitality Management*, Vol 6 No. 4, pp. 3-9.

Prabhu, S. (1996), "Challenges for hospitality and tourism educators: a North American perspective", *International Journal of Contemporary Hospitality Management*, Vol. 8 No. 7, pp. 52-62.

Teare, R. (1995a), "WHATT's available? Hospitality", *Journal of the Hotel and Catering International Management Association*, December 1994/January 1995, No. 147, pp 20-1.

Teare, R. (1995b), "The international hospitality business: a thematic perspective", *International Journal of Contemporary Hospitality Management*, Vol. 7 No. 7, pp 55-73.

Teare, R. (1996), "Hospitality operations: patterns in management, service improvement and business performance", *International Journal of Contemporary Hospitality Management*, Vol. 8 No. 7, pp 63-74.

Trends in hospitality: academic and industry perceptions

Jorge Costa
Research Director designate (South Europe and South America), Worldwide Hospitality & Tourism Trends
Gavin Eccles
Research Manager (Europe), Worldwide Hospitality & Tourism Trends
Richard Teare
Research Director (Europe) Worldwide Hospitality & Tourism Trends

Reviews articles published during 1996 in the *International Journal of Contemporary Hospitality Management, International Journal of Hospitality Management, Tourism Management* and *Travel & Tourism Analyst.* Compares the central themes arising with those identified by a sample of hotel managers working in the UK and in Portugal, with particular reference to aspects of organizational performance. Compares and contrasts themes identified by academics and practitioners with reference to environmental scanning as a supportive process for trends identification and for strategy and decision-making purposes.

Introduction

From the review of the above listed academic journals a number of themes in the areas of hospitality can be identified. Themes like strategy and human resources issues have already been addressed in previous editions of the WHATT Annual Review (*IJCHM*, Vol. 7 No. 7, 1995 and Vol. 8 No. 7, 1996), while others can be seen as new themes highlighting specific tendencies. From the themes identified, the following, owing to their relevance to hospitality and tourism organizations and their pertinence as a research topic, are now presented and discussed. The central studies are summarized in table format, providing the focus of the study and the related sub-themes. These are then used to develop a relationship diagram exploring the existing links and interactions among the themes. Finally, the themes covered by academic research are then compared with those regarded by hotel managers as the most important for their companies' performance. In contextualizing the identification and assessment of business environmental trends, environmental scanning as a tool for strategy and decision making is presented and its role among hospitality organizations evaluated.

Central research themes for academics

In reviewing the academic journals five main themes were identified (Table I):
- Theme 1 – research, strategy and organizational policy.
- Theme 2 – current perspectives in human resource management.
- Theme 3 – new concepts in management and organization.
- Theme 4 – information technology support.
- Theme 5 – finance and investment.

These themes, covering aspects of strategy, human resources, franchising, information technology and finance, are now presented and analyzed.

Theme 1 – research, strategy and organizational policy

A study on the nature of academic research within UK hospitality management, conducted by Taylor and Edgar (1996), highlights the matters regarded as important for the future development of this area. It is the view of these authors that despite the considerable progress made in recent years in terms of the quantity and quality of research, the field has yet to reach a state of maturity. As they contend, increasing pressures are being exerted upon higher education systems to increase their level of research. However, they argue, hospitality research has yet to reach a state of maturity and it seems that no clear articulation exists as to what should be its role, content, and future direction. In order to accelerate the development of this field, Taylor and Edgar (1996) point out three areas they regard as important and as requiring further attention:
1 the role of hospitality research;
2 the scope of hospitality research; and
3 the research approaches and philosophy within hospitality research.

As a concluding remark, they state the need for hospitality researchers to become more discipline oriented.

This discipline-based orientation is already present across the other studies revised, particularly those analyzed in Theme 1. One of the disciplines under investigation is strategic planning, which has been broadly covered in studies by Phillips (1996) and Edgar and Nisbet (1996). In an exploratory investigation of the relationship between strategic planning and business performance, Phillips found a planning-performance relationship at the hotel unit level, and suggests that the core planning process of thoroughness, sophistication, participation, and formality are all important determinants

Jorge Costa,
Gavin Eccles and
Richard Teare
*Trends in hospitality:
academic and industry
perceptions*

Table I
Summary of themes addressed by academic research

Authors	Focus	Sub-theme
Theme 1. Research strategy and organizational policy		
Taylor and Edgar (1996)	The nature of academic research within UK hospitality management	The need for hospitality researchers to become more discipline oriented
Phillips (1996)	The relationship between strategic planning and business performance	Budget-based planning
Edgar and Nisbett (1996)	Strategic planning and chaos in the hospitality industry	Emphasis on innovation and creative practices to sustain competitive advantage
Brown (1996)	Environmental policy in the hospitality industry	Alternative "green" strategies
Camisón (1996)	Total quality management in the hospitality industry	European Foundation for Quality Management (EFQM) model
Theme 2. Current perspectives in human resource management		
Lashley (1996)	How empowered employees will respond to customer needs	Employee involvement or employee participation
Qu and Cheng (1996)	Labour shortages and the employment of older workers	Strengths and weaknesses of older workers
Tracey and Hinkin (1996)	How transformational leaders lead in the hospitality industry	Change-oriented or transformational style of leadership
Watson and D'Annunzio-Green (1996)	How organizations have undertaken the process of cultural change in order to achieve and maintain a competitive advantage	Cultural change through human resources
Barrows, Gallo and Mulleady (1996)	The impact of AIDS on the hospitality industry	Ways in which hospitality organizations can prepare employees to deal with such sensitive problems
Hartman and Yrle (1996)	Hotel employees move from job to job and how this is affected by their degree of "satisfaction"	Voluntary turnover research in the hotel industry
Theme 3. New concepts in management and organization		
McGuffie (1996)	The practice of franchising in the US hotel industry as the route to growth	Franchise development by major hotel chains in Europe
Hing (1996)	Franchising in the food service and lodging sectors of the hospitality industry	Benefits and limitations theoretically associated with purchasing and operating a franchised outlet
Hallam and Baum (1996)	Contracting out food and beverage operations to external operators	The concept of branded restaurant chain as a way to meet hotel guests' needs and attract local customers
Fockler (1996)	The concept of "all-suite hotels" within the US hotel industry	The expansion of all-suites as directly linked to demographic changes
Theme 4. Information technology support		
Harris (1996)	International hospitality marketing on the Internet	The impact of this new technology on the preparation of hospitality students
Sumner and Sellars (1996)	Information gained from computer systems and how much of this is used for marketing purposes	How to improve the use of information systems within the hospitality industry
Cho and Connolly (1996)	The impact of information technology (IT) as an enabler on the hospitality industry	The introduction of new, more powerful and able information systems, and how these will change the way people do business
Theme 5. Finance and investment		
Burgess (1996)	Profile of the hotel financial controller in UK, USA and Hong Kong	Expansion of the hotel controller's role as a result of the emphasis on the profitability of the hotel establishment
Özer (1996)	Educational model to evaluate investment in small hospitality operations	Investment alternatives using discounted cash flow techniques
Langer (1996)	The relationship between traffic noise and hotel profits	Guest reactions to motor-traffic pollution

Jorge Costa,
Gavin Eccles and
Richard Teare
*Trends in hospitality:
academic and industry
perceptions*

of business performance. According to Phillips, an aspect worth careful attention is the fact that, although most of the strategic planning performed in head office is intended to affect individual hotels within the group, competitive advantage in the service sector is determined, to a large extent, at the point of delivery. Another relevant finding from Phillips' study is that what currently passes for strategic planning at the hotel unit level, and in some cases at the head-office level, is no more than extended financial budgeting. The problem with this situation, as regarded by Phillips, is that budget-based planning is more of a control mechanism, and is deficient in that it does not fully consider the immediate strategic questions concerning target market, service levels and competitor analysis, let alone the longer-term strategic issues of environmental change and how these will affect individual hotel units in the future.

A different approach to the study of strategic planning is taken by Edgar and Nisbet (1996). In their study of strategic planning and chaos in the hospitality industry and with reference to the concept of chaos theory, these authors propose that long-term strategic planning is of little benefit to business (especially small businesses) operating in the hospitality industry. As they argue, managerial focus should instead emphasize innovation and creative practices in order to sustain competitive advantages. To achieve this, organizations need to have a clear vision of where they want to be and attempt to achieve this aim by adapting to situations as they arise. They conclude by recommending today's hospitality organizations not to try to overcome their environment by predicting future outcomes but instead engage and adapt with the environment.

Another area deserving attention by academic researchers has been that of environmental policies. In a study of the environmental policy in the hospitality industry, Brown (1996) illustrates alternative "green" strategies to indicate possible reactions of the hotel industry to the environmental issue and the extent of the "greening" process on the control system. Brown concludes that although a number of companies have adopted an environmental policy, in general, the hotel industry is not taking a proactive approach to environmental concerns. This lack of a proactive attitude towards some relevant aspects of the hospitality industry is again confirmed in a study by Camisón (1996) on total quality management in hospitality. This author used the model proposed by the European Foundation for Quality Management (EFQM) to make a cross-analysis of the views of quality from the standpoint of management and external customers in Valencia's hotel industry. Total quality management, according to Camisón, is an essential management technology for laying the foundation of competitiveness for tourism concerns and their search for excellence at the present time. However, he found a great "backwardness" in Valencia's hotel industry on the road towards total quality.

Theme 2 – current perspectives in human resource management

Under the current theme, seven studies were analyzed addressing aspects of empowerment, older workforce, leadership, employee and job satisfaction, change and AIDS. In the first of these studies, Lashley (1996) contends that empowered employees will respond to customer needs as they arise. From his viewpoint, they will react appropriately to customer complaints and develop a sense of ownership, taking personal pride in ensuring that service encounters are a success. According to Lashley, concern to engage employees at an emotional level so as to gain greater commitment, generate greater involvement in service quality and increase labour stability, is not just restricted to organizations operating in the service sector. In fact, firms in all sectors have shown increased interest in initiatives which are based on employee involvement or employee participation. This author also claims that employee empowerment needs to take account of different definitions and meanings used by managers. These different managerial meanings will be shaped by perceptions and concerns about the needs of the particular operation in question. He concludes by saying that whatever the intentions of managers, the effects of empowerment will be mediated by the feelings and experiences of the supposedly empowered. As a consequence, any consideration of the various forms which empowerment takes must be sensitive to the potential tensions between managerial meanings and employees' experiences.

A topic not commonly addressed but of interest owing to demographic trends is that of hotel personnel managers' attitudes towards utilizing older workers aged 55 or above (Qu and Cheng, 1996). The problem of labour shortage in places like Hong Kong has led companies to consider the employment of older workers. In fact, and according to these authors, in the Hong Kong hotel industry, the employment of older workers appears to be widely accepted. Their study identified 92.3 per cent of hotels as employing older workers who were allocated mainly to the food and beverage, housekeeping, engineering and security departments. As viewed by respondents, low absenteeism, low turnover rate,

Jorge Costa,
Gavin Eccles and
Richard Teare
*Trends in hospitality:
academic and industry
perceptions*

diligence and hard work, and a sense of responsibility and co-operative spirit tended to be the strengths of older workers, whereas low productivity, high employment cost and inflexibility tended to be their weaknesses.

Another area deserving the attention of academic researchers is that of leadership. In a study on how transformational leaders lead in the hospitality industry, Tracey and Hinkin (1996) argue that dynamic and changing environments may require a change-oriented or transformational style of leadership. Their findings showed that transformational leadership has a direct impact on perceptions of subordinate satisfaction with the leader and leader effectiveness, as well as an indirect effect on these variables through its impact on openness of communication, mission clarity, and role clarity. These authors conclude by stating that it is unlikely that the hospitality industry will become any more stable or less complex in the future. As a result, transformational leadership, seen as the ability to create and communicate a vision and adapt the organization to a rapidly changing environment, may be the most crucial type of leadership in the years to come.

Cultural change through human resources constitutes another actual theme which has been addressed by Watson and D'Annunzio-Green (1996). These authors examine approaches taken by two UK hotels for survival in the current complex environment in which greater competition, market changes and technological advances are affecting the manner in which the hospitality industry is operating. In their study, Watson and D'Annunzio-Green also examine strategies which have been implemented in an attempt to ensure long-term success. The central aspect of their study is the analysis of the ways in which these organizations have undertaken the process of cultural change in order to achieve and maintain a competitive advantage. This is achieved by focusing on the human resource management within this process.

A pertinent issue needing careful attention is that of AIDS in the place of work. In analyzing the impact of AIDS on the hospitality industry, Barrows *et al.* (1996) suggest a number of ways in which hospitality organizations can prepare employees to deal with such sensitive problem. In fact, and as they argue, a combination of ongoing employee education programmes, in conjunction with a comprehensive policy statement, may be the most effective means of preparing an organization to deal with employees with AIDS.

A final aspect considered under Theme 2 is that of employee turnover. Hartman and Yrle (1996) examined the behaviour of hotel employees who, as they state, even when they say they are "satisfied", move from job to job for reasons unrelated to that "satisfaction". An important reason for this behaviour, as they state, is that such movement may represent an important way to "get ahead". This, they contend, can be seen as a "hobo phenomenon" in the hotel industry. In addressing the limited longitudinal data used to draw their conclusions, Hartman and Yrle (1996) suggest that the hobo phenomenon may have potential as an exploratory variable in voluntary turnover research in the hotel industry. In concluding, they discuss the implications of this phenomenon, emphasizing the need to consider employee perceptions of promotion opportunities, and specifically the importance of considering promotion opportunities separate from promotion fairness, a factor neglected in current job satisfaction.

Theme 3 – new concepts in management and organization

Within Theme 3, aspects such as franchising, contracting out food and beverage and the grading of small hotels are considered. In the first study analyzed, McGuffie (1996) points out the practice of franchising in the US hotel industry as the route to growth and one which has gained wide acceptance from the major institutional investors. With respect to Europe, this author argues that as a result of the predominance of independent, family-run hotels, franchising is less widespread and does not yet have the same recognition by the financial community as in the USA. However, the major hotel chains in Europe have been actively involved in franchise development for some time and are targeting further franchise growth as a primary strategy of extending their presence in Europe's important hotel locations. McGuffie contends that there are advantages and disadvantages of franchising for hotel owners, and that it is not clear as yet whether franchising will secure such major slice of the hotel market as has happened in the USA. On the other hand, the potential exists for a massive expansion in the numbers of franchised hotels in Europe, but it is less clear at what rate they will be able to expand.

A somewhat different perspective on franchising within the hospitality industry is presented by Hing (1996). From her viewpoint, franchising is becoming increasingly prevalent in many Western economies, particularly in the food service and lodging sectors of the hospitality industry. This authors' perspective is that the literature on franchising contains many unsubstantiated claims regarding the advantages and disadvantages of franchising for franchisees. In addressing

Jorge Costa,
Gavin Eccles and
Richard Teare
*Trends in hospitality:
academic and industry
perceptions*

this question, Hing studies the satisfaction of food service franchisees and the benefits and limitations theoretically associated with purchasing and operating a franchised outlet. The findings of this study indicate that, while many of the benefits for franchisees were empirically supported, considerable dissatisfaction was evident with various aspects relating to the financial and contractual controls imposed by franchisers and with the imbalance of power in franchise relationships. However, the conclusions point towards a situation where most franchisees seem willing to accept these limitations as a fair exchange for the substantial benefits they receive in choosing to purchase a franchised, rather than independent, business.

A major change taking place within the hospitality industry with respect to the area of food and beverage (F&B) in hotels, is that of contracting out operations to external operators, whether individual restaurateurs or branded restaurant chain names (Hallam and Baum, 1996). According to these authors, this development is widely regretted by many traditionalists but represents a reality in North America and, increasingly, in the UK. The conclusions of the study undertaken by Hallam and Baum point towards a situation where hotels will continue to distance themselves from their food and beverage operations. As they argue, North America provides the market model for contracting out at the present time but it is a trend which is gaining increasing currency in the UK and other countries. This distancing may be in the form of buying pre-prepared pastries, vegetables, salads and entrées, or as distant as contracting out portions or all of hotels' food and beverage facilities. In concluding, these authors suggest that there are many benefits that come from contracting out portions or all of the food and beverage operation. This may allow managers to provide better service to their guests, it may help attract more lodging guests to the hotel, and it may also help hotel restaurants to compete with the outside market. In advising readers about contracting out their F&B operations, Hallam and Baum state that it should only be for financial reasons and not for any of the previous reasons alone. The idea should be to gain financial stability or financial investment in the operation, or know-how, to gain a proven concept that will meet hotel guest's needs and help attract local customers. These concepts can be a branded restaurant chain, or a local specialty chef.

Within the theme of new concepts in management and organization, a study on the concept of "all-suite hotels" was analyzed (Fockler, 1996). As defined by Fockler, the central idea of "all-suite hotels" is based on the concept of limited service hotels selling two rooms for little more than the price of one. Within the US hotel industry this concept survived the tough years of the early 1990s with better performances than the traditional hotel industry. As stated by this author, despite the fact that industry predictions for the development of the all-suites sector during the first half of the decade were not met, it is now enjoying a resurgence of strong growth with perspectives to continue. The expansion of all-suites is directly linked to demographic changes, especially in the business sector. However, while the early all-suite properties were primarily in the upscale category, the new markets have meant changes in demand, with the current pattern of growth focusing on the extended stay and mid-market properties. Fockler concludes by arguing that, while the major chains are likely to continue to feature among the top all-suite providers, it seems likely that there may be some jostling among leaders for the prime positions.

Theme 4 – information technology support

Theme 4 comprises three studies relating to: hospitality marketing and Internet (Net); computer systems; and information technology. The first of these studies, by Harris (1996), looks at international hospitality on the Net. According to Harris, the use of the Internet in global education is one of unleashed social practice, pedagogical challenge, and investigation of new communication protocol. This technological tool, as he contends, connects cultures with no sense of boundary and is yet uncensored and somewhat uncontrolled. In reality, this release on information and elimination of communication barriers invites a new classroom to educators and students and a world of interactivity to be studied. There are, however, some issues of concern. Harris regards the primary of these issues as including the availability of access, equipment, protection of private information and the funding and management of this tool. A secondary concern will be the management, or lack of, the resources and communication outlets. Looking at this phenomenon from a more positive stance, the Net now provides more information to users and opportunities to communicate and learn from people all over the globe. In evaluating the impact of this new technology, educators and business owners are investigating the use of the Internet and many other forms of technology to improve the learning process and ways to use this tool to compete in a global economy (Harris 1996). Harris' conclusion about the use of the Internet is that, if hospitality educators are to

Jorge Costa,
Gavin Eccles and
Richard Teare
*Trends in hospitality:
academic and industry
perceptions*

prepare their students to be competitive in this economy, they must learn the advantages and disadvantages of this tool and decide how and when it will be used in their professional environments.

The second study analyzed under this theme addresses the area of hotel computer systems and argues whether they can be seen as valuable tools or missed opportunity (Sumner and Sellars, 1996). These authors carried out a survey of the UK hotel industry to establish how much of the information gained from computer systems is used for marketing purposes, and how it is being used. Several hotel groups were contacted, representing a large proportion of the UK hotel industry, to elicit the degree of their use and understanding of three computer systems (guest history, computerized reservation and yield management systems) in improving sales. The results from Sumner and Sellars' study show a mixed use and understanding of the systems, with some degree of under-optimization. These authors conclude that the systems might be better used if management is fully conversant with their applications.

The final study under Theme 4 relates to the impact of information technology (IT) as an enabler on the hospitality industry (Cho and Connolly, 1996). As these authors contend, in the hospitality industry IT is gaining recognition as an enabler for delivering service consistency and establishing employee productivity. They go on to say that absence of technology in today's environment would create hardships in establishing and delivering service consistency. In conclusion, they argue that, with the introduction of new, more powerful and able information systems, it is obvious that these innovations are changing the way people do business in almost every industry, including the hospitality industry.

Theme 5 – finance and investment

For Theme 5, three articles were selected and analyzed. These cover aspects related to the hotel financial controller, investment analysis models; and the relationship between traffic noise and hotel profit. In the first of these studies on the profile of the hotel financial controller in UK, USA and Hong Kong, Burgess (1996) argues that the increasing emphasis on the profitability of the hotel establishment has resulted in an expansion of the hotel controller's role. In this study, Burgess compares the profile and responsibilities of the controller in these three countries and tries to ascertain whether the type of person employed may be generic or specific to a particular area. The results highlight many similarities, which, with the internationalization of hotel groups, may allow the

individual to transfer between countries in order to maintain company standards.

The second study presents an educational model that has been developed to evaluate investment in small hospitality operations (Özer, 1996). The model proposed by Özer was developed in the context of small businesses in Turkey and presents a systematic approach to evaluating the feasibility of small bed and breakfast hotel investments. This model evaluates investment alternatives using discounted cash flow techniques as the user enters inputs with respect to the variables influencing the net cash flow. The use of this model also allows the observation of changes in the value of the investment as any of the input variables are changed or as new scenarios developed. Özer believes that such an approach is expected to increase understanding of investment analysis and contribute to the education and decision process of small investors who usually lack the means for formal feasibility studies.

The final study under Theme 5 reports on an exploratory investigation in Switzerland, Austria and Bavaria relating traffic noise and hotel profits (Langer, 1996). This study shows that traffic-free mountain holiday resorts have an above-average occupancy rate, and resorts where the environmental burden due to traffic is relatively low have a higher occupancy rate than comparable resorts where the burden is much higher. According to Langer, research into guest reactions to motor-traffic pollution and of guest desires for solutions to the traffic problems is necessary as a basis for entire cost-benefit analysis. This basic knowledge, as he argues, is required when dealing with larger investments in transportation, which, among other things, include automobile-free areas or other attractive solutions to the traffic problem. Langer recommends for these investments to be compared with alternative development and investment possibilities for the future of tourist resorts.

Issues affecting hotel companies' performance

As part of the WHATT-CD research project, a series of seminars with hotel managers was conducted in the UK and Portugal. One of the aims of these seminars was to facilitate an ongoing discussion of key market trends and to identify those issues regarded by hotel managers as affecting their company performance. In order to identify these issues, managers were given a list and asked to select the top three factors regarded as most affecting their company performance both for the

Jorge Costa,
Gavin Eccles and
Richard Teare
*Trends in hospitality:
academic and industry
perceptions*

short term and long term. The list provided covered the following factors:
- national economic performance;
- cost of investment;
- inflation;
- interest rates;
- government change;
- new legislation/regulation affecting the sector;
- changing social patterns and behaviour;
- current customer needs;
- competitor pricing strategies;
- re-enforcement of trade action by competitors;
- current cost/availability of raw materials;
- future changes in customer needs and trends;
- potential entrance of new competitors;
- development of new product/services by competitors;
- new technological developments;
- other.

The top three factors selected by managers as most influencing their companies in the short and long term are those given in Table II.

For the short term, the factors selected by both groups are virtually the same with the exception of the last factor where UK managers are more concerned with the national economic performance and Portuguese managers with inflation. The concern, however, is still related with the national economy. The top three factors selected also denote a greater concern for aspects from the operational[1] environment (factors 1 and 2), even though aspects from the general environment are also pointed out. The two most important factors are directly related to the areas where organizations can exert some influence. The factors selected for the short term are also more specific than those selected for the long term. As they seem to impact more strongly on the company operations they deserve the highest attention.

The top three factors ranked by managers as most influencing their companies in the

long term highlight some further differences between UK and Portuguese hotel managers. Even though the first factor is common to both groups, the other two are different. While UK managers show more concern for aspects from the operational environment, Portuguese managers show more concern for those aspects which they cannot influence (national economic performance and new legislation/regulation affecting the sector).

Academic and practitioners' perceptions towards the relevance of themes

In comparing the themes selected for investigation by academics with those regarded by practitioners as affecting their companies' performance, it is clear the broader range of issues is addressed by academics. Hotel managers are essentially concerned with customers, competitors, national economy and legislation. However, this does not mean that they do not pay close attention to other areas both internal and external to the organization. In fact, other factors were identified under the option "other":
- impact of employee retention on customer retention;
- becoming flexible and open to change;
- impact of information on decisions and performance;
- higher degree of concentration on the business.

The reduced areas of concern identified by managers may also reflect a somewhat narrow view about the external business environment. In reality, and despite the fact that environmental scanning[2] helps managers to foresee favourable and unfavourable influences (Olsen *et al.*, 1992), research into this process has also discovered that much of the scanning activity of managers is informal in nature (Fahey *et al.*, 1983). Managers are too concerned with the short term, and for this

Table II
Factors regarded by hotel managers as affecting company performance

Short-term factors	Long-term factors
UK	
Current customer needs	Future changes in customer needs and trends
Competitor pricing strategies	Development of new product/services by competitors
National economic performance	Interest rates
Portugal	
Competitor pricing strategies	Future changes in customer needs and trends
Current customer needs	National economic performance
Inflation	New legislation/regulation affecting the sector

Jorge Costa,
Gavin Eccles and
Richard Teare
*Trends in hospitality:
academic and industry
perceptions*

reason, their main goal is to get information about the economy, financing and customer needs and wants, ignoring other sectors of the general environment (Olsen *et al.*, 1994). One major reason for this behaviour is that any attempt to monitor both the general and operational environments comprehensively is beyond the resources and abilities of any firm.

Improving awareness and identification of trends through environmental scanning

The identification and management of environmental opportunities and threats is fundamental to the competitive positioning of companies. The identification of business environmental trends can be achieved using a

Figure 1
Theme-based relationships

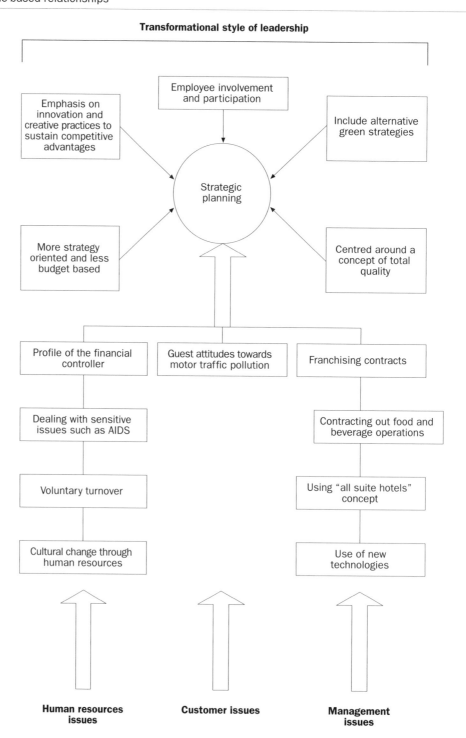

Jorge Costa,
Gavin Eccles and
Richard Teare
*Trends in hospitality:
academic and industry
perceptions*

structured environmental scanning process. The information resulting from this process may assist top management in its task of charting the company's future course of action.

The importance of environmental scanning for organizations can be seen by looking at some of its potential outcomes: identification of events and trends in the external environment, and making sense of the possible relationships between them. By making sense of the data, organizations can extract the main implications for decision making and strategy development.

In reviewing the environmental scanning process, certain aspects emerge as central. When used for organizational development and design, environmental scanning reveals a much broader scope than just the gathering of data for strategic planning and decision making. Besides allowing for early identification of opportunities and threats and providing information on customers, environmental scanning can also provide intellectual stimulation and help in the development of a proactive attitude towards the business environment.

Concluding remarks

From the review of some of the most representative academic journals in the field of hospitality management, it was possible to identify those areas regarded by academic researchers as relevant for this field of study. Themes covering strategic planning, human resources, franchising, information technology and finance were identified and analyzed. From the summary of the studies revised, their focus and the sub-themes addressed, it is possible to develop a relationship diagram (Figure 1) highlighting the links between the concepts and ideas presented.

The theme-based relationship diagram is developed around the concept of strategic planning owing its importance for organizations and the fact that it encompasses all other areas being addressed. The central idea presented considers a transformational style of leadership in the development of the strategic plan. This is then informed by human resources, customer and management issues and at the same time is influenced by aspects such as employee participation, green strategies, total quality concepts, less financial elements, and an emphasis on innovation and creative practices.

These can be seen as much broader issues than those identified by hotel managers. On the other hand, owing to the pace of change in their business environment and the fierce

competition faced by hospitality organizations, it is understandable that only a core group of factors can be closely monitored. However, the need for a better identification of opportunities and threats claims for a different attitude towards the scanning of the business environment. These organizations would explore opportunities and avoid threats better if these could be identified at an early stage. In order to achieve this, managers will have to understand the importance of a formal environmental scanning process in providing decision makers with the supporting information for their managerial activities. Once this first stage of information importance awareness has been achieved, then the identification of the most suitable process, and its development and implementation, will be highly facilitated.

Notes

1 Operational environment is normally considered as the set of suppliers and other interest groups which the firm deals with, while general environment is composed the national and global context of social, political, regulatory, economic and technological conditions.

2 Environmental scanning can be seen as a process of collecting, analyzing and providing information about events and relationships in a company's outside environment which can then be used for strategy and decision making.

References

Barrows, C., Gallo, M. and Mulleady, T. (1996), "AIDS in the US hospitality industry: Recommendations for education and policy formulation", *International Journal of Contemporary Hospitality Management*, Vol. 8 No. 1.

Brown, M. (1996), "Environmental policy in the hotel sector: green strategy or stratagem?", *International Journal of Contemporary Hospitality Management*, Vol. 8 No. 3.

Burgess, C. (1996), "A profile of the hotel financial controller in the United Kingdom, United States and Hong Kong", *International Journal of Hospitality Management*, Vol. 15 No. 1, pp. 19-28.

Camisón, C. (1996), "Total quality management in hospitality: An application of the EFQM model", *Tourism Management*, Vol. 17 No. 3, pp. 191-201.

Cho, W. and Connolly, D. (1996), "The impact of information technology as an enabler on the hospitality industry", *International Journal of Contemporary Hospitality Management*, Vol. 8 No. 1.

Edgar, D and Nisbet, L. (1996), "A matter of chaos – some issues for hospitality businesses", *International Journal of Contemporary Hospitality Management*, Vol. 8 No. 2.

Fahey, L., King, W.R. and Narayanan, V.K. (1983), "Environmental scanning and forecasting in

Jorge Costa,
Gavin Eccles and
Richard Teare
*Trends in hospitality:
academic and industry
perceptions*

strategic planning – the state of the art", in Hussey, D.E. (Ed.), *The Truth About Corporate Planning: International Research Into the Practice of Planning*, Pergamon Press, Oxford, pp. 495-509.

Fockler, S. (1996), "All-suite hotels in the USA", *Travel and Tourism Analyst*, Vol. 3, pp. 44-64.

Hallam, G. and Baum, T. (1996), "Contracting out food and beverage operations in hotels: a comparative study of practice in North America and the United Kingdom", *International Journal of Hospitality Management*, Vol. 15 No. 1, pp. 41-50.

Harris, K. (1996), "International hospitality marketing on the Internet: Project 'Interweave'", *International Journal of Hospitality Management*, Vol. 15 No. 2, pp. 155-63.

Hartman, S. and Yrle, A. (1996), "Can the hobo phenomenon help explain voluntary turnover?", *International Journal of Contemporary Hospitality Management*, Vol. 8 No. 4.

Hing, N. (1996), "An empirical analysis of the benefits and limitations for restaurant franchisees", *International Journal of Hospitality Management*, Vol. 15 No. 2, pp. 177-87.

Langer, G. (1996), "Traffic noise and hotel profits – is there a relationship?", *Tourism Management*, Vol. 17 No. 4, pp. 295-305.

Lashley, C. (1996), "Research issues for employee empowerment in hospitality organisations", *International Journal of Hospitality Management*, Vol. 15, pp. 333-46.

McGuffie, J. (1996), "Franchising hotels in Europe", *Travel and Tourism Analyst*, Vol. 1, pp. 36-52

Olsen, M., Murphy, B. and Teare, R.E. (1994), "CEO perspectives on scanning the global hotel business environment", *International Journal of Contemporary Hospitality Management*, Vol. 6 No. 4, pp. 3-9.

Olsen, M., Tse, E. and West, J. J. (1992), *Strategic Management in the Hospitality Industry*, International Thomson Publishing, London.

Özer, B. (1996), "An investment analysis model for small hospitality operations", *International Journal of Contemporary Hospitality Management*, Vol. 8 No. 5.

Phillips, P. (1996), "Strategic planning and business performance in the quoted UK hotel sector: results of an exploratory study", *International Journal of Hospitality Management*, Vol. 15 No. 4, pp. 347-62.

Qu, H. and Cheng, S. (1996), "Attitudes towards utilizing older workers in the Hong Kong hotel industry", *International Journal of Hospitality Management*, Vol. 15 No. 3, pp. 245-54.

Sumner, J. and Sellars, T. (1996), "Hotel computer systems: valuable tool or missed opportunity?", *International Journal of Contemporary Hospitality Management*, Vol. 8 No. 2.

Taylor, S. and Edgar, D. (1996), "Hospitality research: the emperor's new clothes?", *International Journal of Hospitality Management*, Vol. 15 No. 3, pp. 211-27.

Tracey, J. and Hinkin, T. (1996), "How transformational leaders lead in the hospitality industry", *International Journal of Hospitality Management*, Vol. 15 No. 2, pp. 165-76.

Watson, S. and D'Annunzio-Green, N. (1996), "Implementing cultural change through human resources: the elusive organization alchemy?", *International Journal of Contemporary Hospitality Management*, Vol. 8 No. 2.

WHATT Annual Review (1995 and 1996), *International Journal of Contemporary Hospitality Management*, Vol. 7 No. 7 and Vol. 8 No. 7.

Performance management: processes, quality and teamworking

Hadyn Ingram
Research Manager (Europe) Worldwide Hospitality and Tourism Trends

Reviews journal articles and worldwide hospitality and tourism trends research entries relating to three themes: business performance and performance measurement, process and quality improvement and teamworking. Draws on generic and industry specific material to identify "best practice" approaches adopted in other industries that might be applied in the context of hospitality and tourism settings.

Introduction

The purpose of this article is to review the journal and research material, primarily in the WHATT-CD database, concerning three themes: business performance and performance measurement, process and quality improvement and teamworking in the hospitality industry. The literature is summarized in tables and interrelationships between the themes are shown in the form of diagrams. The second part of the article draws on generic material from a range of industries with the aim of identifying other approaches which may be worthy of further examination in the hospitality context.

Theme 1: business performance and performance measurement

Business performance is related to success and the construct of "excellence" as proposed by Peters and Waterman in the 1980s. Caruana *et al.* (1995) comment that, although these so-called excellent firms in that study revealed themselves to be rather ordinary performers, the modelling technique called EXEL is able to be used in service firms with reliability and validity. Peacock (1995), like many other authors, emphasizes that there is no correct definition of good job performance and suggests that the conflicts between managerial perspectives of success should be recognized. A more holistic approach is offered by Staw (1986) who contends that performance may be staged at the level of the individual, group or the organization. The performance implications of perceptual differences between these levels is referred to as "a strategic gap" by Edgar (1996) in his study of hotels in the short-break market. The results showed considerable variation between average hotel performance but that locational strategies might optimize performance. For example, in primary locations segmentation/packaging strategies work best while optimal performance is achieved with promotional strategies in hotels located in secondary and tertiary locations.

In 1989, Witt and Witt (1989) remarked that productivity in the hotel sector is low and

that hospitality managers are reluctant to use analytical tools to monitor performance. Since then, technological advances have made information technology (IT) more widely accessible to business users. Liu's (1995) research concludes that the effective use of IT has the ability to increase overall revenue, improve customer services and to increase manpower productivity in hotel operations. The key factor is that there should be positive user attitudes to the potential advantages of the use of IT. Information technology can also be used to compare the performance of hotels and their managers. Morey and Dittman (1995) have developed a computer model to benchmark general manager performance and to take into account environmental variables which contribute to profitability. Benchmarking is an important adjunct to continuous quality improvement in which the role of upper management is crucial. Yasim and Zimmerer's (1995) model of the benchmarking of hotel operations focuses on the need to match customer requirements with hotel service quality to achieve superior performance.

Business performance may be viewed from the perspectives of a number of stakeholders and hospitality research has focused primarily on consumers and producers. Gu's (1994) study reviews US performance from the investor viewpoint in a ten-year comparative measurement of the risks and returns from hotel, casino and restaurant operations. He concludes that the casinos offers greater investment opportunities and uses two performance measures to compare the sectors. Brander-Brown and McDonnell (1995) review the use of Kaplan and Norton's "balanced score-card" to measure performance in the hospitality industry. The score-card offers an even-handed approach to performance management based on four perspectives: customer, financial, internal and innovation and learning, as shown in Figure 1.

The literature emphasizes greater concerns for those performance outcomes which can lead to organizational success in competitive hospitality environments and the challenges which are posed for management. Although "bottom line" performance measurement is important, "softer" indicators may offer

[61]

Figure 1
The four perspectives of the balanced score-card

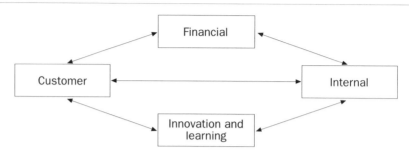

Source: Kaplan and Norton (1992)

Table I
Business performance and performance measurement

Authors	Focus	Sub-theme
Caruana (1995)	Assesses the use of a construct called EXEL to measure excellence in UK service firms and links it to business performance	Overall business performance
Peacock (1995)	Reports on a survey of the perceptions of "success" exhibited by hospitality managers	Difficulty in defining effective performance
Edgar (1996)	This study finds a "strategic gap" between intended and implemented corporate strategy which affects organizational performance	Proposes locational and sector-specific strategies
Witt and Witt (1989)	Suggests that productivity in the hotel sector is low and that it is difficult to measure	Reluctance to use analytical techniques
Liu (1995)	Investigates the relationship between information technology (IT) and business performance and suggests a positive correlation between user attitudes and the potential advantage in the use of IT	Effective management of IT
Morey and Dittman (1995)	Offers a computer model which evaluates the performance of hotel general managers against environmental variables	Measures managerial efficiency
Yasim and Zimmerer (1995)	Provides a conceptual framework of benchmarking for hotels and guidelines to assist in implementing a benchmarking programme	Primary role of upper management
Gu (1994)	Reports on a study which focuses on performance from the viewpoint of investors. Reviews risk and return in hotels, casinos and restaurants over a ten year period	Oversupply situation in USA and Europe
Brander-Brown and McDonnell (1995)	The assessment of Kaplan and Norton's "balanced scorecard" as a means of performance measurement for hotels	Performance measurement is more than profitability

greater opportunities for organizational effectiveness in the longer term. A central strategy in hospitality performance management is to focus on customer satisfaction through quality improvement.

Theme 2: process and quality improvement

Dodwell and Simmons (1994) posit that quality in hospitality services is concerned with "delighting the customer". It may be argued that this has always been the maxim of successful hospitality companies, but the need to create and maintain high quality standards could be said to be greater than ever. Day and Peters (1994) submit that a shared understanding of quality is a necessary antecedent to setting standards and that quality may be said to have static and dynamic components. Static quality is that which is normally expected by the customer such as a

Table II
Process and quality improvement

Authors	Focus	Sub-theme
Day and Peters (1994)	Argues that quality should be analysed from "static" and "dynamic" dimensions	A holistic view of quality is required
Coyle and Dale (1993)	Chronicles a study of the determinants of quality from the viewpoints of customer and provider and questions traditional methods of determining customer needs may be inadequate	Re-evaluating quality
Heymann (1992)	Sets out a quality management model which can be tailored to any organization and serves as a guideline for future action based on a holistic approach	Integrative quality management
Atkinson (1994a)	Proposes six ingredients for a successful continuous improvement programme based on employee involvement and teamworking	Organizational improvement in teams
Sparrow and Wood (1994)	This study holds that sophisticated psychological techniques are necessary to elicit employees' views as a basis for quality improvement. Increased reflection and disclosure can enhance feelings of self-worth and trust	More mature human resource strategies
Kirk (1995)	Reviews the applicability of the soft systems approach to problem solving in hospitality operations management. An open rather than a prescriptive approach is more likely to yield benefits	Involvement is related to success
Jones and Lockwood (1995)	Suggests that hospitality operations management can be characterized by a four-level model	Reconciles process and output analysis
Orgonyi (1995)	A study which considers the use of statistical process control (SPC) as a means of achieving continuous quality improvement in hospitality	Process monitoring techniques
Jienpetivate (1995)	This research used critical incident technique (CIT) to study the hotel service encounter. The investment of time and effort can yield benefits	Managing the service encounter
Breiter *et al.* (1995)	Describes the quality strategies of Bergstrom Hotels which have been practised since 1989. Emphasizes the centrality of teamworking and human resource support systems	Quality management techniques

bed free of cockroaches, while dynamic quality represents "moments of truth" of human interaction. According to Coyle and Dale (1993), quality failures are often the result of gaps in perceptions between customers and providers. They contend that more effort should be expended by providers in determining the needs and expectations of customers and that traditional methods such as questionnaires are inadequate for this purpose.

Models of quality management for hospitality are proposed by Heymann (1992) and Atkinson (1994a). Heymann's holistic approach requires organizations to develop a positive, adaptive culture to ensure continuous improvement based on systematic planning and the judicious use of people. This theme of programmed and sustained change is echoed by Atkinson's (1994a) "mix of six" approach to continuous improvement. The maintenance of quality over time requires commitment from every grade of employee and not just management. Sparrow and Wood (1994) advance the proposition that experienced food servers have a far richer picture of customers than do training manuals and that

their perceptual "maps" can assist in providing quality service. Further, such techniques produce enhanced feelings of trust and self-worth in employees as well as reducing absenteeism and waste.

The task of setting of standards requires hospitality organizations to reflect carefully on the relationship between production and service processes to customer satisfaction. Kirk (1995) reviews the applicability of soft systems methodology to hospitality operations and concludes that it is necessary to take a holistic approach in which technical sub-systems are integrated with human activity sub-systems. Catering systems, for example, require technical objectives of safety, customer satisfaction and cost control as well as recognizing the importance of human relationships in implementing these plans. Hospitality systems too, can benefit from holistic approaches and Jones and Lockwood (1995) propose a hotel operations management model which integrates the analysis of process and outputs. Techniques for analysing processes in hospitality environments are offered in postgraduate studies by

Orgonyi and Jienpetivate. Orgonyi's (1995) MSc thesis looked at the success of statistical process control (SPC) in manufacturing as a continuous quality improvement strategy for reducing variability and improving the production process. He concluded that there are differences between manufacturing and service products, but SPC can be used in hospitality as a means of monitoring measured processes. Jienpetivate (1995) studied the service encounter through the methodology of critical incident technique (CIT) and concludes that the investment of effort into managing the service encounter can lead to an enhanced understanding between the server and the served.

It is interesting to review the extent to which hospitality quality initiatives are reflected in the literature and the different approaches which are taken by firms. Breiter *et al.* (1995) remark that total quality management in hotels is becoming commonplace and recount the case in the USA of Bergstrom Hotels who have been practising quality principles since 1989. Bergstrom's "quality commitment" has evolved into continuous improvement based on systematic decision-making, teamwork and human resource support systems. Also in the USA, Ritz-Carlton Hotel company have produced "Gold Standards" which include a credo, motto and 20 "Ritz-Carlton Basics" in the quality management programme. Their initiative has led them to be the first hotel group to win the Malcolm Baldrige National Quality Award (Partlow, 1993). In the UK, the Sutcliffe Group of contract caterers seeks to define quality as a means of sustaining growth, improving client retention and focusing employees on providing a quality service (Page, 1994). Callan (1992) reports the case of the Avant Hotel in Oldham, which was the first UK hotel recipient of the British Standard BS 5750. BS 5750 is a set of documented operational quality standards that is accepted by the British Standards Institution (BSI) and regularly monitored by them. Benefits of BS 5750 for the Avant Hotel include a keener focus on staff training, reduced staff turnover, waste reduction, and widespread publicity as the first registered for BS 5750. There is, however, little evidence that BSI standards of quality have been widely espoused by hospitality firms.

The literature indicates that the setting and maintenance of quality standards is an increasingly important activity for hospitality firms, but that those techniques used in manufacturing may not be entirely applicable to the service context. The very act of process analysis is, in itself, useful, but to maintain the impetus of continuous improvement requires commitment from management and staff.

Theme 3: teamworking

Much of the literature on performance and quality management emphasizes that hospitality organizations can continuously improve their businesses through more effective analytical techniques and through people. Teamworking is a force for co-ordination and communication and is of particular use to the hotel sector where inter-departmental conflict is a characteristic feature (Dann and Hornsey, 1986) and negative images of employees affect job performance (Palmer and Lundberg, 1995). Although hotels are traditionally grouped into functional departments, Nebel *et al.* (1994) propose a re-engineering approach in which hotels group tasks into coherent business processes such as customer communication, product development and problem resolution. Hotels may not wish to espouse such radical solutions, but the literature suggests that empowerment can offer benefits for hotels. Lashley (1995) advances teamworking in hospitality as a means of empowerment and continuous improvement and cites examples such as the Accor Group (quality circles), Harvester Restaurants (autonomous work groups), the former Scott's Hotels (whatever-it-takes training), Hilton Hotels (team briefing).

Brymer (1991) suggests that empowerment can affect guest satisfaction, employee satisfaction and bottom line profits.

A natural development to teamworking initiatives is the formation of self-managed teams to solve problems and drive continuous improvement (CI). Atkinson (1994b) argues that the foundation to CI is workplace improvement teams which probably started as quality circles and may have evolved into self-managed work teams. Their aim is continuously to seek improvements within their own remit and they are supported by corrective action teams. Actual hospitality examples of self-managed teams are scarce, but Newton (1992) reports the efforts of Harvester Restaurants who formed teams according to Belbin's typology and asked them to formulate unit strategies and personal objectives over a two-day brainstorming period. Operational teams are led by an elected leader, self-managing and accountable for team recruitment and selection. Performance contracts are reviewed at meetings held bi-monthly and are supported by reward and recognition systems.

To date, there is little evidence that teamworking has been as widely espoused in hospitality as in manufacturing. Ingram *et al.* (1997) contend that much of the literature on the subject is inconclusive and anecdotal and they propose a descriptive model of effective

Table III
Teamworking in hospitality services

Authors	Focus	Sub-theme
Palmer and Lundbert (1995)	The results of this study of metaphors or mental images of hospitality employees found that negativity is more prevalent. Many metaphors relate to organization structure	Job performance influences
Nebel et al. (1994)	Proposes a hotel re-engineering approach in which traditional departments are replaced by task-driven groups. Managers are able to be leaders and facilitators rather than checkers and arbitrators	Changing role of management
Lashley (1995)	Describes the extent of teamworking in hospitality as a means of empowerment and continuous improvement	The power and benefits of teamworking
Brymer (1991)	Argues that the results of empowerment programmes in hotels can be measures in terms of guest and employee satisfaction as well as increased profits	Empowerment should cascade down the organization
Atkinson (1994b)	Suggests that the foundation of continuous improvement is self-managed work teams supported by customer feedback	Maximizing customer satisfaction
Newton (1992)	Reports on the formation of self-managing teams in Harvester Restaurants, formed according to Belbin's typology	Reward and recognition systems
Ingram et al. (1997)	Proposes a system model as the conceptual basis for teamworking research	Teamworking processes may be the greatest determinant of team effectiveness

teamworking as a basis for future research. The comparative success of quality assurance schemes such as the government-led Investors in People scheme (Ball, 1993) suggests that hospitality firms are seeking new approaches to people which can address problems such as internal conflict and staff turnover.

Thematic interrelationships

Having reviewed some dimensions of business performance and performance measurement, process and quality improvement and teamworking, it seem clear there are links between the three themes. This part explores some of these interrelationships and illustrates them in a relationship diagram shown in Figure 2.

An integrated process/people approach must specify balanced standards of performance and empower staff to perform more effectively by working together in teams. This will enable organizations to operate a quality assurance programme which is accompanied by improved customer satisfaction and performance improvement.

Figure 2
A people/process driven approach

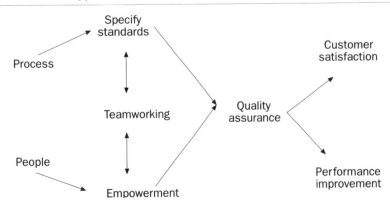

Patterns from the generic literature

Outside the hospitality industry there are many examples from around the world which indicate that teamworking has the power to improve the way that firms operate and their outputs. This section reviews literature evidence from other industries and the world of sport and considers the benefits of teamworking. Suggestions about appropriate structures and team development will be applied to the context of hospitality firms.

Evidence from other industries

There is a considerable body of evidence which demonstrates that teamworking strategies are being applied in a range of industries with apparent success. Teare *et al.* (1997) have documented case study evidence which demonstrates the increasing role of teamworking in the new process paradigm approach to attaining higher levels of service and responsiveness. They cite examples of the role of continuous improvement and self-directed teams in identifying problems and applying solutions themselves. Brown (1996) reports evidence which concludes that a quarter of UK employers recognize teamworking in their pay systems and that another 17 per cent are actively planning its introduction.

The power of teamworking

The literature suggests that teamworking has the potential to provide such benefits as improved and sustained organizational outputs (Harris and Harris, 1996) and to act as an effective agent of change, especially with the trend towards horizontal structures (Stewart and Kleiner, 1996). Teams can refocus product design processes on the customer (Valdez and Kleiner, 1996) and help develop competitive advantage (Twomey and Kleiner, 1996). A major benefit of teamworking is greater co-ordination of departments (Nurmi, 1996) and the synergy that creates. The advantages for the teams and team members include greater job satisfaction and camaraderie (Elloy and McCombs, 1996) as well as self esteem and self-actualization (Stainforth, 1996).

Shonk and Shonk (1988) submit that business teams can learn from the factors that make sports teams successful. These characteristics of unitary behaviour and "team spirit" in sports teams include, according to Syer (1986), morale, cohesion, confluence and synergy. Morale is an emotive term which refers to the contentment of the team, military unit or the organization as a whole. Cohesion is used by behaviourists who believe that an individual acts only according to the threat of a promise or reward and cohesive forces include commitment to success or task motivation, difficulty of withdrawing (due to

inertia or fear of letting down the team) or social needs (Festinger *et al.*, 1950). It may be argued that cohesion is the result rather than the cause of improved performance. This is often demonstrated in football teams who, as a result of above average performance, derive what Syer describes as confluence or "peak experiences of intense concentration and awareness when it seems impossible to do wrong". This leads to a synergy, or a sense of additional energy, strength or creative ability which is available when teams work harmoniously together for each other and themselves.

Teamworking structures

In order to succeed, teams need structures which enable them to develop and flourish. Elloy and McCombs (1996) describe a programme of greater employee participation in a US manufacturing plant based on the open systems concept. The process involved completely re-structuring the plant to form self-governing teams which were responsible for their own cost control, absenteeism, safety training, discipline and employee selection and in which leadership emerged naturally. Strachan (1996) reports on the formation of environmental action teams by such firms as Kodak, BT and Apple Computers and contends that traditional management structures may impose certain constraints on the way the team operates. He contends that "organic" cultures supported by participative styles of management best allow teamwork to flourish.

Building teams

Practical advice about building teams is plentiful in the literature. McDonald and Keys (1996), for example, identify seven major errors in teambuilding programmes from real life episodes. They stress the mutual nature of teams, which they describe as "learning and sharing systems for organization". The point that is most often stressed is the need for upper management support, without which failure is likely. An example of an empowerment effort that "came undone" is recorded by Rothstein *et al.* (1995), who report the case of a sportswear manufacturer who attempted to establish self-managed work teams but, in the absence of whole-hearted management support, the scheme fell at the first hurdle. If the teamworking ethic is to permeate down an organization, it must first be fully espoused at the top and the commitment of middle management secured. This was the case at the First National Bank of Chicago in the mid 1980s, where there was a development from a staid culture to one which showed more risk-taking and innovation through team management (Harris and Harris, 1996).

Table IV
Generic teamworking patterns

Authors	Focus	Sub-theme
Teare et al. (1997)	Interprets case study examples of 14 UK and US-based manufacturing and service firms and assesses the contribution of work-based teams to quality improvement	Teamworking can be used in single problem and team-directed projects
Elloy and McCombs (1996)	Applies open systems theory to the redesign of organization processes in a manufacturing plant. Involvement of the workforce helped to raise commitment, production and job satisfaction	Practical application of theory
Twomey and Kleiner (1996)	Defines the essential factors of effective teams and describes the process of team development. Teamwork can promote camaraderie	Developing competitive advantage
Nurmi (1996)	Examines four team leadership styles: dictatorial, compromise, integrative teamwork and synergistic teamwork	Creating optimum new solutions
Higgs (1996)	Discusses the literature on cross-cultural diversity on teambuilding in a global context and outlines a framework for building cultural awareness. International teambuilding strategies take account of different personal styles and behaviours	Increasing globalization
Strachan (1996)	Highlights the creation of environmental "green" teams by large firms who champion environmental excellence	Teamworking structures
McDonald and Keys (1996)	Identifies seven major errors found in teambuilding programmes and offers guidelines for overcoming them	Team/organization relationships
Stewart and Kleiner (1996)	Outlines the benefits of teamworking to the change process in the information technology industry and the trend to the horizontal organization	Democracy in business
Brown (1996)	Reports on real life and research findings on team rewards and condenses them into the advice to be strategic, flexible and open	Designing equitable team rewards
Valdez and Kleiner (1996)	Reports on the development of integrated product teams in redesigning the processes of firms in the defence industry	Empowerment of cross-functional teams
Wilson (1996)	Describes the process of team development and especially the importance of "catalyst" team members	Team focus
Harris and Harris (1996)	Discusses the creation of an effective team culture which is necessary to achieve and maintain high output at a time of fast growth	Self-managed teams
Stainforth (1996)	Argues that effective teamworking requires relevant organizational systems and practices rather than those designed for the employment of individuals	Benefits of teamworking to self-actualization
Esquivel and Kleiner (1996)	Focuses on the different types of conflict that characterize team development and argues that the ability to manage it successfully will give work teams the competitive edge	Mature team leadership

While it is important that top management set the scene and focus the goals, they must allow the teams the space to develop themselves because, as Fred Wilson (1996) suggests, "great teams build themselves". An important contributory factor to teams' success is a suitable leadership style which enables synergy to take place. Nurmi (1996) contends that synergistic teams can be "fertilized" by management, but after that, management has little to say in igniting the process. Another role of the leader is to manage the team processes effectively towards the goals and in a mature and supportive atmosphere. Esquivel and Kleiner (1996) stress the importance of conflict management in which the focus is on the issues and not individuals and in which teams develop "a sense of family". Team members must feel that they can contribute "safely" in an ambience of trust and confidence.

Conclusions and applications to hospitality services

The generic literature suggests that many firms, particularly in manufacturing, have successfully implemented teamworking strategies and have derived benefits from doing so.

Hadyn Ingram
Performance management: processes, quality and teamworking

As with any leading edge management strategy, its longer term value can only be speculated on; longitudinal studies, and eventually hindsight, will help in this respect. Teamworking certainly seems to provide a means whereby organizations can focus on the key contemporary imperatives of managing quality and processes to improve performance and customer satisfaction. While improvements in systems or technology are incremental, the capacities of people seem to know no bounds.

It is more difficult, however, to apply these lessons from other industries to the hospitality context. Part of the problem may be the traditional nature of hospitality management and its attendant functional departmental structure which can contribute to inertia, conflict and lacklustre performance. Another difficulty arises in matching a generic team strategy to hospitality units of diverse sizes, cultures and product offering, many of whom are struggling with the challenge of brand identity. One hospitality firm who has consistently tried to reconcile the opposing tensions of standardization and empowerment is the Accor Group of France. From earlier experiments with quality circles, their Novotel chain of three-star hotels has developed a new approach to developing staff and ensuring standard brand quality. Susan Segal-Horn (1995) reports that flexible working patterns have broken down the staff demarcation normal within hotels and has enabled the creation of an "open space" approach to organizational learning. Firmly at the helm of this initiative is the unit general manager, whose role has been redefined much closer to the social role of a ship's captain. As a result, Segal-Horn reports greater collaboration between levels and an increased autonomy which has added value for staff and customers alike. The success of Novotel's approach may encourage other hospitality firms to follow their example.

In conclusion, teamworking may be seen, not so much as a discrete force for change, but more as the social mechanism through which improvement may take place. In order for a teamworking programme to be successful management must have the vision to inspire and the courage to withdraw and let the process gain it own impetus. Teamworking may not come easily, but its potential rewards are improved process and quality management as well as enhanced individual and organizational improvement.

References

Atkinson, C. (1994a), "Continuous improvement: the ingredients of change", *International Journal of Contemporary Hospitality Management*, Vol. 6 Nos. 1/2, pp. 6-8.

Atkinson, C. (1994b), "Continuous improvement the total teamwork way", *International Journal of Contemporary Hospitality Management*, Vol. 6 No. 3, pp. i-ii.

Ball, S. (1993), "Investing in people", *Voice*, July/August, pp. 22-4.

Brander-Brown, J. and McDonnell, B. (1995), "The balanced score-card: short term guest or long-term resident?", *International Journal of Contemporary Hospitality Management*, Vol. 7 Nos. 2/3, pp. 7-11.

Breiter, D., Tyink, S.A. and Corey-Tuckwell, S. (1995), "Bergstrom Hotels: a case study in quality", *International Journal of Contemporary Hospitality Management*, Vol. 7 No. 6, pp. 14-18.

Brown, D. (1996), "Team rewards: lessons from the coal-face", *Team Performance Management*, Vol. 2 No. 2, pp. 6-12.

Brymer, R.A. (1991), "Employee empowerment: a guest-driven leadership strategy", *Cornell Hotel and Restaurant Administration Quarterly*, Vol. 32 No. 1, pp. 56-8.

Callan, R.J. (1992), "Quality control at Avant Hotels – the debut of BS 5750", *Service Industries Journal*, Vol. 12 No. 1, pp. 17-33.

Caruana, A., Pitt, L.F. and Morris, M.H. (1995), "Are there excellent service firms and do they perform well?", *Service Industries Journal*, Vol. 15 No. 3, pp. 243-56.

Coyle, M.P. and Dale, B.G. (1993), "Quality in the hospitality industry: a study", *International Journal of Hospitality Management*, Vol. 12 No. 2, pp. 141-53.

Dann, D.T. and Hornsey, T. (1986), "Towards a theory of interdepartmental conflict in hotels", *International Journal of Hospitality Management*, Vol. 5 No. 1, pp. 23-8.

Day, A. and Peters, J. (1994), "Rediscovering standards: static and dynamic quality", *International Journal of Contemporary Hospitality Management*, Vol. 6 Nos. 1/2, pp. 81-4.

Dodwell, S. and Simmons, P. (1994), "Trials and tribulations in the pursuit of quality improvement", *International Journal of Contemporary Hospitality Management*, Vol. 6 Nos. 1/2, pp. 14-18.

Edgar, D.A. (1996), "The strategic gap: a multi-site, short break perspective", in Johns, N. (Ed.), *Productivity Management in Hospitality and Tourism*, Cassell, London, pp. 38-54.

Elloy, D. and McCombs, T (1996), "Application of open systems theory in a manufacturing plant", *Team Performance Management*, Vol. 2 No. 3, pp. 15-22.

Esquivel, M.A. and Kleiner, B.H. (1996), "The importance of conflict in work team effectiveness", *Team Performance Management*, Vol. 2 No. 3, pp. 42-8.

Festinger, L., Schachter, S. and Back, K. (1950), *Social Pressures in Informal Groups: A Study of a Housing Project*, Harper and Row, New York.

Gu, Z. (1994), "Hospitality return, risk and performance indexes: a ten-year examination", *Hospitality Research Journal*, Vol. 17 No. 3, pp. 17-26.

Harris, P.R. and Harris, K.G. (1996), "Managing effectively through teams", *Team Performance Management*, Vol. 2 No. 3, pp. 23-6.

Heymann, K. (1992), "Quality management: a ten-point model", *Cornell Hotel and Restaurant Administration Quarterly*, Vol. 33 No. 5, pp. 50-60.

Higgs, M. (1996), "Overcoming the problems of cultural differences to establish success for international management teams", *Team Performance Management*, Vol. 2 No. 1, pp. 36-43.

Ingram, H., Teare, R., Scheuing, E. and Armistead, C. (1997), "A systems model of effective teamworking", *The TQM Magazine*, Vol. 9 No. 2, pp. 118-27.

Jienpetivate, M. (1995), "The management of service encounters", MSc dissertation, University of Surrey, Guildford.

Jones, P. and Lockwood, A. (1995), "Hospitality operating systems", *International Journal of Contemporary Hospitality Management*, Vol. 7 No. 5, pp. 17-20.

Kaplan, R.S and Norton, D.P., (1992) "The balanced scorecard – measures that drive performance", *Harvard Business Review*, Vol. 70 No. 1, pp. 71-9.

Kirk, D. (1995), "Hard and soft systems: a common paradigm for operations" , *International Journal of Contemporary Hospitality Management*, Vol. 7 No. 5, pp. 13-16.

Lashley, C. (1995), "Towards an understanding of employee empowerment in hospitality services", *International Journal of Contemporary Hospitality Management*, Vol. 7 No. 1, pp. 27-32.

Liu, M-C.B. (1995), "Information technology and management of hotel operations: an examination of the link between the effective use of IT, managerial effectiveness and improvement in business performance", MSc dissertation, University of Surrey, Guildford.

McDonald, J.M. and Keys, J.B. (1996), "The seven deadly sins of teambuilding", *Team Performance Management*, Vol. 2 No. 2, pp. 19-26.

Morey, R.C. and Dittman (1995), "Evaluating a hotel GM's performance", *Cornell Hotel and Restaurant Administration Quarterly*, Vol. 36 No. 5, pp. 30-2.

Nebel, III, E.C., Rutherford, D. and Schaffer, J.D. (1994), "Reengineering the hotel organization", *Cornell Hotel and Restaurant Administration Quarterly*, Vol. 35 No. 5, pp. 88-95.

Newton, S. (1992), "Customer obsession". *Managing Service Quality*, pp. 269-74.

Nurmi, R. (1996), "Teamwork and team leadership", *Team Performance Management*, Vol. 2, No. 1, pp. 9-13.

Orgonyi, V. (1995), "An exploratory study into the applicability of statistical process control (SPC) in the hospitality industry", MSc dissertation, University of Surrey, Guildford.

Page, C. (1994), "Sutcliffe Catering's approach to continuous improvement", *International Journal of Contemporary Hospitality Management*, Vol. 6 Nos. 1/2, pp. 19-24.

Palmer, I. and Lundberg, C.C. (1995), "Metaphors of hospitality organizations", *Cornell Hotel and Restaurant Administration Quarterly*, Vol. 36 No. 3, pp. 80-5.

Partlow, C.G. (1993), "How Ritz-Carlton applies 'TQM'", *Cornell Hotel and Restaurant Administration Quarterly*, August, Vol. 34 No. 4, pp. 16-24.

Peacock, M. (1995), "A job well done: hospitality managers and success", *International Journal of Contemporary Hospitality Management*, Vol. 7 Nos. 2/3, pp. 48-51.

Rothstein, L.R., Hackman, J.R., Pascual, E., Gelinas, M.V., James, R.G. and Randolph, W.A. (1995), "The empowerment effort that came undone", *Harvard Business Review*, January/February, Vol. 73 No. 1, p. 20.

Segal-Horn, S. (1995), "Core competence and international strategy in service multinationals", in Teare, R. and Armistead, C. (Eds), *Service Management: New Directions, New Perspectives*, Cassell, London.

Shonk, W. and Shonk, J.H. (1988), "What business teams can learn from athletic teams", *Personnel*, June, Vol. 65 No. 6, p. 76.

Sparrow, J. and Wood, G. (1994), "You're stopping me from giving quality service", *International Journal of Contemporary Hospitality Management*, Vol. 6 Nos. 1/2, pp. 61-7.

Stainforth, D. (1996), "Teamworking, or individual working in a team?", *Team Performance Management*, Vol. 2 No. 3, pp. 37-41.

Staw, B.M. (1986), "Organizational psychology and the pursuit of the happy/productive worker", *California Management Review*, Summer, Vol. 4, pp. 40-53.

Stewart, G.R. and Kleiner, B.H. (1996), "The enabling power of teams and information technology", *Team Performance Management*, Vol. 2 No. 2, pp. 13-18.

Strachan, P.A. (1996), "Achieving environmental excellence through effective teamwork", *Team Performance Management*, Vol. 2 No.1, pp. 25-9.

Syer, J. (1986), *Team Spirit: The Elusive Experience*, The Kingswood Press, London, pp. 13-14.

Teare, R, Ingram, H., Scheuing, E. and Armistead, C. (1997), "Organizational teamworking frameworks: evidence from UK and US-based firms", *Journal of Service Industry Management*, Vol. 8, No. 3 (forthcoming).

Twomey, K. and Kleiner, B.H. (1996), "Teamwork: the essence of the successful organization", *Team Performance Management*, Vol. 2 No. 1, pp. 6-8.

Valdez, R. and Kleiner, B.H. (1996), "How to build teamwork in the defence industry", *Team Performance Management*, Vol. 2 No. 2, pp. 41-8.

Wilson, F. (1996), "Great teams build themselves", *Team Performance Management*, Vol. 2 No. 2, pp. 27-31.

Witt, C. and Witt, S.F. (1989), "Why productivity in the hotel sector is low", *International Journal of Contemporary Hospitality Management*, Vol. 1 No. 2, pp. 28-33.

Yasim, M. and Zimmerer, T.W. (1995), "The role of benchmarking in achieving continuous service quality", *International Journal of Contemporary Hospitality Management*, Vol. 7 No. 4, pp. 27-32.

Supporting managerial learning in the workplace

Richard Teare
Research Director (Europe) Worldwide Hospitality and Tourism Trends

Suggests that more and more organizations are attempting to establish a culture of learning that values the knowledge that employees have derived from learning how to perform effectively in the workplace. Reviews recent contributions to the literature on aspects of managerial learning and addresses the question "how do managers learn best in the workplace?" Draws from articles published between 1994-1996 in eight journals: *Executive Development; Journal of Management Development; Journal of Organizational Change Management; Leadership & Organization Development Journal; Management Development Review; Team Performance Management; The Journal of Workplace Learning; The Learning Organization.* Focuses on four themes: managerial learning and work; coaching, mentoring and team development; competences, managerial learning and the curriculum; work-based action learning. Concludes with a summary of the implications for managerial learning.

Introduction

Evidence suggests that more and more organizations are attempting to establish a culture of learning that values the knowledge that employees have derived from learning how to perform effectively in the workplace. However, an organizational initiative to "learn more and do better" is unlikely to flourish if it is imposed and the contention here is that it is necessary to begin by encouraging and motivating individuals to learn and to take the initiative in identifying their own learning needs. This article reviews recent contributions to the literature on aspects of managerial learning and addresses the question "how do managers learn best in the workplace?" The review is drawn from articles published between 1994-1996 in eight journals: *Executive Development; Journal of Management Development; Journal of Organizational Change Management; Leadership & Organization Development Journal; Management Development Review; Team Performance Management; The Journal of Workplace Learning; The Learning Organization.* The review focuses on four themes: managerial learning and work; coaching, mentoring and team development; competences, managerial learning and the curriculum; work-based action learning and concludes with a summary of the implications for managerial learning.

Theme 1: managerial learning and work

The relationships between managerial learning and work are wide-ranging and Table I identifies a number of sub-themes that reflect this. The variables include: how managerial work is defined and how individual work preferences influence work styles, managers' use of their time and interpersonal communications; identifying and realizing the potential for development and the means of achieving it through formal and informal learning goals.

Shenhar and Renier (1996) see the main task of management as "getting results through the work of others for the benefit of the client". They depict a parallel process of questioning and applying skills and knowledge, drawn from four sub-domains – technical, human, operational and strategic. The key tasks stem from the "what" and "how" of managing:

- What is management? – spans aspects of science and art; encompasses people, technology and money; relates to the systemized use of resources, processes, situations and relations; involves taking responsibility for achieving results, for people and for organizational activity.
- How to manage? – requires information gathering, decision-taking and action; uses and develops interpersonal skills, involves planning, organizing, staffing, leading and controlling.

Commenting on the patterns and interactions associated with managerial work, Oshagbemi (1995) observes that:

...not only are managerial functions varied, but also the locations where these are performed, the people managers interact with and the duration of managerial activities. In addition, managers experience different forms of fleeting contacts and interruptions during the course of their working day. This is a feature that may hinder their creative work, if care is not taken (p. 32).

His findings suggest that improvements in the use of managerial time can be obtained by focusing attention on: the management of meetings; the management of paper and desk work activities; delegation and supervision and the management of fleeting contacts and interruptions.

McKenna (1994) reviews the changes that are affecting managerial work – he sees increasing discontinuity, uncertainty, ambiguity and complexity – and believes that traditional approaches to management development are not sufficiently flexible to cope with these conditions. Instead, he proposes a forum for "generative learning" so that managers can challenge assumptions and paradigms; enable participants to challenge themselves and achieve "higher order" learning that enlightens rather than merely refreshes. Personal learning needs are central to the forum concept so that "value added" initiatives are generated from the

Table I
Managerial learning and work

Authors	Focus	Sub-theme
Shenhar and Renier (1996)	Applies a modular approach to defining managerial work and roles so that managers can assess the complexities of their own jobs and related development needs	Defining managerial work
Margerison and McCann (1996b)	Outlines the eight main types of work in organizations (advising, innovating, promoting, developing, organizing, producing, inspecting, maintaining) and advocates self-profiling or work preferences so as to understand and work effectively with others	Preferences and managerial work
Oshagbemi (1995)	Discusses the nature and the reality of managerial work and how managers spend their time	Managers' use of their time
Margerison and McCann (1996a)	Profiles five key communication skills – enquiring, diagnosing, summarizing, proposing and directing. Relates these skills to either a problem-centred or solution-centred focus and describes a self-assessment resource for use in personal and team development	Communication skills and managerial work
Dixon (1995a, 1995b)	Summarizes a study undertaken in 46 privatized firms concerned with middle managers and their attitudes towards the culture change they had experienced during the privatization process	Middle management potential and development
Megginson (1994)	Considers the challenges posed by helping managers to learn when they are reluctant to take responsibility for the direction of their own development or seem unable to learn from their own experiences	Planned and emergent managerial learning
Mumford (1994)	Investigates how managers learn from experience with reference to a study of 21 directors in 15 UK organizations and proposes four approaches (intuitive, incidental, retrospective and prospective)	Learning from managerial experience
Barclay (1996)	Emphasizes the value of real world experience in learning about management – especially interpersonal skills development, learning about one's organization and industry and learning how to manage personal development and self-understanding	Learning from experience with learning logs

reality of the middle manager's own world. In order to capture own world realities, McKenna advocates the use of a "complexity map". The complexity map seeks to portray a personalized view of reality for each participant attending the forum and a snapshot of how their learning needs are woven into it and might be deduced from it. In particular, the map helps to identify some of the personal paradigms and assumptions that need to be challenged in order to "stretch" the participant. In so doing, the map provides a basis for action by depicting the reality-based "real plays" that confront participants, together with the patterns and interrelationships on which they need to act in order to leverage personal development and business improvement gains from the complexities that surround them. This form of cognitive mapping offers a dynamic and personalized means of enabling managers to assess their current capabilities and learning needs. Set in the context of a generative learning forum, it provides a diagnostic tool for self-managed learning and development.

Dixon (1995a, 1995b) relates a study of privatized firms to the culture change needed to "release" the potential of middle managers working in newly privatized organizations. She outlines her findings with reference to the views of managers on the need to: invest in education and training; create, translate and share the "new" strategic vision; establish constructive channels for communicating with senior managers; develop incentives and rewards; and break with tradition by encouraging middle managers to initiate and lead. Dixon observes that: "The overwhelming demand from middle managers was for the organization to invest in education for all levels of employee. There was an implication that the organization needed to be creative in the type of training and education provided as the 'traditional' approaches were no longer appropriate…" (Dixon, 1995b, p. 11).

Mumford (1994) examines the proposition that managers learn in hindsight by reviewing the experiences they have had and, less frequently, learn by identifying in advance how to use opportunities for learning as a means of self-development. He uses evidence from a study conducted over a three-month period by personal interview, with 21 directors from 15 UK organizations to characterize four approaches to learning. The purpose of the interviews was to discuss the respondents' experiences at work and what they had learned from them so as to explore how they might use alternative ways of analyzing experiences and ultimately enhance their capacity to learn at work. The four approaches defined by Mumford are:

- *The intuitive approach* – learning from experience, but not through a conscious process. Learning or developmental issues are rarely, if ever, mentioned, as this approach sees managing and good business practices as synonymous with learning.
- *The incidental approach* – learning by chance from activities that prompt the individual to reflect and review. Typically, this includes unusual occurrences and planned activities with unanticipated or undesirable outcomes.
- *The retrospective approach* – learning from experience by reviewing what happened and reaching conclusions about it. Prompted mainly by mishaps or mistakes, but those who use this approach are more inclined to draw lessons from unexpected variances.
- *The prospective approach* – includes retrospective components and an element of planning to learn before an event takes place. Here, future events are seen not merely as things to be successfully completed but as opportunities to learn.

Mumford adds: "Individuals using this approach are expectant learners with their antennae constantly tuned in to the possibility of learning from a whole variety of experiences" (p. 6).

Theme 2: coaching, mentoring and team development

The learner support provided for managers – whether it be individual coaching and mentoring or work group related, plays an integral role in workplace learning. Table II lists a set of sub-themes that spans: the role of coaching in developing managers (including the application of sports coaching techniques to team-building in business); mentoring and other forms of organizational support; learning and team development; work group dynamics; and learning and cross-functional team development.

Phillips (1996) examines the possibilities for using coaching as a management tool and considers its part in the management process. He identifies a number of applications and outlines the roles and responsibilities of both the coach and those being coached. He sees flexibility as the key with the coach acting as an enabler. Bloch (1995) relates "soft" skills development in the workplace to enabling employees to achieve their potential and she uses evidence from a study to emphasize the perceived value of internal coaching to organizations:

> Individuals who are given ownership of their own development and career management are usually more highly motivated than those whose paths are mapped out for them. *Yet the survey found that only around one-third of the companies surveyed encouraged individuals to take responsibility for their own development.* Over half said the development of future top managers should be the joint responsibility of the individual, his or her line manager, and the company. However, what actually happens in practice is sometimes very different. As one respondent remarked: "Responsibility for development is meant to be tripartite, but we spend out lives trying to get the line manager involved" (pp. 20-21).

Forret *et al.* (1996) review the issues involved in the development and implementation of in-company mentoring programmes, with reference to interviews with managers in five organizations who had established their own programmes. Scandura *et al.* (1996) address the question: "Why do mentors engage in mentoring?" and discuss the role of leadership in the development of leader-supported mentoring processes. They offer an array of insights on the process of mentoring and the

Figure 1
Interrelationships between personal and organizational development

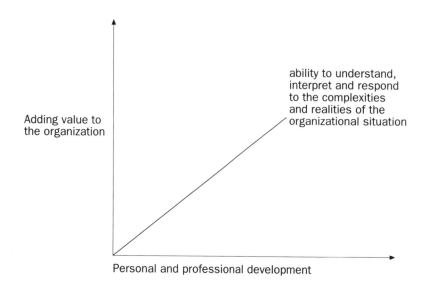

Adding value to the organization

ability to understand, interpret and respond to the complexities and realities of the organizational situation

Personal and professional development

Source: adapted from McKenna (1994, p. 9)

Table II
Coaching, mentoring and team development

Authors	Focus	Sub-theme
Bloch (1995)	Reports that 14 respondents (from a survey of 39 firms) cited internal coaching as a key method used to develop managers; more than 25 per cent of the sample were using external consultants as mentors	The role of coaching in developing managers
McNutt and Wright (1995)	Observes numerous parallels between sport and business and suggests that the methods used by successful sports coaches might be used to improve employee performance	Applies sports coaching techniques to team-building in business
Veale and Wachtel (1996)	Describes Coca-Cola Foods' coaching and mentoring programmes and relates mentoring to human resource development strategy	An integrated approach to coaching and mentoring
Forret, Turban and Dougherty (1996)	Provides a "how to" overview on the steps involved in setting-up a mentoring programme and outlines the benefits of such a programme for the organization and for the mentees and mentors	A practical guide to mentoring
Booth (1996)	Contrasts mentoring with typical employee/manager relationships and considers the advantages and disadvantages and how gender influences the mentoring process with reference to a case study of two supervisory mentoring relationships	Mentoring and other forms of organizational relations
Beeby and Simpson (1995)	Describes a non-prescriptive means of assisting managers to recognize and work on change issues. The approach uses a cognitive mapping technique to draw on the experiences of managers and to define causal problems and appropriate responses	Cognitive mapping and learner development
Strachan (1996)	Reviews the organizational literature and identifies the role of teamworking in building a learning organization	Learning and team development
Kur (1996)	Depicts patterns of team behaviour using a series of temperaments. Reflects the dynamic qualities of groups of individuals working separately and interacting together to achieve agreed tasks	Work group dynamics and learning
Proehl (1996)	Reviews the effectiveness of cross-functional teams in tackling broad-scale organizational problems. Identifies some of the difficulties in sustaining cross-functional team effort and considers the implications for team development	Cross-functional team development

range of relationships that need managing if the programme is to yield benefits for mentors, mentees and the organization as a whole. Clawson (1996) presents mentoring as a valuable form of social development and raises questions about how mentoring might be shaped by the era of electronic communications. He views mentoring as a vital support mechanism in the information age and poses a number of questions for mentors to address in the information age:

- How will people find their protégé or mentor counterparts in the new era? Will they continue to work through face-to-face meetings or will there be forums set up on the Internet like the personal ad columns in newspapers?
- How long will these relationships last? (With e-mail providing worldwide support, there is no proximity reason for breaking

them off when the mentee is promoted or transferred).
- How can companies take advantage of the new technologies and the new insights about mentoring to foster and encourage healthy, working developmental relationships among their employees?
- How will cross-cultural mentoring work out? Will there be early examples to encourage and guide subsequent generations?

Theme 3: competences, managerial learning and the curriculum

The extent to which workplace learning can be formalized and even measured in relation to specific outcomes is considered here. Table III depicts an array of sub-themes relating to: the attainment of core competences and their relationship to individual performance; open

Table III

Competences, managerial learning and the curriculum

Authors	Focus	Sub-theme
Lane and Robinson (1995)	Reviews aspects of the management charter initiative (MCI) and its aim of establishing standards of good practice for managers in the UK	Competences for managers
Ashton (1996)	Reports on how Holiday Inn Worldwide has implemented competency-based human resource strategies which provide a direct link between individual performance and business objectives	Core competences and individual performance
Davies (1996)	Surveys the literature on open and distance learning (includes flexible, self-paced and resource-based learning) and identifies a gap that might be partially filled by a more comprehensive model of open learning in management development	Open and distance learning in management
King (1996)	Describes IKEA's self-managed learning programme which is being used to support its expansion plans and to strengthen its competitive position	Self-managed learning
Kilcourse (1995)	Decries the rapid proliferation of business schools and asserts that dynamic, continuous change poses new challenges for managers, requiring a different form of management development	Relating management development to current and future needs
Critten (1996)	Makes a case for a new kind of partnership between universities and their local communities within which organizational as well as individual learning can be recognized, developed and accredited	University and community learning networks
Carnall (1995)	Examines the changes which are likely to occur in MBA programmes during the coming decade. Predicts that the "third generation" MBA will place more emphasis on the learning process than its curriculum and content	The future orientation of MBA programmes
Zuber-Skerritt (1995)	Explores ideas and issues related to management education and development for the new learning organization and presents an example of a course design for experienced managers which is work-based	Relating course design to organizational learning

Figure 2

Cycle of key strategic actions and decisions

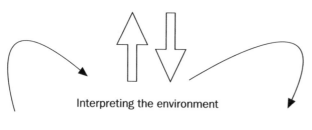
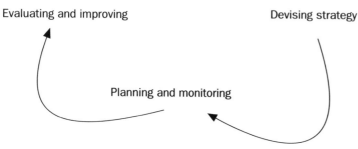

Interpreting the environment

Evaluating and improving

Devising strategy

Planning and monitoring

Source: adapted from Lane and Robinson (1995, p. 7)

and distance learning in management; self-managed learning; relating management development to current and future needs; university and community learning networks; the future orientation of MBA programmes and relating course design to organizational learning.

Lane and Robinson (1995) report on a study undertaken on behalf of the Management Charter Initiative (MCI). The study sought to determine the main areas of decision taking and action which are of strategic importance to organizations and need to be implemented effectively.

These are:

• *Understanding and influencing the environment*. Identifying and evaluating opportunities and threats or obstacles for the organization in relation to its internal and external environments.

• *Setting the strategy and gaining commitment*. Contributions to developing and communicating the mission, objectives,

goals, values and policies of the organization and its units.
• *Planning, implementing and monitoring.* Developing and implementing programmes, projects and operating plans for the organization.
• *Evaluating and improving performance.* Reviewing and evaluating objectives and policies and their implementation.

Pierce *et al.*'s (1995) follow-up survey confirms the significance of these core competence areas and they report a high level of agreement and acceptance among senior managers from a wide range of organizations.

Loan-Clarke (1996) reviews aspects of the debate about the merits of implementing MCI standards and questions whether a national standards-based approach can, in fact, deliver improved managerial performance. The most fundamental criticism concerns the claim regarding the relevance of the management standards to all organizations. Loan-Clarke argues that it is not possible for the standards to have specific contextual relevance so as to reflect organizational culture and industry sector requirements. He believes that it may be more appropriate for the MCI to emphasize the exchange value national standards, rather than its specific value to individual employers. A CBI review of NVQs in 1994 recommended that a core set of competences, with choices from a range of options, may be the best way of tailoring competence-based development to specific individual and organizational needs. Yet, the emphasis of management NVQs still places greater value on being assessed for a qualification than the process of learning and development.

Ashton (1996) explains how a series of core competences were identified and defined by Holiday Inn Worldwide (HIW). High and low performers were selected by management for behavioural event interviews with external consultants and this activity yielded details of career highlights, job challenges and difficulties. After this, high performance role models were constructed around nine core competences viewed by HIW as effective predictors of job performance, relative to key organizational criteria.

The competence areas are:
• *Customer service orientation.* Understanding and acting on the needs of others to serve them better.
• *Flexibility.* The ability to adapt and work effectively in varied groups and situations.
• *Commitment to organizational values.* Acting consistently, in accordance with corporate values and standards.
• *Achievement orientation.* A desire to improve performance, related to challenging objectives and standards of excellence.
• *Initiative and proactivity.* Self-motivation, persistence and reaching beyond the job description for potential outcomes.
• *Organizational influence.* Influencing others effectively.
• *Creative problem solving.* Identifying patterns in problem situations that are not obviously related and achieving solutions.
• *Enablement.* Inspiring acceptance of added responsibilities and accountabilities.
• *Developing others.* To enhance talent or performance.

The competence model is viewed as an integral approach, spanning selection, training and development and performance management. During selection, applicants are assessed on two business unit criteria – position requirements stated in the form of knowledge, skills and abilities (KSAs). These are the basic qualifications for a given job, together with the core competences and applicants must meet the minimum threshold in both areas before a job offer is made. In relation to performance management, specific KSAs are agreed between managers, supervisors and operatives at the beginning of each year, with appraisals twice annually at mid-year (optional) and at year-end (compulsory). Managers are expected to seek inputs from an employee's peers, customers or, if applicable, subordinates so as to ensure that the review is as rounded and accurate as possible. The review process is meant to be open, discursive and encompass aspects of negotiation and task clarification.

Hilgert (1996) reasons that for a working executive, the decision to pursue an advanced academic degree is a major choice that involves a significant commitment of time and effort as well as an array of implications for family, social and professional commitments. Hilgert investigates the reasons why executives take this decision and identifies differences by age group. For respondents in their 30s, the meaning of pursuing advanced study centres on issues of increased self-confidence and growth, authority and status. For the late 40s respondent, education goals tend to reflect a considered view of "what next" in life and a reaffirmation of self; these considerations also affect respondents embarking on a course of study in their 50s, with the added incentive of a planned career change and/or preparation for a post-retirement career. Almost all the study respondents said that support and encouragement from workplace colleagues was important to them and in the majority of cases, represented a significant source of positive meaning for educational activities.

Hilgert (1995) poses a series of questions relating to the outcomes of an executive MBA programme: Does the significant investment of time, self and economic resources result in a substantial broadening of perspectives? Have the graduates moved towards a more global, integrative view of their organizations? Are the graduates more flexible and better equipped to deal with change? And how are these outcomes reflected through the various aspects of self? His study uses survey and interview techniques and his data reveal a number of "life changing" developmental outcomes. The data showed that the educational experience impacted on the personal self, the career self and the self in significant relationships. More specifically, the study revealed that developmental changes had occurred in that there appeared to be evidence of increasingly complex thinking processes and cognitive structures, changes in world view, perceptions of self, and approaches to problem solving. Baruch and Leeming (1996) present the results of a study concerned with the design of a business school MBA curriculum. They explain how the views of its past students were sought. Graduates saw adaptability and flexibility as key considerations in building a programme that could cater for both generalization and specialization and provide the appropriate learning skills to equip future graduates with the competences seen as desirable in business.

Kilcourse (1995) observes that the scale and pace of change that managers in most industries must now respond to is both unprecedented and discontinuous in nature. The responsive organization is now leaner and flatter than ever before and Kilcourse believes that: "...teams in tomorrow's commercial maelstrom will need 'hands on' help in turning 'here and now' problems into learning opportunities. In short, they will need the kind of help at present available from only a handful of business schools". Bolton (1996) sees the problem as but one form of criticism levelled at existing business school curricula and describes an initiative to re-position an MBA programme in collaboration with human resource professionals so as to produce a more innovative, international, practical and reflective study experience. A further example of collaborative programme development comes from Blackburn and Fryer (1996) who describe a management development course that encompasses work-based learning, mentoring and accreditation of prior learning.

Lorange (1996) advances the proposition that business schools should be learning organizations with the faculty member as the learner and contributing to various modes of organizational learning. Osborne (1995) makes a similar set of points and, using the analogy of expensive trains heading off the rails, asserts that business schools must learn to do what they teach – i.e. become learning organizations – if they are to stay relevant in a rapidly changing world. Zuber-Skerritt (1995) profiles an approach that she views as highly relevant to personal and organizational learning. She describes an executive MBA course by action learning which is work-integrated, learner-centred, problem-focused, interdisciplinary in nature and founded on adult learning principles. It aims to facilitate organizational learning and development as well as the personal and professional development of senior managers, who are able to upgrade their knowledge and skills and exchange their work experience and ideas with fellow executives in small groups.

Theme 4: work-based action learning

Work-based action learning seeks to relate the curriculum to learner needs and aspirations and to the organizational setting. In so doing, it is seen to be relevant and to deliver benefits for individuals (managerial learning) and for the sponsor (organizational learning). The sub-themes in Table IV relate to articles that address the steps involved in: using action learning in the learning organization; relating action research to managerial development; action learning and its impact on corporate culture; using action learning and research skills in the workplace; contributions from the learning set in action learning and measuring return on investment from management education.

Cusins (1996) defines action learning as a "dynamic syndrome" or flowing together of four primary activities, each of which enhances the others. These are experiential learning, which is problem oriented and with problem solving it is augmented by the acquisition of additional relevant knowledge and the support of a co-learner group. O'Neill (1996) believes that a willingness to "learn how to learn" and the ability to learn from experience are among the best ways of coping with continuous change. She views action learning as an effective means of helping individuals to acquire new learning skills and the learning adviser plays an instrumental role in this process. In contrast to the

Table IV
Work-based action learning

Authors	Focus	Sub-theme
Harrison (1996)	Critically examines the concepts of action learning (AL) and the learning organization and concludes that AL offers the potential to develop strategic awareness and thinking even in turbulent environmental conditions	Using action learning in the learning organization
Chan (1994)	Relates an action learner's experience of action research and discusses how AL and action research deliver a balance of knowledge and action, academic rigour and managerial relevance	Relating action research to managerial development
Reeves (1996)	Compares two companies' use of action learning, one primarily for individual staff development, and a second where action learning's questioning, problem-solving ethos had pervaded corporate life	Action learning and its impact on corporate culture
Howell (1994)	Presents a case study of the International Management Centres (IMC) and shows that its graduate managers can operationalize AL and action research to bring about organizational, professional and personal development as well as productivity improvements	Using action learning and research skills in the workplace
Mumford (1996)	Identifies a gap in the current literature on action learning re: drawing contributions from set members as distinct from facilitators. Offers a method that might be used to overcome this bias	Contributions from the learning set in action learning
Wills and Oliver (1996)	Report on a four-year impact analysis of action learning MBA programmes. The findings reveal an array of benefits for employing organizations and show that individual managers gained a variety of "soft" benefits	Measuring return on investment from management education

traditional business curriculum, a "dynamic" syllabus for work-based action learning seeks to address specific, relevant questions for the organization and its members, rather than following a prescribed, "static" list of topics. A dynamic curriculum guides individuals to draw from the body of knowledge and an array of other sources (such as company literature and other contextualized information). Dilworth (1996) sees a need to interrelate academic and workplace domains and argues that by addressing either domain in relative exclusion from the other risks creating a workplace context where learners are able to grasp real-world problems but lack the underlying academic knowledge to solve them.

Limerick *et al.* (1994) consider the characteristics of an action learning organization in terms of its bias for reflection-in-action, formation of learning alliances, development of external networks, multiple reward systems, the creation of meaningful information, individual empowerment, leadership and vision. They conclude that the knowledge-generating organization that engages in these kinds of activities is more likely to be able to survive in turbulent market conditions.

McNulty and Canty (1995) foresee that tomorrow's managers will have be: "...simultaneously and consecutively specialists and generalists, team players and self-reliant, able to think for themselves as a business of one and plan accordingly". They believe that to succeed, managers will have to commit themselves to a lifelong learning career, at the heart of which will be: "...knowing one's self and knowing what one has to offer in the 'de-jobbed' marketplace". This new emphasis demands different kinds of development programmes: those which emphasize learning not teaching, action not theory and business results not classroom results.

Wills and Oliver (1996) describe how action learning's focus on company-specific issues makes it easier to review the "hard" return on investment for the enterprise. They conclude that training and development managers can and should measure the "value added" by evaluating the organizational and financial impact of their own organization's investment in management education. In so doing, they feel that a "budgetarily supportive culture" is more likely to emerge. This approach would also help to highlight the range of "softer" personal benefits derived by individual participants. These include: changed behaviours, growth in confidence and learning from fellow members of the small action learning group or set. Peters and Smith (1996) also consider ways of achieving the best return on a learning investment. They suggest that the organization should identify its self-motivated, high-potential managers and sponsor them to explore the learning agenda for tomorrow's leaders and change agents. Key issues are likely to include: getting things done within the organization's cultural and political norms; taking risks within a psychologically safe environment; learning how to act with others, how to act alone and how to self-develop; comprehending and shaping the present and future strategic agenda for the organization. Peters and Smith argue that the best way to address this kind of company-specific agenda is by formalizing a work-based or action learning programme of study:

> Success in an organization depends on far more than acquiring technical knowledge and management concepts. It comes from an understanding of and a feel for factors such as organizational politics and culture, the art of influencing others, the ability to delegate, the skills of timing, presentation and selling ideas, not just having them. These are the qualities we expect from organizational leaders, and without them, and without a developmental approach to gaining such qualities, the emergence of effective leaders will continue to be a hit-and-miss affair (p. 8).

Implications for managerial learning

In designing and implementing a programme for managerial learning in the workplace it is helpful to consider the following points:

1 How are the participants roles defined (scope, tasks, responsibilities, relationships), how do they currently enact their roles (gather information, take decisions and action, contribute to key activities such as planning, organizing, staffing, leading and controlling) and what improvements would participants like to achieve for themselves, their work group and the wider organization?

2 What are the external variables affecting managerial work (e.g. related to sources of discontinuity, uncertainty, ambiguity, complexity) and how might the programme enable parallel, on-going learning to occur so that managerial skills and knowledge keep pace?

3 How can the programme encourage participants to enhance their capacity to learn from work by using a variety of ways of analyzing experiences (e.g. intuitive, incidental, retrospective, prospective approaches) so that learning becomes self-sustaining?

4 What forms of learner support should be used (e.g. coaching, mentoring, team

development) so as to help people to learn, widen and strengthen organizational participation and embed a culture of learning?

5 Who will coach and mentor and what are the resource and development implications?

6 What are the core and specialist levels of competence, how will these by built-in to the programme and measured for attainment? How will these considerations affect the form(s) of learning and the methods of delivery?

7 How will the efforts of participants be recognized – formally (e.g. accredited learning and the completion of an academic award), informally (e.g. support, encouragement, study time) and professionally (e.g. enhanced career prospects)?

8 How will programme outcomes "add value" for participants and the organization as a whole? How can the programme encourage others to take responsibility for recognizing and responding to their own development needs?

9 How can the benefits of workplace learning be readily identified and "sold" to participants, their superiors and subordinates? How can the reactions of sceptics and opponents be anticipated and effectively dealt with?

10 How might "return on investment" (time, resources, individual and organizational effort) be measured and monitored?

References

Ashton, C. (1996) "How competencies boost performance", *Management Development Review*, Vol. 9 No. 3, pp 14-19.

Barclay, J. (1996) "Learning from experience with learning logs", *Journal of Management Development*, Vol. 15 No. 6, pp 28-43.

Baruch, Y. and Leeming. A. (1996), "Programming the MBA programme – the quest for curriculum", *Journal of Management Development*, Vol. 15 No. 7, pp 27-36.

Beeby, M. and Simpson, P. (1995), "Developing strategic processes for change in top management teams", *Executive Development*, Vol. 8 No. 1, pp 20-2.

Blackburn, P. and Fryer, B. (1996), "An innovative partnership in management development", *Management Development Review*, Vol. 9 No. 3, pp 22-5.

Bloch, S. (1995), "Coaching tomorrow's top managers", *Executive Development*, Vol. 8 No. 5, pp 20-2.

Bolton, A. (1996), "Joint architecture by HR specialists and business schools", *Management Development Review*, Vol. 9 No. 1, pp 22-4.

Booth, R. (1996), "Mentor or manager: what is the difference? a case study in supervisory mentoring", *Leadership & Organization Development Journal*, Vol. 17 No. 3, pp 31-6.

Carnall, C. (1995), "The third-generation MBA: global reach and 'local' service", *The Learning Organization*, Vol. 2 No. 2, pp 18-27.

Chan, K. C. (1994), "Learning for total quality an action learning approach", *The Learning Organization*, Vol. 1 No. 1, pp 17-22.

Clawson, J.G. (1996), "Mentoring in the information age", *Leadership & Organization Development Journal*, Vol. 17 No. 3, pp 6-15.

Critten, P. (1996), "A learning community in the making – Middlesex University's new MA in personal and organizational development", *The Learning Organization*, Vol. 3 No. 5, pp 14-17.

Cusins, P. (1996), "Action learning revisited", *The Journal of Workplace Learning*, Vol. 8 No. 6, pp 19-26.

Davis, H.J. (1996), "A review of open and distance learning within management development", *Journal of Management Development*, Vol. 15 No. 4, pp 20-34.

Dilworth, R. L. (1996), "Action learning: bridging academic and workplace domains", *The Journal of Workplace Learning*, Vol. 8 No. 6, pp 45-53.

Dixon, P. (1995a), "Releasing middle management potential: Part 1", *Executive Development*, Vol. 8 No. 5, pp 23-5.

Dixon, P. (1995b), "Releasing middle management potential: Part 2", *Executive Development*, Vol. 8 No. 7, pp. 11-13.

Forret, M.L., Turban, D.B. and Dougherty, T.W. (1996), "Issues facing organizations when implementing formal mentoring programmes", *Leadership & Organization Development Journal*, Vol. 17 No. 3, pp 27-30.

Harrison, R. (1996), "Action learning: route or barrier to the learning organization?", *The Journal of Workplace Learning*, Vol. 8 No. 6, pp 27-38.

Hilgert, A. D. (1995), "Developmental outcomes of an executive MBA programme", *Journal of Management Development*, Vol. 14 No. 10, pp 64-76.

Hilgert, A. D. (1996), "The working executive: the developmental role of executive degree programmes", *Journal of Management Development*, Vol. 15 No. 7, pp 47-61.

Howell, F. (1994), "Action learning and action research in management education and development: a case study", *The Learning Organization*, Vol. 1 No. 2, pp 15-22.

Kilcourse, T. (1995), "The business of business schools", *The Learning Organization*, Vol. 2 No. 2, pp 32-5.

King, S. (1996), "European cases of self-managed learning", *Management Development Review*, Vol. 9 No. 2, pp 8-10.

Kur, E. (1996), "The faces model of high performing team development", *Leadership & Organization Development Journal*, Vol. 17 No. 1, pp. 32-41.

Lane, G. and Robinson, A. (1995), "The development of standards of competence for senior management", *Executive Development*, Vol. 8 No. 6, pp. 4-8.

Limerick, D., Passfield, R. and Cunnington, B. (1994), "Transformational change: towards an action learning organization", *The Learning Organization*, Vol. 1 No. 2, pp 29-40.

Loan-Clarke, J. (1996), "The management charter initiative – a critique of management standards/NVQs", *Journal of Management Development*, Vol. 15 No. 6, pp 4-17.

Lorange, P. (1996), "A business school as a learning organization", *The Learning Organization*, Vol. 3 No. 5, pp 5-13.

Margerison, C. and McCann, D. (1996a), "Five skills to improve performance", *Team Performance Management*, Vol. 2 No. 1, pp 14-16.

Margerison, C. and McCann, D. (1996b), "Men and women at work", *Team Performance Management*, Vol. 2 No. 1, pp 22-4.

McKenna, S. D. (1994), "Leveraging complexity: the middle manager's dilemma", *The Learning Organization*, Vol. 1 No. 2, pp 6-14.

McKenna, J.F., Cotton, C.C. and Van Auken, S. (1995), "Business school emphasis on teaching, research and service to industry: does where you sit determine where you stand?", *Journal of Organizational Change Management*, Vol. 8 No. 2, pp 3-16.

McNulty, N.G. and Canty, G.R. (1995), "Proof of the pudding", *Journal of Management Development*, Vol. 14 No. 1, pp 53-66.

McNutt, R. and Wright, P.C. (1995), "Coaching your employees: applying sports analogies to business", *Executive Development*, Vol. 8 No. 1, pp 27-32.

Megginson, D. (1994), "Planned and emergent learning: a framework and a method", *Executive Development*, Vol. 7 No. 6, pp 29-32.

Mumford, A. (1994), "Four approaches to learning from experience", *The Learning Organization*, Vol. 1 No. 1, pp 4-10.

Mumford, A. (1996), "Effective learners in action learning sets", *The Journal of Workplace Learning*, Vol. 8 No. 6, pp 3-10.

O'Neill, J. (1996), "A study of the role of learning advisers in action learning", *The Journal of Workplace Learning*, Vol. 8 No. 6, 1996, pp. 39-44.

Osborne, R.L. and Cowen, S.S. (1995), "Business schools must become learning organizations – or else", *The Learning Organization*, Vol. 2 No. 2, pp 28-31.

Oshagbemi, T. (1995), "Management development and managers' use of their time", *Journal of Management Development*, Vol. 14 No. 8, pp. 19-34.

Peters, J. and Smith, P. (1996), "Developing high potential staff: an action learning approach", *The Journal of Workplace Learning*, Vol. 8 No. 3, pp. 6-11.

Phillips, R. (1996), "Coaching for higher performance", *The Journal of Workplace Learning*, Vol. 8 No. 4, pp. 29-32.

Pierce, C., Hannon P. and Wilson, L. (1995), "The standards of competence for senior management: field test results", *Executive Development*, Vol. 8 No. 6, pp 9-12.

Proehl, R.A. (1996), "Enhancing the effectiveness of cross-functional teams", *Leadership & Organization Development Journal*, Vol. 17 No. 5, pp 3-10.

Reeves, T. (1996), "Rogue learning on the company reservation", *The Learning Organization*, Vol. 3 No. 2, pp 20-9.

Scandura, T.A., Tejeda, M.J., Werther, W.B. and Lankau, M.J. (1996), "Perspectives on mentoring", *Leadership & Organization Development Journal*, Vol. 17 No. 3, pp 50-6.

Shenhar, A.J. and Renier, J. (1996), "How to define management: a modular approach", *Management Development Review*, Vol. 9 No. 1, pp 25-31.

Strachan, P.A. (1996), "Managing transformational change: the learning organization and teamworking", *Team Performance Management*, Vol. 2 No. 2, pp 32-40.

Veale, D.J. and Wachtel, J.M. (1996), "Mentoring and coaching as part of a human resource development strategy: an example at Coca-Cola foods", *Leadership & Organization Development Journal*, Vol. 17 No. 3, pp 16-20.

Wills, G. and Oliver, C. (1996), "Measuring the ROI from management action learning", *Management Development Review*, Vol. 9 No. 1, pp 17-21.

Zuber-Skerritt, O. (1995), "Developing a learning organization through management education by action learning", *The Learning Organization*, Vol. 2 No. 2, pp 36-46.

Enabling organizational learning

Richard Teare
Research Director (Europe) Worldwide Hospitality and Tourism Trends

It is clear from studies of organizations and a considerable body of anecdotal evidence that organizational life is strongly influenced by organizational leaders. In particular, the vision, style of leadership and motivation that enables them to "make things happen" and inspire others to follow their direction. Reviews recent contributions to the literature on aspects of organizational learning and considers how organizational processes might encompass effective learning support for individuals and groups of learners. Draws from articles published between 1994-1996 in seven journals: *Executive Development; Journal of Organizational Change Management; Journal of Management Development; Leadership & Organization Development Journal; Management Development Review; The Journal of Workplace Learning; The Learning Organization.* Concentrates on three areas: organizational vision; leadership and motivation; organizational change and performance. Concludes with a summary of the implications for organizational learning.

Introduction

It is clear from studies of organizations and a considerable body of anecdotal evidence that organizational life is strongly influenced by organizational leaders. In particular, the vision, style of leadership and motivation that enables them to "make things happen" and inspire others to follow their direction. In seeking to release the potential that exists inside the organization in order that it might perform well and respond to change, the contention here is that individuals need to learn and develop at least as quickly as the pace of external change. If this is to be achieved, the structures, processes and procedures adopted by organizations must encourage and support personal growth rather than impeding or even discouraging it. In essence, organizations "learn" from individuals and groups or teams as they share insights and experiences and in so doing, capture "new" knowledge and understanding. This article reviews recent contributions to the literature on aspects of organizational learning and considers how organizational processes might encompass effective learning support for individuals and groups of learners. The review is drawn from articles published between 1994-1996 in seven journals: *Executive Development; Journal of Organizational Change Management; Journal of Management Development; Leadership & Organization Development Journal; Management Development Review; The Journal of Workplace Learning; The Learning Organization.* The review concentrates on three areas: Organizational vision; Leadership and motivation; Organizational change and performance and concludes with a summary of the implications for organizational learning.

Theme 1: Organizational vision

Allen (1995) sees "vision" as the starting-point, the anchor and the means of communicating a sense of organizational direction to its members. In practical terms, he suggests that a vision statement can provide an organizational road map to guide its future development – providing it is: coherent enough to create a recognizable picture of the future; powerful enough to generate commitment to performance and that it emphasizes what realistically can be and clarifies what should be. Among other sources, he bases his interpretation on the Old Testament view that without a vision the people will perish (Proverbs 29:18 and Hosea 4:14). Richardson and Thompson (1995) describe some of the characteristics of modern business environments and relate these to a vision of the strategic competences that organizations are likely to need in the future. These are summarized in Table I.

Richardson and Thompson observe that organizations will need to rethink their vision if they are to equip themselves with the competences needed to succeed in the future, not least because of the preoccupation with financial performance indicators and related information systems in the past. For instance, to remain competitive, the organization must accept the need for challenge and change and the right of others to have their say. Similarly, customer responsiveness is more likely to be achieved by empowered staff and goals and performance measures that reflect the "new" competences that the organization is seeking to develop.

Table II highlights some of the issues that influence the concept and application of organizational vision. These include the need for regular up-dating and review (with reference to current and future planning and organizational direction); the need to consider the interrelationships between organizational complexity, information, organizational structure and learning and the evolutionary role of organizational vision (encompassing future scenarios for organizational development).

Benbow (1995) observes that business leaders do recognize the seriousness of the external threats from increased global competition and greater regulatory and/or political intervention. Coupled with this they are also aware of the need to broaden their future social agenda and foresee that their responsibility is likely to be broader and more complex. Paradoxically, chief executives tend to look inwards for advice and the majority seem to rely on colleagues as the most valued

Table I

Business trends: envisioning strategic responses

Trend	Response	Implications
Towards larger operating arenas	Organizations will need to draw on and assimilate information from a wider range of external sources	Competence in environmental surveillance; empowered personnel; productive strategic alliances and learning communities
Towards more, and more diverse, influences.	Skill in developing "helicopter vision" to facilitate a strategic overview and planning for the organization's future development	Competence in strategic analysis; enabling fast, effective communications; contingency planning, crisis avoidance and management
Towards greater speed of change	The ability to reflect the dynamics of external change internally so that strategy, communications and decision making keep pace	Competence in listening to the issues raised by stakeholders; envisaging successful futures; adapting the organizational vision; changing course if necessary
Towards greater external power and threat	Organizational readiness to respond to the laws of chaos and catastrophe theory: a change in one part of a system can ricochet through the whole system, often in a seemingly random and unpredictable way	The ability to: respond and adapt to the aspirations of powerful stakeholders; change direction to meet new demands as they arise; monitor for new market phenomena; devise political strategies and negotiate expertly
Towards greater competitiveness	Acceptance that free market policies attract more competitors providing more choice for customers. Realization that competitiveness may mean new processes, products and services and/or reduced costs of production	Willingness to: improve competitive, innovative, product quality and customer responsive competences; make effective choices about when to leave marketplaces and about which new ones to enter
Towards resource depletion and life-threatening pollution	Willingness to re-consider beliefs about what organizations should be and what they should do to protect ecosystems	Plan to be "greener" more environmentally responsive, productive in resource usage, collaborative and socially responsible

Source: Adapted from Richardson and Thompson (1995, pp. 17-19)

source of ideas and inspiration rather than seeking views from customers or consultants. This is apparently because they are sceptical about the value of external experts, preferring to rely on coaching by those in post and on personal experience. In contrast, Bell and Tunnicliff (1996) describe the activities of a "future search" conference where a sizeable number of stakeholders are brought together to explore the past, agree the present and draw up action steps for the future. They see this as a forum for learning where stakeholders can identify common problems and explore higher order solutions.

Gault and Jaccaci (1996) note that successful businesses are, of necessity, using their complex environments to become planned cultures of learning and creativity. Here, "successful" companies are the ones that understand the connection between learning on the one hand and creativity and profitability on the other.

Smith and Saint-Onge (1996) outline an approach to influencing management thinking that encourages managers to think and act responsively, thereby promoting the concept of an "evolutionary organization" (EVO). They contend that the wellspring of real learning lies within the organization itself

and that it can be released by channelling aspirations, imagination and experimentation. To achieve EVO status, they say it is necessary to create an organizational climate that accords with a particular ideal or vision – that learning is integral to the roles of all employees. In changing the rules and emphasizing the learning imperative, all employees are forced to change their habits of thinking and learning without necessarily knowing that this is happening. To acquire new insights and learn from them, frequent interaction among members of the organization must occur. In so doing, people understand more and begin to depend on one another to a greater extent. Further, the EVO structures the organization so that employees are forced to solve their own problems and so expertise is enhanced and reinvested. "Experts" learn to become even more expert as they take incrementally bigger risks and, when they succeed, they acquire the kind of knowledge that increases the likelihood of future success. In this way, Smith and Saint-Onge believe that around 75 per cent of the organization's members will become active learners (They estimate that around 15 per cent of managers in any given organization are likely to be active, continuous learners, that

Table II
Organizational vision

Authors	Focus	Sub-theme
Allen (1995)	Presents a visioning action plan that represents all organizational stakeholders. The model promotes participative agreement throughout the visioning process. Observes that organizational members should agree with the vision and put it into daily practice.	Defining organizational vision
Richardson and Thompson (1995)	Assess a number of related trends occurring in business environments and considers the implications for developing requisite strategic competences in organizations	Relating future impacts to organizational competence
Benbow (1995)	Reports on a study of how organizational leaders view their development, responsibilities and succession, together with their vision on social issues	Implementing and updating organizational vision
Bell and Tunnicliff (1996)	Examines how companies plan ahead and argues that current strategic planning and re-engineering approaches alone will not enable them to compete in the future. Promotes an inclusive stakeholder approach to pooling knowledge and resources	Future planning and organizational direction
Gault and Jaccaci (1996)	Suggests how periodicity can be used with complexity theory to enable businesses to understand their position in the periodic cycle of gather, repeat, share and transform	Interrelating complexity, information, organizational structure and learning
Smith and Saint-Onge (1996)	Contends that in dealing with change, the mindsets of the organization's managers are the most critical factor. Suggests that the best way to deal with mindsets is to prevent them from hardening by promoting a culture of active learning	Establishing an evolutionary organization
Theobald (1996)	The pace of change and divergent views about "what next" suggests no "safe" future. Those who advance the maximum growth model assume ecological adaptability (among other variables) and are likely to place decision-makers under greater stress because of this	Future scenarios for organizational development
McDermott and Chan (1996)	Argues that corporate commitment to stakeholders is not an option but a necessity for companies aiming to build competitive advantage. Asserts that customer loyalty is obtained through trust and this must be won by paying equal attention to all stakeholders	Towards "flexible, intelligent relationship management strategy"

60 per cent possess the potential to learn if they are convinced of the need to do so and that the remaining 25 per cent are unlikely to respond.) Senior management's main role in an EVO is to provide leadership, look outwards, create a business vision and strategy, and build the organization's intellectual capital.

McDermott and Chan (1996) observe the passing of an organizational era – one which is characterized by the shift from the command-and-control type to the information-based type. The new form of structure involves a fundamental re-shaping of managerial responsibilities, of communication and information flows, and of interpersonal relationships. Chan (1994) emphasizes the importance of relationships built on "sincerity, trust and integrity" (see Figure 1). The principle and values of "flexible intelligent relationship management strategy" (FIRMS) is seen as a means by which the chain of relationships linking customers, workers, suppliers, distributors and even competitors might

be managed. Action learning is presented as the guiding philosophy of FIRMS for achieving world-class performance. Ultimately learning is related to action, for without activity, the authors assert, there is no feedback.

Theme 2: Leadership and motivation

The role of organizational leadership is a multifaceted one that draws on an array of professional skills and personal qualities. Table III reflects this and provides an indicative list of articles relating to topics such as: the role of the company director; the attributes of organizational leadership; leadership contexts and roles for learning; political awareness; executive leadership development; the leadership of a cultural change process and learning from leadership.

Tait (1996) identifies the self-reported attributes of effective leadership from a sample of 18 business leaders. The interviewees

[83]

formed two sub-groups – those in their mid-50s or older with reputations among their peers and the public as outstanding managers/leaders ($n = 9$) and a second group of younger chief executives who had been five years or less in the role. Reflecting on the group's responses, Tait believes that the qualities of effective leaders will remain largely unchanged in the future.

Figure 1
Relating corporate vision to core business activities

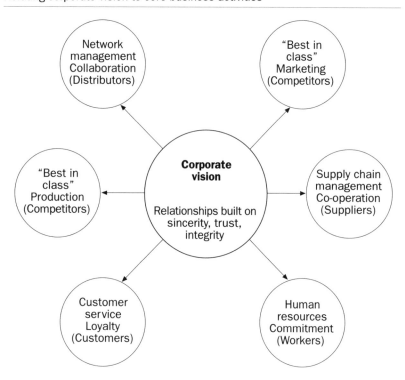

Source: adapted from Chan (1994, p. 20)

The "recipe" for effective leadership encompasses: clarity of vision (derived from the ability to reduce a complex reality to the critical essentials); credible communication and interpersonal skills (to sell the vision and inspire people to action); sincerity, generosity and self-mastery (to inspire trust and withstand the loneliness of leadership) and high levels of motivation and physical energy (to achieve the extraordinary). Tait adds:

> These qualities, combined with a self-critical, open, flexible and lifelong learning approach that draws on a track record of broad functional experience, early successful line management experience, international experience (increasingly) and the lessons to be learned from managing in diversity and adversity in fast-changing conditions, will continue to be what it takes to reach the top in the new millennium (p. 31).

Taylor and Taylor (1996) note that leaders are largely responsible for setting the tone for an organization and this is reflected in how they approach given tasks, how company guidelines are interpreted and how employees are treated. The sum total of senior executive behaviour and beliefs ultimately becomes the organization's "philosophy" on how it conducts its business. If organizational members are to interpret the action of senior managers, it is helpful to understand the organizational priorities that drive their actions. Knippen and Green (1996) provide a stepwise approach for discerning the motivations of organizational superiors and suggest ways in which these might be explored. They also observe that the priorities that influence motives and behaviours frequently change in relation to circumstances, events and other factors.

Richardson (1995a) explores the spectrum of learning-related leadership tasks, ranging from classically administered ("hard") to facilitated self-organized, learning networks ("soft") approaches. He concludes that the learning organization of the future will be a place in which networks of learning communities thrive, despite the influence of "maverick" groupings of employees. To maintain these networks, the organizational leader must deploy "harder" planned approaches and "softer" political, social and cultural approaches at the same time. The network of learning communities within the organization is the knowledge resource of the enterprise, vested in its workforce and their individual and collective expertise. McCrimmon (1995) considers the prospects for what he calls "knowledge workers" in organizations, linked to the trend towards knowledge-intensive businesses. He argues that the development of new products and services will depend increasingly on leadership from knowledge workers who are at the leading edge of their technical field. This development, he feels, threatens the traditional role of the "generalist" manager who holds a formal leadership role in the organizational hierarchy. He believes that the solution is to elevate the status of the knowledge workers and reward them accordingly so that they might exert informal influence through their singular performance or innovation-led contribution without burdening them with too much unnecessary managerial and administrative work. If those with leadership potential in knowledge-based projects and generalist roles are to perform well, they must receive appropriate development. Klagge (1996) presents a generalized process for defining, discovering and developing personal leadership in organizations. He

Table III
Leadership and motivation

Authors	Focus	Sub-theme
Kenton (1995)	Considers the company director's role and questions conventional thinking about the myopic pre-occupation with short-term cost cutting and rationalization. Asserts that directors should possess a strong sense of purpose and a vision for the long-term	The role of the company director
Tait (1996)	Reports on in-depth interviews with 18 business leaders, focusing on the qualities and skills they felt to be essential for success in directing and guiding a large organization	The attributes of organizational leadership
Richardson (1995a)	Relates the job of learning organization leader to prescriptions for implementing classically administered productivity improvement and an alternative approach to facilitating self-organizing learning networks	Leadership contexts and roles for learning
Richardson (1995b)	Examines the dangers of "self-enacted reality" strategic drift and the need for planning and control systems that reflect the harsh realities of the marketplace	The politically aware leader
Kur and Bunning (1996)	Describes a three-track process for executive leadership development intended to develop a cadre of strategic business leaders for the next decade	Executive leadership development
Brooks (1996)	Explores the role of leadership in initiating and sustaining a major process of change. Finds that leadership of cultural change requires leaders to think culturally and to be guided by a cognitive model of change while focusing on the politics of acceptance	Leadership of a cultural change process
Carr (1996)	Questions whether individuals, using psychoanalytic insights, can learn from their experience of leadership. Believes that leaders can develop insights in an experiential manner and concludes that most develop them by listening, hearing and responding	Learning from leadership
Carling (1995)	Argues that leadership is the main factor in enhancing human performance and is the all-important key to unlocking the latent potential of individuals, both in business and in sport	Harnessing individual and team potential

advocates the use of 360 degree performance evaluations to detect leadership qualities and suggests that employees with the potential to assume leadership roles need to be encouraged by a combination of recognition, rewards and training.

Theme 3: Organizational change and performance

The literature relating to organizational change and performance seems to converge wherever organizational imperatives for change are considered. Typically this means that organizations change because they have to remain competitive and perform well and consistently over time, not from choice. Table IV considers some of the implications of this for human resources (adapting to the needs of flexible working); for making structural adjustments (e.g. relationships between information flow and organizational performance, integrating intelligence systems and learning) and for decision-making (organizational self-reflection; using decision rules to guide organizational decision-making). The

methods used to measure performance are in themselves an indicator of how far and how quickly an organization has been able to adapt to change and there are many strategic issues and options to consider. These include: the prospects for using "learning partnerships" to leverage improved organizational performance; promoting diversity as a means of enhancing organizational performance and using "soft systems" to relate strategic change to career and management development planning.

Coping with change in the workplace
Old (1995) argues that what she calls "whole system" organizational change occurs on three levels: transactional (observable ongoing work); systemic (strategy, structure, culture, rewards, technology, information) and "deep" structure (underlying patterns). Old reasons that a well integrated change methodology is needed if organizations are to respond well to change and embed new thinking and a change orientation in the organization's "deeper" systems and interactions. Field (1996) observes that many workplace changes are occurring because of

Table IV
Organizational change and performance

Authors	Focus	Sub-theme
Field (1996)	States that flexible working methods have become an enduring feature of the modern employment market and estimates that by the year 2000 one quarter of the UK working population will be involved in flexible working	Adapting to the needs of flexible working
Kock, McQueen and Baker (1996)	Discusses the relationships between knowledge, information and data and relates these to the concept of knowledge organizations which rely on knowledge workers and intense information flow	Information flow and organizational performance
Venugopal and Baets (1995)	Examines the capabilities of information technology as a support function for organizational learning and presents a framework for integrating intelligent systems with "real time" learning events	Integrating intelligence systems and learning
Keating, Robinson and Clemson (1996)	Describes a process for facilitating organizational self-reflection and advocates the use of action research to design, enact and observe aspects of organizational performance	Organizational self-reflection
Lyles (1994)	Shows that firms develop decision rules that help future decision-makers to distinguish between similar and dissimilar situations. Findings from a study also reveal attempts to maintain flexibility and to encourage innovative responses to "new" events	Using decision rules to guide organizational decision making
Lorange (1996)	Describes a managerial approach for creating or strengthening organizational learning through partnership with external partners	Learning partnerships and organizational performance
Harung and Harung (1995)	Suggests that to benefit from "unity in diversity" it is necessary to encourage empowerment, decentralization and self-management and then seek to integrate differences of view, guided by the organizational vision and a shared set of values	Diversity as a means of enhancing organizational performance
Bolton and Gold (1995)	Explains how the Nationwide Building Society used soft systems methodology to analyze career aspirations and map them against personal development needs and organizational development and performance criteria	Career and management development using a soft systems approach
Stone (1996)	Reviews the literature that points to a "revolution" in business performance measurement and the greater use of "soft" employee-related measures. Study findings reveal that fewer companies than predicted are using or developing alternative performance measures	Performance measurement

developments in technology and especially the convergence of computer and telecommunication technologies:

> In the age of the virtual office, global networking and cyberspace meeting rooms, IT is increasingly defining workforce systems and the control of management information. The medium is, in a sense, becoming the management message where E-mail, desktop conferencing and workgroup software are tomorrow's everyday management tools (p. 7).

Field argues that the pervasive influence of "instant" communications in the workplace presents a significant opportunity for human resource managers. He believes that they should be shaping an organizational response by building and managing "in-house" expertise in this sphere of change management. As and when human resource departments grasp this opportunity they will play a key role in determining the success (or failure) of the organization's ability to come to terms with new working practices. Macadam (1996) offers some guidance on how to overcome the barriers associated with organizational change. In particular, he suggests ways in which negative attitudes such as resentment, depression, distrust, stress, disloyalty and lack of productivity – often manifest in staff who are about to experience a major change – might be channelled in a more productive way.

Lacey (1995) reviews the role of internal consultants in organizational change and development and compares the role with that traditionally played by external consultants. She finds that internal consultants frequently have to cope with problems associated with role confusion, compartmentalization, marginality, unclear career paths, lack of continuity, varying client expectations and departmental jealousies. She adds that internal consultants would be able to perform more effectively if these pressures were clearly identified and better understood.

Learning from experience

Lyles (1994) observes that organizations do learn from their experiences and can remember incidents from the past that may influence future actions. This assumes that they consciously seek to develop the necessary skills to discriminate effectively between actions that have been successful and the appropriateness of deploying a "tried and tested" course of action in "new" circumstances. Kransdorff (1996) notes that while most organizations use post-project reviews, internal audits and/or oral post-mortems to learn from their own experiences, the problem with these techniques is that they rely on retrospection, which makes them susceptible to partial and selective memory recall by managers who, after the event are unlikely to be neutral or objective. Kransdorff offers a prescription for tackling the uncertainties of memory recall and defensive reasoning and helping managers to use the benefits of hindsight more effectively. Learning from experience and organizational "self-reflection" can in themselves generate opportunities for organizational learning as depicted in Figure 2.

Gustavsson and Harung (1994) argue that the level of collective consciousness determines the quality of life and the level of performance of an organization. They suggest that organizational learning is mainly restricted to the "surface areas" of awareness: action, senses, active thinking, but at deeper levels of consciousness (such as feeling and intuition), much less progress has occurred. They propose a concept of learning that aims to facilitate a greater awareness of the capacity for organizational development. Their study findings reveal that it is possible to achieve the transformation of both individual and collective consciousness by using Eastern style meditation techniques to heighten awareness of the capacity for continued growth. Srikantia and Pasmore (1996) also consider the concept of awareness, focusing on the roles of conviction and self doubt in organizational learning processes. They explore how these negative feelings and emotions impede the individuals' development and how they might be overcome so that learning processes might enable individuals to contribute more effectively to the corporate effort.

Organizational learning and performance

Fulmer (1995) describes MIT's Center for Organizational Learning and its four main areas of activity: learning laboratory projects related to generic management issues; team-related "dialogue" projects; a CEO leadership project and a learning organization curriculum project. Roth and Senge (1996) say that more collaboration between researchers and practitioners is needed to establish "best practice" models of organizational learning. To do this, they suggest that more needs to be done to establish consensus about the research territory, research methods and goals, and how meaningful field projects can be designed and conducted. McDougall and Beattie (1996) report on a two-year project designed to evaluate the processes and outcomes of learning groups and suggest that lessons learned from this project can be applied to help to maximize learning and performance in groups in a wide range of organizational contexts.

Mirvis (1996) and Ford and Ogilvie (1996) present a broad review of theory and research about organizations and show how alternative schools of thought explain the different outcomes from routine and creative action in organizations. Mirvis contends that knowing "how" and "why" these different outcomes are achieved makes it easier to help people to "unlearn" old habits and develop new behaviours. Mirvis also considers the extent to which holistic thinking and work arrangements can be used to promote organizational learning and how measures to enhance collective consciousness might enable people to learn how to learn.

Lorange (1996) suggests that a learning partnership between an organization and one or more external catalysts should be founded on four propositions:

P1: organizational learning depends on complementary factors: the discovery of new knowledge and the ability to adapt to the subsequent changes required.

P2: organization learning takes place in two complementary places: inside the organization (a closed system) and outside (an open system) in a joint effort with other corporations – in a benchmarking mode.

P3: organizational learning is a deliberate process.

P4: external catalysts can play a critical, positive role in the organizational learning process.

Lorange proposes a number of partnership activities, each with performance-related benefits for the host organizations. These include: joint discovery and research projects; workshop and benchmarking activities;

in-company tailored partnership programmes and organizational network activity assessments. The potential benefits to be derived from intra and inter-organizational learning are shown in Figure 3.

Lewis (1996a, 1996b) argues that, while total quality management had separate origins from the "culture" movement, the two fields have, in effect, converged as the desire to achieve "excellence" and "quality improvement" imply either "change" or "working with the prevailing culture of the organization". In order to investigate the range of business performance measures used by UK companies, Stone (1996) conducted a survey of the *Times* Top 500 companies. The study sought to probe the issues relating to the use of so called "soft" employee-related performance measures, such as employee satisfaction, morale and commitment. The results, derived from 45 companies, indicated that few of the companies reporting were using or even developing innovative "soft" measures as a counterbalance to "harder" financially-related measures. The findings suggest that the "balanced scorecard" approach is impeded by lack of company evidence that "soft" performance measures yield similar benefits to financially-led ones.

Implications for organizational learning

To enable organizational learning to occur as effectively as possible, as an outcome of both formal programmed learning and informal self-reflection, it is helpful to consider the following points:

1 How can the organization equip itself to detect and respond appropriately to market trends? What processes and procedures are needed to isolate any given pattern of external events, devise suitable responses and ensure that the implications for re-aligning resources and competences are addressed? How should the organization assimilate the "new" knowledge that it acquires from this continuous cycle of adjustment and re-alignment?

2 Should the organization make a deliberate attempt to interrelate complex internal and external environments to planned organizational cultures for learning and creativity? If so, how might the concept of an "evolutionary organization" (EVO) be launched? What are the organization's ideals or vision for an EVO? How can organizational members be encouraged to think and act responsively and without unnecessary constraint so that natural curiosity drives workplace learning?

3 What kind of organizational structure is appropriate now and in the future? To what extent could and should the organization move towards facilitated self-organized learning networks so that budgets, resources, targets and goals for learning are "released" to groups of employees,

Figure 2
Opportunities for organizational learning

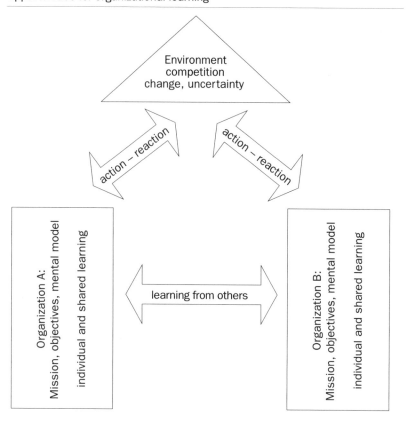

Source: adapted from Venugopal and Baets (1995, p. 24)

Figure 3
Dimensions of organizational learning

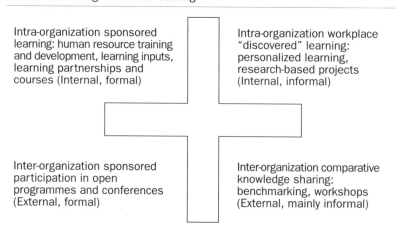

Intra-organization sponsored learning: human resource training and development, learning inputs, learning partnerships and courses (Internal, formal)

Intra-organization workplace "discovered" learning: personalized learning, research-based projects (Internal, informal)

Inter-organization sponsored participation in open programmes and conferences (External, formal)

Inter-organization comparative knowledge sharing: benchmarking, workshops (External, mainly informal)

Source: adapted from Lorange (1996, p. 14)

each "managing" enterprise activities? How will the differing roles of "knowledge workers" and generalists be reconciled if this approach is adopted?

4 How should the organization adjust its information flows so as to take advantage of real time communications (virtual office, global networking via internet and intranet) for transacting its business? How could communications technologies be used to create a searchable knowledge network within the organizations to support the learning effort?

5 What action is needed to ensure that learning from experience is "captured" and that opportunities for organizational learning from self-reflection (individual and shared learning) and from studying other organizations are acted upon?

6 How might learning partnerships with external catalysts be used to organize joint discovery and research projects, workshop and benchmarking activities, in-company tailored partnership programmes and organizational network activity assessments?

7 What performance measures does the organization currently use most often and why?

8 Should "soft" employee-related performance measures (e.g. commitment, employee satisfaction, self-development, morale) be given more emphasis? How might the full range of organizational performance measures be related to improvements arising from the organizational learning effort?

References

Allen, R. (1995), "On a clear day you can have a vision: a visioning model for everyone", *Leadership & Organization Development Journal,* Vol. 16 No. 4, pp. 39-44.

Bell, M. and Tunnicliff, G. (1996), "Future search for stakeholders", *Management Development Review*, Vol. 9 No. 1, pp. 13-16.

Benbow, N. (1995), "Preparing for tomorrow", *Executive Development,* Vol. 8 No. 7, pp. 29-30.

Bolton, R. and Gold, J. (1995), "Career management at Nationwide Building Society using a soft systems approach", *Executive Development*, Vol. 8 No. 4, pp. 22-5.

Brooks, I. (1996), "Leadership of a cultural change process", *Leadership & Organization Development Journal,* Vol. 17 No. 5, pp. 31-7.

Carling, W. (1995), "Winning through leadership", *The Journal of Workplace Learning,* Vol 7 No. 4, pp. 27-30.

Carr, W. (1996), "Learning for leadership", *Leadership & Organization Development Journal,* Vol. 17 No. 6, pp. 46-52.

Chan, K.C. (1994), "Learning for total quality an action learning approach", *The Learning Organization*, Vol. 1 No. 1, pp. 17-22.

Field, R. (1996), "The flexible workforce: redefining the role of HR", *Management Development Review*, Vol. 9 No. 1, pp. 5-7.

Ford, C.M. and Ogilvie, D.T. (1996), "The role of action in organizational learning and change", *Journal of Organizational Change Management*, Vol. 9 No. 1, pp. 54-62.

Fulmer, R.M. (1995), "Building organizations that learn: the MIT Center for organizational learning", *Journal of Management Development*, Vol. 14 No. 5, pp. 9-14.

Gault, S.B. and Jaccaci, A.T. (1996), "Complexity meets periodicity", *The Learning Organization*, Vol. 3 No. 2, pp. 33-9.

Gustavsson, B. and Harung, H.S. (1994), "Organizational learning based on transforming collective consciousness", *The Learning Organization*, Vol. 1 No. 1, pp. 33-40.

Harung, H.S. and Harung, L.M. (1995), "Enhancing organizational performance by strengthening diversity and unity", *The Learning Organization*, Vol. 2 No. 3, pp. 9-21.

Keating, C., Robinson, T. and Clemson, B. (1996), "Reflective inquiry: a method for organizational learning", *The Learning Organization,* Vol. 3 No. 4, pp. 35-43.

Kenton, B. (1995), "What is a director's role?", *Executive Development,* Vol. 8 No. 2, pp. 16-18.

Klagge, J. (1996), "Defining, discovering and developing personal leadership in organizations", *Leadership & Organization Development Journal*, Vol. 17 No. 5, pp. 38-45.

Knippen, J.T. and Green, T.B. (1996), "What motivates your boss?", *The Journal of Workplace Learning*, Vol. 8 No. 3, pp. 15-18.

Kock, N.F., McQueen, R.J. and Baker, M. (1996), "Learning and process improvement in knowledge organizations: a critical analysis of four contemporary myths", *The Learning Organization*, Vol. 3 No. 1, pp. 31-41.

Kransdorff, A. (1996), "Using the benefits of hindsight – the role of post-project analysis", *The Learning Organization*, Vol. 3 No.1, pp. 11-15.

Kur, E. and Bunning, R. (1996), "A three-track process for executive leadership development", *Leadership & Organization Development Journal*, Vol. 17 No. 4, pp. 4-12.

Lacey, M.Y. (1995), "Internal consulting: perspectives on the process of planned change", *Journal of Organizational Change Management*, Vol. 8 No. 3, pp. 75-84.

Lewis, D. (1996a), "The organizational culture saga – from OD to TQM: a critical review of the literature. Part 1 – concepts and early trends", *Leadership & Organization Development Journal*, Vol. 17 No. 1, pp. 12-9.

Lewis, D. (1996b), "The organizational culture saga – from OD to TQM: a critical review of the literature. Part 2 – applications",

*Leadership & Organization Development
Journal*, Vol. 17 No. 2, pp. 9-16.

Lorange, P. (1996), "Developing learning partnerships", *The Learning Organization*, Vol. 3 No. 2, pp. 11-19.

Lyles, M.A. (1994), "An analysis of discrimination skills as a process of organizational learning", *The Learning Organization*, Vol. 1 No. 1, pp. 23-32.

Macadam, C. (1996), "Addressing the barriers of managing change", *Management Development Review*, Vol. 9 No. 3, pp. 38-40.

McCrimmon, M. (1995), "Bottom-up leadership", *Executive Development*, Vol. 8 No. 5, pp. 6-12.

McDermott, M.C. and Chan, K. C. (1996), "Flexible intelligent relationship management: the business success paradigm in a stakeholder society", *The Learning Organization*, Vol. 3 No. 3, pp. 5-17.

McDougall, M. and Beattie, R.S. (1996), "Learning from learning groups", *The Journal of Workplace Learning*, Vol. 8 No. 3, pp. 26-30.

Mirvis, P.H. (1996), "Historical foundations or organization learning", *Journal of Organizational Change Management*, Vol. 9 No. 1, pp. 13-31.

Old, D.R. (1995), "Consulting for real transformation, sustainability, and organic form", *Journal of Organizational Change Management*, Vol. 8 No. 3, pp. 6-17.

Richardson, B. (1995a), "Learning contexts and roles for the learning organization leader", *The Learning Organization*, Vol. 2 No. 1, pp. 15-33.

Richardson, B. (1995b), "The politically aware leader: understanding the need to match paradigms and planning systems to powerful, turbulent fields, environments", *Leadership &*

Organization Development Journal, Vol. 16 No. 2, pp. 27-35.

Richardson, B. and Thompson, J. (1995), "Strategy evaluation in powerful environments: a multi-competence approach", *Leadership & Organization Development Journal*, Vol. 16 No. 4, pp. 17-25.

Roth, G.L. and Senge, P.M. (1996), "From theory to practice: research territory, processes and structure at an organizational learning centre", *Journal of Organizational Change Management*, Vol. 9 No. 1, pp. 92-106.

Smith, A.C. and Saint-Onge, H. (1996), "The evolutionary organization: avoiding a Titanic fate", *The Learning Organization*, Vol. 3 No. 4, pp. 4-21.

Srikantia, P. and Pasmore, W. (1996), "Conviction and doubt in organizational learning", *Journal of Organizational Change Management*, Vol. 9 No. 1, pp. 42-53.

Stone, C.L. (1996), "Analysing business performance: counting the 'soft' issues", *Leadership & Organization Development Journal,* Vol. 17 No. 4, pp. 21-8.

Tait, R. (1996), "The attributes of leadership", *Leadership & Organization Development Journal,* Vol. 17 No. 1, pp. 27-31.

Taylor, R. and Taylor, C. (1996), "Trouble at the top: assessing the upper-level executive", *The Journal of Workplace Learning*, Vol. 8 No. 7, pp. 13-15.

Theobald, R. (1996), "The inevitably surprising future", *The Learning Organization,* Vol. 3 No. 2, pp. 30-2.

Venugopal, V. and Baets, W. (1995), "Intelligent support systems for organizational learning", *The Learning Organization*, Vol. 2 No. 3, pp. 22-34.

Empowerment and organizational change

Margaret Erstad
Research Manager (Europe) Worldwide Hospitality and Tourism Trends

Among the many fashionable management terms, empowerment refers to a change strategy with the objective of improving both the individual's and the organization's ability to act. Reviews the various themes of empowerment with particular reference to articles published between 1994-1996 in the journal *Empowerment in Organizations*. The main themes are: creating an empowerment culture; empowerment as a management strategy; training and development for empowered employees; empowered teams and implementation techniques and empowerment and organizational change in the hospitality industry

Introduction

Empowerment is a topic that appears frequently in human resource, business, and management literature but more infrequently in the hospitality and tourism literature. This article aims to review the various themes of empowerment primarily in the specialized publication, *Empowerment in Organizations*, during 1994-1996 in order to expose empowerment theories and practices of potential value to the hospitality and tourism industries. The empowerment literature is divided into key themes which are subsequently summarized separately by subject in table form. The themes are then linked in a diagram in order to construct a larger image of empowerment as a change strategy. The article concludes with a discussion of the implications that empowerment research has for the hospitality industry.

Defining empowerment

Empowerment has been described as a means to enable employees to make decisions (Bowen and Lawler, 1992) and as a personal phenomenon where individuals take responsibility for their own actions (Pastor, 1996). The first definition relates to how management facilitates and implements the empowerment culture, while the second emphasizes the importance of the individual in the truly successful application of empowerment. Wing (1996) uses the term personal empowerment in relation to business consultants and views it as a strong self-analytical tool which allows them to understand and address their personal biases, differences of opinions, and experiences with clients in order to be successful in change efforts. Whatever the definition of empowerment used, the end goal is to develop the performance and potential of the individual as well as that of the organization (Long, 1996).

Lashley (1996) defines empowerment in relation to an organization's purpose for using the strategy. Is empowerment deployed to achieve greater employee commitment, to gain information from employees and improve the bottom-line, or to increase responsiveness to customers? While the pursuit of one objective does not automatically exclude the others, organizations may focus on a specific empowerment aim at the expense of potential gains from seeking other empowerment goals.

Creating an empowerment culture

Why the concern for empowerment? Nixon (1994) sees empowerment arising from external and internal challenges for organizations. External challenges have resulted as a result of higher levels of competition, changes in the composition of the workforce, and higher expectations from customers. Internal challenges relate to employee retention, motivation, and development.

According to Beach (1996), empowerment remains with the individual and cannot be imposed from above. How then can an environment conducive to empowerment be created? Organizations wishing to instill a culture of empowerment must find a way of establishing systems and processes that do not restrict employees. By concentrating on what behaviour is considered optimal for the employees and what they do well, management can adapt, develop and change the organizational structure to produce the sought after behaviour: employees dedicated to learning, growing, and developing; employees who are self-managed; leadership not only existing at the top; a high level of trust between management and employees as well as among employees; employee participation in decision making; a high level of vertical and horizontal communication; and employees able to deal with conflict management and resolution effectively and efficiently.

To bring all this about, a shift in management thinking and management strategy are necessary. Collins (1996a) looks at historical debates on democracy to gain insight on how a radical change to organizational culture for empowerment can be developed. He looks at reasons why people fail to participate in a democratic system and attributes this to either a lack of education and knowledge for groups to be able to participate or a failure to see the connection between participation and political decisions. From this historical analysis, there appear to be two essential ingredients for a successful implementation of empowerment in organizations: education and participation in the decision-making process, particularly for decisions influencing the individual's sphere of influence.

Parry (cited by Collins, 1996a) delves deeper into participation theory and outlines three ways of viewing it:

1 how participation takes place (direct or indirect);
2 to what degree participation occurs (intensity and frequency); and
3 the quality of participation (and resulting impact or change).

Traditionally, and even today, collective bargaining has been the strongest form of employee participation. Could empowerment change this?

An empowered organizational culture relies on the involvement of everyone, including both management and employees, to bring about its success. Simmons (1995) illustrates the overlapping or disappearance of boundaries between formal and informal leadership to that of an inclusive organization where there are "leaders of leaders".

Empowerment may take the form of so-called empowered subcultures of low and mid-level managers cut off from the top echelons of an organization (Logan *et al.*, 1996). The commitment and participation of top management, the strategy and policy makers of an organization, are necessary for a truly comprehensive culture of empowerment to exist. Empowering employees does not mean disempowering managers but rather permits time and energy to be used more efficiently and productively by all players.

Why should empowerment be taken seriously as a management strategy or organizational philosophy? Empowerment offers the potential for guaranteeing employee performance through a higher level of self-control (Collins, 1996b). In an organization such as Mazda, where there is an extremely thorough selection process to establish the prospective employee's fit with the organization, the worker selected has demonstrated a willingness to commit to the organization and subsequently becomes an active member of an empowered system of processes geared to stimulate and encourage his or her participation.

Empowerment as a management strategy

A five-point empowerment strategy is described by Nixon (1994) in order to develop an organization where people can work as individuals and also in teams towards common goals. The strategy consists of:

1 establishing a vision;
2 prioritizing and acting only where most impact is possible;
3 developing strong relationships with colleagues;
4 expanding networks;
5 using internal and external support groups.

To create a synergy of outcomes, people should be channelled to work together on workshops and projects directly connected with organizational issues affecting them. Once the skills to work together on projects have been learned, the same process can be further embedded in the organization by cascading the workshops throughout the organization.

Cook (1994) summarizes essential stages in the empowerment process in a diagram that includes the vision, values, management role as facilitator, teamwork, training support and process improvement which are all reviewed and monitored at the end of the process.

For Long (1996), achieving an empowerment objective for a company is closely linked to three important concepts: an annual strategic plan, annual personal performance-related appraisals, and training and development. Höpfl (1994) concurs in the need for goal setting with employee participation in determining individual and organizational objectives, courses of action, problem solving, and company policy.

A programme at Ashworth Hospital used competence development through the accreditation of work-based learning with a support structure based on action learning sets as the foundation of the empowerment project (Newton and Wilkinson, 1994). Project

Figure 1
The empowerment process

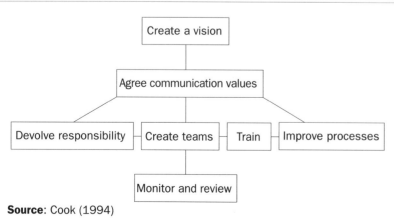

Source: Cook (1994)

MORALE used Mentorship, Ownership, Responsibility, Accountability, and Learning in order to achieve Empowerment.

Although empowerment was not the term used initially to describe the changes undertaken at a publishing enterprise (Gore *et al.*, 1994) to deal with internal and external challenges, it is a very appropriate way of describing the resulting package of strategies. Organizational change was brought about by concentrating on: management action learning (10 per cent of payroll is now dedicated to above-the-line training investment); systems development; mentoring and coaching; and structural change including profit-related pay. The end result has been an organization where employees have grown and developed their response to change.

With the background of an empowered organizational culture and management strategy, tools and techniques are needed by both management and employees if unrealized potential and individual entrepreneurship are to be created. The articles under the next topic heading describe some of the programmes and methods used to provide higher levels of participation and empowered employees.

Training and development for empowered employees and employee participation

Jones *et al.* (1996) stress the need to shift away from controlling to enabling in order for employees to contribute more. This requires new management skills to maximize employee potential. These skills relate to co-ordination, facilitation, commitment and trust, communication, knowing more

precisely what your people can and cannot do, and promoting learning and employee ownership of what they do. Identification with organizational values, competence building, employee self esteem, delegation, and coaching are fundamental qualities for employee participation (Potter, 1994).

A three-stage training structure for managers which begins at the bottom is advocated by Nicholls (1995). In the first stage, an analysis is made of current capabilities and employees are helped to work to their full potential. Next, managers need to use coaching techniques to get employees to work beyond their present capabilities. Third, the commitment of the employees is obtained through the sharing of visions and values. When the last stage has been completed, then full empowerment has been achieved.

When the training needs of the organizaion as a whole have been attended to, it may be necessary to identify any special areas or disadvantaged groups that would benefit from further preparation. Equal opportunity exists by law at the recruitment level, yet once selected, employees from recognized disadvantaged sectors may require special efforts to allow them to participate at the same level as other employees (Echiejile, 1994).

Kappelman and Richards (1996) advocate allowing employees to participate early on in change programmes. Their study was undertaken in bank branches during the implementation of a data system. Some employees were able to decide the dates when they would undergo training, and data from this group were compared to employees who were not able to decide on the dates. The empowered employees from the first group were 88 per cent more motivated, 146 per cent more satisfied with their training, and 99 per cent more satisfied with the change process.

The suggestion method of employee participation was used at Nissan where employees were expected to submit a pre-determined number of suggestions each month (Rodrigues, 1994). Employee participation was developed at British Gas through the implementation of an employee suggestion programme designed to allow employees to recognize problems and possible solutions (Lloyd, 1996). Over a three year period, British Gas received more than 11,000 suggestions of which approximately 10 per cent were implemented for an added value to the organization of £10 million. In order to obtain employee input, the organization must provide an atmosphere which encourages and rewards employee participation. Essential in this process is the need for managers to stimulate, communicate, and encourage

Figure 2
The second stage of empowerment – as a coaching enabler

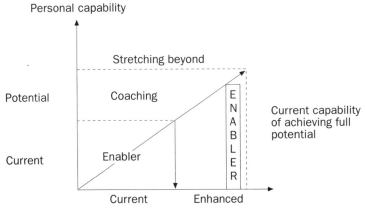

Source: Nicholls (1995)

Table I

Creating an empowerment culture and management strategy

Authors	Focus	Sub-theme
Beach (1996)	Relates the experience of one organization in establishing an empowerment culture through non-traditional management	Practical examples of changes through focusing on employee performance and commitment are given
Collins (1996a)	Links the concept of empowerment to participation and democracy to show the complexity of theory and debate in this field	The lack of more frequent debate on empowerment in management literature is also reflected in the absence of discussion on empowerment within businesses
Collins (1996b)	Views empowerment as a part of a greater whole, that is a part of management control systems	Management control and governance are reviewed by using the examples of Nissan and Mazda
Cook (1994)	Reflects on the impact of empowerment on organizational culture when employees are able to influence their work	Training and teamwork support are important components of an empowered culture
Gore, Toledano and Wills (1994)	Looks at an empowered leadership strategy for MCB publishing to include management action learning; systems development; mentoring and coaching; and structured change	How use of action learning as a management strategy can facilitate change
Höpfl (1994)	Considers the relationship between management development and self-development for empowered management	Gaps may often spring up between management objectives and everyday practices
Logan *et al.* (1996)	Reflects on the subject of empowerment as members of the Editorial Advisory Board of *Empowerment in Organizations*	Empowerment seen not only from a professional role but also from a personal one
Long (1996)	Follows a case study over four years primarily in health-care companies	Empowerment requires top to bottom involvement with employee appraisals an intricate part of the process
Newton and Wilkinson (1994)	Examines an empowerment project for 80 first-line and middle managers at a hospital in the UK to enable them to take ownership of their jobs and ultimately improve the hospital's performance	Organizational change is only possible with the firm commitment and dedication of management
Nixon (1994)	Sees empowerment as a function of leadership and organizational culture and tries to apply practical strategies for achieving this state	Difficulties associated with empowerment and learning are discussed in order to revise existing programmes and processes
Simmons (1995)	Calls for a partnership between workers and management as a means of encouraging workers to give their energy and commitment	Employee motivation is not only materialistic but non-material strategies can be effective motivational tools

employees to participate in the flatter organization.

The British Gas suggestion process relies on a closely defined structure to ensure successful implementation of the empowerment concept. At the time of submitting a suggestion, all employees are offered a scratch card with a maximum prize value of £5. This incentive was developed as a way to get people to participate. Each suggestion is given careful consideration with the maximum time between suggestion submission and a management decision regarding the added value of the suggestion limited to 72 hours. Those suggestions adding value and in line with business objectives receive an award of 10 per cent of the added value minus any costs accrued during the first year it is implemented. When awards are implemented for the business unit as a whole, the maximum is increased a further 10 per cent or up to a maximum of £2,500. Critical to the success of the evaluation and suggestion stages of the programme is the fact that these have become items on which managers are measured in their performance appraisals. Each year an award presentation attended by top management and line managers is held where the best award receives a trip to the value of £5,000.

Table II

Empowerment in training and development and employee participation

Authors	Focus	Sub-theme
Davis and Stocking (1996)	Empowerment used as a tool to transform the culture of a typical local authority bureaucracy	The learning organization and staff development
Echiejile (1994)	Gives examples of empowerment programmes where the needs of disadvantaged employees are considered	Special programmes viewed not as a burden for organizations but a win-win opportunity
Jones *et al.* (1996)	Looks at how to get the most out of people and see people as the key to organizational change and success	Information technology is not a substitute for human qualities and capabilities
Kappelman and Richards (1996)	Examines how a small degree of empowerment in a change programme positively affected the success of the programme	Empowerment becomes a way individuals can exert control in a change situation
Lloyd (1996)	The flatter organizational structure at British Gas required new suggestion systems in order for employees to participate and influence change	Organizaional culture and a participative environment
Nicholls (1995)	Interprets empowerment as a state or frame of mind requiring training and not something merely passed on from one person to the next	The broadening of an individual's work challenges employees and enhances personal development
Nykodym *et al.* (1994)	Employee participation through empowerment can take many forms and employ many management techniques	Some of the potential negatives with empowerment strategies are illustrated
Potter (1994)	Describes how empowerment has changed the role and activities of managers and defines a ten-point action plan	Empowerment and employee participation linked to the mission statement
Rodrigues (1994)	Raises the difficulties involved in empowerment programmes in order to bring about organizational effectiveness	Empowerment requires ongoing training and development

Legislative and policy changes forced one local authority to look at how the organization was functioning and take action geared to customer needs. All staff participated in key activities: the formulation of a statement of purpose, a communication charter, and performance appraisal with the outcome being a high level of energized creativity and innovation throughout the organization. Seminars and questionnaires were used to launch the empowerment programme with input from employees on what areas they felt the organization was actually hindering their work. Quick win situations were created with an award system, communications working group, and organizaional learning. To ensure managers were responsive to their employees, performance reviews of managers included employee development, 360 degree appraisal, and managers' achievements through delegation and the use of man-management skills.

Employee participation may happen in the form of employees taking part in decisions and making their own individual contribution, employees working together with management, or employees collaborating with co-workers in project or work groups (Nykodym *et al.*, 1994). The next section reviews the literature on empowerment in the context of empowerment implementation with the purpose of gaining knowledge of ways to put empowerment theory into practice effectively in general and more specifically through the use of teams.

Empowerment implementation techniques and empowering teams

The term "catalytic empowerment" is used by Dickmeyer and Williams (1995) to refer to techniques applied to unprofitable companies in order to make them profitable. When the empowerment process is set in motion, a chain reaction occurs drawing employees, suppliers, customers, and stakeholders into the transformation.

One method of putting empowerment into practice is by creating self-managed project or product work groups (Marguilies and Kleiner, 1995). These teams have the ability to make decisions regarding the project and input information impacting on organizational strategy. Built into the empowerment of teams is a reward system recognizing the

Table III

Empowerment implementation techniques and empowering teams

Authors	Focus	Sub-theme
Born and Molleman (1996)	Rewarding employees for empowered behaviour is complex in traditional pay systems thus requiring more flexible systems of reward	The character of the job often determines the degree of empowerment possible
Brower (1995)	Delves into the issue of empowerment in teams and develops a model of empowerment	In order to achieve empowerment, basic development tools are required
de Burgundy (1996)	Critiques the use of management consultancies and advocates organizations use their own workers to understand how the organization functions	Management techniques used by consultants are reviewed
Cleary (1995)	Exposes empowerment as a way to improve quality by using the plan-do-study-act theory of Deming	The process of empowerment brings about unknown and unknowable benefits for the organization
Dickmeyer and Williams (1995)	Discuss the term catalytic empowerment where consultants turn around unsuccessful companies	Performance measurement is necessary to test the success of empowerment
Harley (1995)	Cites the need for balancing operational and human issues for empowerment and describes eight key principles to accomplish this	Organizational authority, if used properly, can unleash hidden human potential
Logan (1995)	Includes empowerment in the larger framework of actions driving quality within an organization	Human quality is often neglected in the drive for superior technological quality
Marguilies and Kleiner (1995)	Describes empowerment in terms of how work groups are designed and highlights the concept of self management for these groups	Empowerment seen as a package of behavioural and support attributes
Miller (1996)	Advocates the use of humour as a way to stimulate empowered cultures	Positive feedback and stroking can do much to raise employees' self-esteem
Morley (1995)	Theorizes about the use of empowerment in the public sector	Empowerment can be misused as a manipulative technique by management.
Pearson and Chatterjee (1996)	Assess the implementation of empowerment in a study of its introduction in an organization and presents a model for implementation	Empowerment viewed as it is cascaded throughout the organization
Pence and Lunderman (1995)	Gives a practical example of an empowerment programme with impacting employee participation at lower management levels	Article is concluded with a short review and critique of the programme that was implemented
Pence (1996)	Uses a technique of self-assessment to measure an organization's commitment to empowered teams	Support systems are fundamental to the success of empowered teams

contribution of the team as a unit. Working on a group project develops bounds between team members and employee motivation rises through greater job satisfaction and self actualization. Organizational communication also benefits since group projects stimulate lateral exchanges as opposed to vertical communication. Self-management does require certain conditions to function properly. These are a level of task differentiation, the degree to which the group has control over its project, and the level of empowerment in the decision-making process.

Pence (1996) has designed a self-diagnostic questionnaire to determine an organization's commitment to teams. The 15 questions cover pertinent issues and the company's relationship with teams including top management commitment, recruitment, management appraisals, training, standards, rewards and recognition, communication, policies and procedures, and facilities. For Brower (1995), empowerment consists of four A's which must be aided by suitable information, support from within the organization, and several types and levels of leadership to be successful (Figure 3).

In a survey of 600 companies in diverse sectors covering 12 employee characteristics of quality, empowerment was ranked as very important by 53 per cent of respondents (Jolton cited in Logan, 1995). Responses for the 12 dimensions ranged from 43 per cent for development to 76 per cent for customer orientation. For Cleary (1995), empowerment is also closely linked with quality improvements.

Empowering employees who possess first-hand knowledge of their work can take place by using quality guru Edward Deming's plan-do-study-act cycle. Cleary demonstrates how response time was reduced for support calls to a software and training organization as a result of a team of employees' analysis of the process and actions to improve it.

Miller (1996) sees humour as a powerful empowerment tool to stimulate the communication and creativity processes as well as relieving stress. Empowered organizations should also be fun environments for management and employees.

The inherent difficulties of traditional pay and reward systems to recognize and incorporate empowerment has led Born and Molleman (1996) to conclude that more flexible pay systems would be needed to deal appropriately with rewarding individual and/or team empowered performance. Figure 4 illustrates the elements of empowerment, beginning with the concept of a change strategy and ending with results.

Empowerment and the hospitality industry

Lashley (1996) writes of the gap between management's intention in using empowerment strategies and employees' experiences with empowerment in the hospitality sector. If employees interpret empowerment as added responsibility and an increased workload without a corresponding reward, whether monetary or nonmonetary, they are unlikely to respond positively to it. Empowerment should be a matter of choice and not obligation. A five-dimensional model of empowerment for hospitality operations was developed by Lashley and McGoldrick (1994, p. 31) to include: "the task dimension, the task allocation dimension, the power dimension, the commitment dimension and the cultural dimension".

The work of Huang *et al.* (1996) looked at how different cultures react to poor hotel service. They found that in the case of American customers with complaints, these customers sought out higher-level management to address their problem. Empowerment may therefore need to take into account the customer's attitude towards empowered employees and some form of educating the customers might be required to inform them as to what the empowered employees are entitled to do and what issues these employees can address. At Radisson Hotels in Sweden, a brochure entitled "No Excuses" is found in each room which sets out 12 attributes of the room that must be in perfect

Figure 3
Building blocks of team empowerment

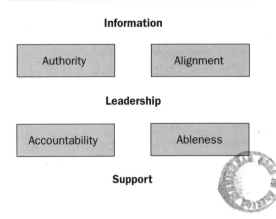

working order or repaired within one hour. If the problem is not resolved, the customer will be moved to a new room. If there is no other room available, the customer will be not be charged for the room. The customers and the employees know exactly what the conditions of the guarantee programme are and can act accordingly.

Maxwell's (1997) case study of empowerment at the Glasgow Marriott, which used an employee questionnaire, discovered that employees had a positive approach to empowerment although advantages and disadvantages were also clearly stated. Advantages for the employees included higher levels of job satisfaction, better customer service, more rapid decision making, and personal development. Some of the deficits employees found in empowerment related to communication difficulties, unclear work practices, higher levels of pressure on staff, and increased competition among employees. Equally important was the need to support the early stages of the empowerment process with training to clarify the extent and implications of its use.

In the service sector, and more specifically the hotel industry, empowerment is often seen as a way to gain competitive advantage with the consumer. However, the true potential of empowerment is broader. Dickmeyer and Williams' (1995) article on turning around unprofitable companies demonstrates the impact of empowerment and change on six performance measures: employee turnover (a decline with empowerment), increase in sales per employee, a higher profit margin, lower material cost as percentage of sales, lower labour cost as a percentage of sales in two out of four cases, and higher net profit dollars. Empowerment can thus be linked to soft measures of performance exposed by Brander-Brown and McDonnell

Figure 4
Empowerment and organizational change

(1995) with the use of the balanced score-card concept in the hotel sector.

Conclusions

Empowerment has been explored in the context of articles from a journal specializing in this area. The concept can be approached from many angles, and organizations wanting to embrace this approach to business must be fully aware of its complexity. Empowerment is not something which can be passed over from management to employees as a pen is handed from one person to another. It is a complex process which requires a clear vision, a learning environment both for management and employees, and participation and implementation tools and techniques in order to be successful. While the hospitality industry has been quick to latch on to the potential of empowerment for a sector so reliant on human capital, many lessons can be learned from research and experience in other business sectors in order to achieve a truly entrepreneurial culture throughout all levels of the organization.

References

Beach, A.J. (1996), "Empowerment to the people: creating an atmosphere for growth", *Empowerment in Organizations*, Vol. 4 No. 1, pp. 29-33.

Born, L. and Molleman, E. (1996), "Empowerment and rewards: a case study", *Empowerment in Organizations*, Vol. 4 No. 3, pp. 30-3.

Bowen, D.E. and Lawler, E.E. (1992), "The empowerment of service workers: what, why, how and when", *Sloan Management Review*, Vol. 33 No. 3, pp. 31-9.

Brander-Brown, J. and McDonnell, B. (1995), "The balanced score-card: short term guest or long-term resident?", *International Journal of Contemporary Hospitality Management*, Vol. 7 Nos 2/3, pp. 7-11.

Brower, M.F. (1995), "Empowering teams: what, why, and how", *Empowerment in Organizations*, Vol. 3 No. 1, pp. 13-25.

de Burgundy, J. (1996), "Shoot the messenger! Crazy management fads and faddish management 'crazies'", *Empowerment in Organizations*, Vol. 4 No. 4, pp. 28-35.

Cleary, B.A. (1995), "Supporting empowerment with Deming's PDSA cycle", *Empowerment in Organizations*, Vol. 3 No. 2, pp. 34-9.

Collins, D. (1996a), "Whither democracy? Lost debates in management empowerment", *Empowerment in Organizations*, Vol. 4 No. 1, pp. 12-24.

Collins, D. (1996b), "Control and isolation in the management of empowerment", *Empowerment in Organizations*, Vol. 4 No. 2, pp. 29-39.

Cook, S. (1994), "The cultural implications of empowerment", *Empowerment in Organizations*, Vol. 2 No. 1, pp. 9-13.

Davis, J.E. and Stocking, B.A. (1996), "Unearthing buried treasure", *Empowerment in Organizations*, Vol. 4 No. 2, pp. 8-15.

Dickmeyer, M. and Williams, B. (1995), "Gordon Gecko versus Tom Sawyer: catalytic empowerment techniques", *Empowerment in Organizations*, Vol. 3 No. 1, pp. 32-9.

Echiejile, I. (1994), "Empowering disadvantaged employees", *Empowerment in Organizations,* Vol. 2 No. 1, pp. 31-7.

Gore, L., Toledano, K. and Wills, G. (1994), "Leading courageous managers on", *Empowerment in Organizations*, Vol. 2 No. 3, pp. 7-24.

Harley, W.B. (1995), "Eight critical principles of empowerment", *Empowerment in Organizations,* Vol. 4 No. 3, pp. 16-25.

Höpfl, H. (1994), "Empowerment and the managerial prerogative", *Empowerment in Organizations*, Vol. 3 No. 1, pp. 5-12.

Huang, J-H., Huang, C-T. and Wu, S. (1996), "National character and response to unsatisfactory hotel service", *International Journal of Hospitality Management*, Vol. 15 No. 3, pp. 229-43.

Jones, P., Palmer, J., Whitehead, D. and Osterweil, C. (1996), "Performance through people", *Empowerment in Organizations,* Vol. 4 No. 4, pp. 23-7.

Kappelman, L.A. and Richards, T.C. (1996), "Training, empowerment, and creating a culture for change", *Empowerment in Organizations,* Vol. 4 No. 3, pp. 26-9.

Lashley, C. (1996). "Research issues for employee empowerment in hospitality operations", *International Journal of Hospitality Management*, Vol. 15 No. 3, pp. 283-98.

Lashley, C. and McGoldrick, J. (1994), "The limits of empowerment a critical assessment of human resource strategy for hospitality operations", *Empowerment in Organizations,* Vol. 2 No. 3, pp. 25-38.

Lloyd, G.C. (1996), "Fostering an environment of employee contribution to increase commitment and motivation", *Empowerment in Organizations*, Vol. 4 No. 1, pp. 25-8.

Logan, L. (1995), "McGraw-Hill/London House studies the human side of TQM", *Empowerment in Organizations,* Vol. 3 No. 3, pp. 44-5.

Logan, L., Harley, W.B., Pastor, J., Wing, L.S., Glasman, N., Hanson, L., Collins, D., Cleary, B.A., Miller, J. and Hegedahl, P. (1996), "Observations on the state of empowerment in today's organization", *Empowerment in Organizations,* Vol. 4 No. 1, pp. 6-11.

Long, R.F. (1996), "Empowerment – a management style for the millennium?", *Empowerment in Organizations*, Vol. 4 No. 3, pp. 5-15.

Marguilies, J.S. and Kleiner, B.H. (1995), "New designs of work groups: applications of empowerment", *Empowerment in Organizations*, Vol. 3 No. 2, pp. 12-18.

Maxwell, G.A. (1997), "A critique of empowerment in the UK hospitality industry", *6th Annual Hospitality Research Conference Proceedings,* pp. 52-66.

Miller, J. (1996), "Humor – an empowerment tool for the 1990s", *Empowerment in Organizations*, Vol. 4 No. 2, pp. 16-21.

Morley, L. (1995), "Theorizing empowerment in the UK public services", *Empowerment in Organizations*, Vol. 3 No. 3, pp. 35-41.

Newton, R.J. and Wilkinson, M.J. (1994). "Project MORALE: the empowerment of managers in their everyday work", *Empowerment in Organizations,* Vol. 2 No. 1, pp. 25-30.

Nicholls, J. (1995), "Getting empowerment into perspective: a three stage training framework", *Empowerment in Organizations*, Vol. 3 No. 2, pp. 6-11.

Nixon, B. (1994), "Developing an empowering culture in organizations", *Empowerment in Organizations*, Vol. 2 No. 1, pp. 14-24.

Nykodym, N., Simonetti, J.L., Nielsen, W.R. and Welling, B. (1994), "Employee empowerment", *Empowerment in Organizations,* Vol. 2 No. 3, pp. 45-55.

Pastor, J. (1996), "Empowerment:what it is and what it is not", *Empowerment in Organizations*, Vol. 4 No. 2, pp. 5-7.

Pearson, C.A.L. and Chatterjee, S.R. (1996), "Implementing empowerment through sub-unit clusters: a Western Australian case study", *Empowerment in Organizations*, Vol. 4 No. 3, pp. 16-25.

Pence, P. (1996), "Is your organization really committed to teams? A self-test for measuring your organization's commitment", *Empowerment in Organizations,* Vol. 4 No. 2, pp. 22-8.

Pence, P. and Lunderman, K. (1995), "AMD's journey to excellence", *Empowerment in Organizations*, Vol. 3 No. 3, pp. 19-24.

Potter, J. (1994), "Tapping the iceberg: how to get the best out of your people through empowerment", *Empowerment in Organizations,* Vol. 2 No. 1, pp. 4-8.

Rodrigues, C.A. (1994), "Employee participation and empowerment programs: problems of definition and implementation", *Empowerment in Organizations*, Vol. 2 No. 2, pp. 29-40.

Simmons, M. (1995), "Building an inclusive organization", *Empowerment in Organizations,* Vol. 3 No. 3, pp. 11-18.

Wing, L.S. (1996), "Personal empowerment: self as tool", *Empowerment in Organizations*, Vol. 4 No. 3, pp. 34-6.

A market-driven approach to business development and service improvement in the hospitality industry

John T. Bowen
Research Director (North America) Worldwide Hospitality and Tourism Trends

Reviews hospitality research relating to the themes of business development and service improvement. Relates this to five sub-theme areas: market sensitivity and competitiveness; segmentation; branding and service customization; service quality and customer retention; product design and internal marketing.

Introduction

The purpose of this article is to review hospitality research concerning the broad theme of business development and service improvement. This theme is divided into five sub-themes: market sensitivity and competitiveness; segmentation, branding and service customization; service quality and customer retention; product design and internal marketing. Journal articles from 1990 to June of 1997 were used in this study. Abstracts of most of the articles can be found on the WHATT CD.

The objective of the study is to provide practitioners with suggestions and ideas for business improvement. Millions of dollars of research are referenced in this article. The results of the research are not proprietary, but available for all to use. For practitioners, the article will explain the management implications of the research. For academics, the article provides an overview of current research by area and presents suggestions for future research.

Theme 1: Market sensitivity and competitiveness

The research in the area of market sensitivity and competitiveness tended to be on yield management and positioning. The yield management research was grouped into two general issues, pricing systems to increase yield and the choice of market segments that would create the highest yield. The positioning articles discussed the use of perceptual maps as a strategic tool. The methodology used in the positioning articles could be applied to most hospitality companies, giving good information for strategic planning.

Yield management

The yield management articles are broken up into conventional yield management articles and methods for choosing the market segments that will create the highest yield. Griffin (1995) provided an overview of yield management and identified a number of critical success factors for yield management systems. Among these are several environmental factors that relate to booking patterns, price sensitivity of market segments, and the distribution channel's tolerance for differential pricing. Jeffrey and Hubbard (1994) developed a model of occupancy performance that can be easily applied by hotel managers and others with access to hotel occupancy data. The model looked at two fundamental aspects of a hotel's occupancy performance: the proportionality component, which includes the effects of regular and periodic demand fluctuations, and the competitive components, which include local and unique forces.

Bull (1994) investigated the contribution a hotel's location makes to the market value of the hotel's rooms. This methodology makes it possible to put implicit price-location contours on an area map. The study also has implications for area growth that may affect the contribution of a property's location to its room rate. Weatherford (1995) cited the importance of incorporating a guest's length of stay into the room allocation decisions. He claimed proper use of the length of stay dimension can increase revenue by up to 3 per cent. One of the problems with most yield management systems is that they only look at room revenue. Quain (1992) introduced profit analysis by segment (PABS). PABS takes into account room and non-room revenue to determine the value of different market segments. As yield management matures in the hotel industry, more robust models will be developed that take into account total guest expenditures and the long-term value of the guest. In developing yield management systems it is important that customer retention be included in the model. Maximizing revenue today has little value if it drives off tomorrow's customers.

Positioning/perceptual maps

Dev et al. (1995) cited the need for managers to monitor the implications of their marketing strategies. The authors stated that managers need to examine the attributes that consumers use to differentiate one hotel brand from another and illustrated how managers can do this by using multidimensional scaling to build perceptual maps. Kim (1996) used perceptual maps to show how customers perceive food and beverage at competing

[100]

Table I
Market sensitivity and competitiveness

Authors	Focus	Sub-theme
Kim (1996)	Positioning of food and beverage outlets in competing hotels	Positioning/ perceptual maps
Dev, Morgan and Shoemaker (1995)	Used multi-dimensional scaling to build perceptual maps	Positioning/ perceptual maps
Mazanec (1995)	Shows how self-organizing maps can be used to analyse a hotel's position	Positioning/ perceptual maps
Shaw (1992)	Pricing from a strategic positioning viewpoint	Positioning/ perceptual maps
Lewis (1990)	Focus on customers rather than objective positioning	Positioning/ perceptual maps
Knutson, Malk and Schmidgall (1995)	Looks at when it may be profitable to turn business away	Yield management
Weatherford (1995)	Length of stay as a variable in yield management	Yield management
Bull (1994)	Contribution of location to the price of a hotel's rooms	Yield management
Quain (1992)	Including non-room revenue in yield management	Yield management

hotels. Kim also developed ideal points to show how a hotel can change its attributes to gain a better position *vis-à-vis* its competitors. The methodology used in the study could be used to position different product or product groups of a hotel or restaurant.

Shaw (1992) investigated price from a strategic positioning viewpoint. She explained how price has both a strategic component and a tactical component. Shaw stated a positioning approach focuses first on price levels, then on actual price decisions for a specific product. Shaw's approach to pricing could help a brand achieve a desired position, which then could be validated through one of the perceptual mapping techniques.

Theme 2: segmentation, branding, and service customization

It is no secret that different customer segments want different product attributes. Commissioned sales people want hotel rooms with a free telephone, while upscale business travellers want expedited check-in. Thus, one of the first decisions for a company is to decide what segments it wants to target. This will determine the company's marketing mix. As segments grow and decline, a company must constantly review its segmentation strategy, looking for viable segments that are compatible with the company's objectives and products. After a company chooses a target market, the company must position itself in the marketplace *vis-à-vis* the other companies that are going after the target market. Two ways of accomplishing this positioning are through branding and service customization.

This section looks at research on segmentation, branding, and service customization.

Segmentation

The segmentation research identifies product attributes that create value for market segments. This information is useful to companies targeting these segments or companies who may have a marketing mix that is valuable to these segments. It is always advisable to replicate segmentation studies using data from customers. Owing to time and regional differences, the wants of customer segments can vary. The segmentation research also presents a variety of research techniques that can be used to give greater insight into what the segments desire and the importance they put on different product attributes.

Shaw *et al.* (1991) investigated product attributes of hotel convention services that create satisfaction among meeting planners. The authors went beyond just looking at the mean ratings of the attributes. They developed a multivariate approach to analysing the data, which could be applied to similar survey data to provide rich information.

Several studies looked at specific segments. For example, Wight (1996) researched ecotourism and divided it into two market segments: general consumers interested in ecotourism and experienced ecotourism travellers. Her findings are useful for resorts that are interested in catering to this market. Callan (1996) compared UK leisure travellers with business travellers on their importance ratings of hotel attributes. Makens (1992) investigated catering to the family market at resorts. The article provides some case studies of resorts that have children's

John T. Bowen
*A market-driven approach to
business development and
service improvement in the
hospitality industry*

programmes. For more studies that looked at specific segments, see Table II.

Conjoint analysis gives insight to the importance that customers place on different product attributes. Several studies provided examples of how conjoint analysis can be used in segmentation studies. Hu and Hiemstra (1996) used hybrid conjoint analysis to measure meeting planners' preferences in hotel selection. Becker-Suttle *et al.* (1994) used conjoint analysis to explore restaurant benefits sought by seniors and non-seniors.

The use of neural networks, a type of artificial intelligence, is becoming a popular segmentation technique. It is often used in data mining tools to discover relationships between customers, identifying customer segments that might not be apparent to the marketer. Mazanec (1992) illustrated the usefulness of neural networks by segmenting tourists.

Branding
Customers develop brand images, or a set of beliefs, about where each brand stands on different product attributes. One of the trends in the hospitality industry is to use brands that have a positive brand image, rather than a company's own products which may have little brand image. For example, many hotels and catering companies in the USA are using kiosks to sell Starbucks Coffee, which has a strong brand image. ARAMARK, a contract food service company, franchises Burger King and Pizza Hut outlets even though they have the ability to produce products that have a similar quality. Hotels are contracting out their food service to local providers and chains that have a strong image. Thus, brand management is an area that is emerging as an important marketing area.

The research on branding was scarce, indicating a need for future research in this area. Hallam and Baum (1996) surveyed hotel managers in North America and the UK to gain perceptions of why hotels may contract out portions or all of their food and beverage operations. One of the major reasons cited in the study was that a branded or well-known operator could help attract more accommodation guests. Thus, managers saw a branded restaurant as an amenity that was valued by the lodging guests. Connell (1992) looked at the benefits and problems of branding in the hotel industry. He used the rebranding of Forte after the acquisition of Crest as a case study.

Customization
Effective guest history systems now make it possible to customize guest service. Unpublished research by Bowen and Shoemaker found that customized services were one the most important attributes to luxury hotel customers. Ritz-Carlton used guest history very effectively to produce customized services (Partlow 1993). Dev and Ellis (1991) presented a guest history management model

Table II
Segmentation, branding and service customization

Authors	Focus	Sub-theme
Callan (1996)	Leisure and business travellers	Segmentation
Hu and Hiemstra (1996)	Conjoint analysis as a segmentation tool – benefits sought by meeting planners	Segmentation
Oh and Jeong (1996)	Expectation based segmentation	Segmentation
Wuest, Tas, and Emenheiser (1996)	Assessed the importance of services provided by hotels/ motels as perceived by mature travellers	Segmentation
Wight (1996)	Ecotourism	Segmentation
Becker-Suttle, Weaver and Crawford-Welch (1994)	Conjoint analysis as a segmentation tool – benefits sought by seniors and non-seniors	Segmentation
Weaver and Oh (1993)	Service requirements of frequent and infrequent business travellers	Segmentation
Ananth, DeMicco, Moreo and Howey (1992)	Conjoint analysis as a segmentation tool benefits sought by seniors and non-seniors	Segmentation
Makens (1992)	Families with children at resorts	Segmentation
Mazanec (1992)	Use of neural networks to segment	Segmentation
Hallam and Baum (1996)	Leasing of hotel food and beverage operations	Branding
Connell (1992)	Problems and benefits of branding in the hotel industry	Branding
Partlow (1993)	Ritz-Carlton	Service customization
Sparks (1993)	Using guest history to customize services	Service customization

John T. Bowen
A market-driven approach to business development and service improvement in the hospitality industry

and explained how it could be used to customize service for repeat guests. Customization of services can create a competitive advantage by increasing guest loyalty.

Theme 3: service quality and customer retention

What is service quality?

A distinction can be made between two types of quality: product features that enhance customer satisfaction and freedom from deficiencies that increase customer satisfaction. The first type of quality, product features, adds to the cost of the product. Customers must be willing to pay for either the added costs of additional product features or these features must make them more loyal. For example, lettuce and tomato is found only on McDonald's more expensive hamburgers. Hotel rooms on concierge floors have more features than standard rooms and command a higher price. La Quinta Inns offers free local telephone calls to encourage loyalty among salespeople.

The expectations of guests are formed by company image, word of mouth, the company's promotional efforts, and price. A guest paying $35 for a room at a Motel 6 or Formula 1 will have different expectations from a guest paying $250 for a room at a Four Seasons Hotel. The person staying at the budget hotel may be perfectly satisfied. The room features meet their expectations. The first type of quality, product features, relates to guest expectations. People staying in a budget hotel may perceive it as the best quality motel for less than $40. They are not comparing it to a Four Seasons Hotel. Both the guests of a Motel 6 or Formula 1 and a Four Seasons Hotel will expect the room to be free from deficiencies. For example, guests at the Four Seasons and those at the budget hotel are both likely to get upset if they return in the evening to rooms that have not been made up.

There is another way to view quality. A distinction can be made between technical and functional quality. Technical quality refers to what the customer is left with after the customer-employee interactions have been completed. For example, technical quality relates to the guest room in the hotel, the meal in the restaurant, and the car from the rental agency. Functional quality is the process of delivering the service or product (Grönroos, 1982). While the service is being delivered, customers go through many interactions with the firm's employees. A guest makes a reservation, is greeted by the door attendant, is escorted to the front desk by a bellperson, checks in with the desk clerk, and is escorted to the room. The experience of checking into a hotel is an example of functional quality. Excellent functional quality may make up for a room that is not quite up to expectations. If functional quality is unpleasant, a high-quality room might not overcome the guests' previous dissatisfaction.

Models of quality management

For a good introduction to service quality see a series of articles by Johns (1992a, 1992b, 1993). In these articles he presented a comprehensive overview of quality management in the hospitality industry. Partlow (1993) provided a comprehensive overview of how Ritz-Carlton won the Malcolm Baldrige Award. In the article, Partlow presented an overview of Ritz's quality management program. Later, Partlow (1996) focused on the human resource practices that support TQM. Heymann (1992) provided a ten-point model for quality management.

Measuring service quality

A service quality audit can identify problems when a firm is first developing a quality management programme or it can be used to audit an existing programme. Luchars and Hinkin (1996) developed a service quality audit that can be used to identify errors and determine their frequency, assign costs of fixing (or not fixing) the errors, and identify steps to prevent them. They provided a case study of a New York hotel to illustrate their service-quality audit.

SERVQUAL developed by Parasuraman *et al.* is one of the most popular instruments for measuring service quality. Knutson *et al.* (1991) adapted SERVQUAL into a specific instrument for hotels. They tested the reliability of their instrument, LODGSERV, and found it to be a reliable instrument. Later Stevens *et al.* (1995) developed DINESERV for measuring service quality in restaurants. Barsky (1992) discussed a theoretical model of customer satisfaction and then tested the model using a survey instrument. Using his survey instrument, he was able to support his hypothesis that intent to return will be positively related to customer satisfaction.

Customer retention

One desired outcome of service quality is customer retention. The following research investigated customer retention. Dube *et al.* (1994) used conjoint analysis to show the overall utility of seven service-quality attributes that all bear significantly on customers' intent to return. The authors' methodology provides managers with information that will help justify (or not justify) the costs of

John T. Bowen
A market-driven approach to business development and service improvement in the hospitality industry

Table III

Customer retention and service quality

Authors	Focus	Sub-theme
Partlow (1996)	Human resource practices that support TQM	Models of quality management
Yasin and Zimmerer (1995)	Benchmarking	Models of quality management
Page (1994)	Case study of Sutcliffe Catering's approach to continuous improvement	Models of quality management
Partlow (1993)	Overview of Ritz Carlton's TQM programme	Models of quality management
Heymann (1992)	TQM model	Models of quality management
Johns (1992a, 1992b,1993)	Overview of quality management in hospitality industry	Models of quality management
Watson, McKenna and McLean (1992)	Barriers to successful implementation of TQM and ways to overcome these barriers	Models of quality management
Lee and Hing (1995)	Use the SERVQUAL instrument to measure quality in restaurants	Measuring quality
Stevens, Knutson and Parton (1995)	Developed DINERSERV to measure consumer's perception of quality in restaurants	Measuring quality
Almanza, Jaffe and Lin (1994)	Measuring satisfaction and importance of product attributes	Measuring quality
Barsky (1992)	Customer satisfaction and retention	Measuring quality
Knutson, Stevens, Wullaert, Patton and Yokoyama (1992)	Developed LODGESERV, a 26 item index to measure consumer's perception of quality in the hotels	Measuring quality
Knutson *et al.* (1990)	LODGESERV	Measuring quality
Callan (1990)	Found a wide diversity of opinions among travel industry journalist's measurement on the value of qualitative award schemes as a measure of service quality	Measuring quality
Buttle and Bok (1996)	Used theory of reasoned action model to predict intention to return	Customer retention
Dube, Renaghan and Miller (1994)	Investigated service attributes that are related to intention to return	Customer retention
Reid and Reid (1993)	Communication strategies relating to customer retention	Customer retention
Toh, Rivers and Withiam (1991)	Frequent guest programmes	Customer retention

improving quality. Toh *et al.* (1991) researched the effectiveness of frequent-guest programmes in hotels. They found many of the programmes were not effective in creating repeat customers. The authors provide insights on how the programmes could be improved. Buttle and Bok (1996) provided an overview of Fishbein's theory of reasoned action. They found two predictor constructs: attitude towards the act, and subjective norm jointly explain about 65 per cent of the intention to stay in a hotel on the next trip.

Theme 4: product design

A company must build a service delivery system that provides product attributes desired by its target market. The articles on service design were on both the macro and micro level. Some articles looked at the overall design of a hospitality operation, while other articles looked at specific issues. This section will first review the macro articles and then discuss the micro articles.

Comprehensive design models

Pannell Kerr Forster Associates (1993) concluded that hotel design factors can be summarized into three areas: market factors including customer requirements, competitive influences and trends; impact of new technology enabling new services or increased levels of comfort to be available

John T. Bowen
A market-driven approach to business development and service improvement in the hospitality industry

Table IV
Product design

Authors	Focus	Sub-theme
Verma and Thompson (1995)	Design model using discrete choice analysis	Comprehensive design model
Elliott and Johns (1995)	Trends in resort designs	Comprehensive design model
Pannell Kerr Forster Associates (1993)	Hotel design	Comprehensive design model
West and Purvis (1993)	Looks at hotel design effectiveness	Comprehensive design model
Miner (1996)	Menu items	New product design
Shoemaker (1996)	Importance of scripts in new product development	New product design
Jones (1995)	Applies a model for new product development to airline catering	New product design
Makens and Bowen (1996)	Restaurant merchandizing	Specific products
Bowen and Morris (1995)	Menu design	Specific products
Goldman (1993)	Restaurant concept selection	Specific products
Monteson and Singer (1992)	Spa at resorts	Specific products

and leading to improvements in construction techniques and choice of materials used; and statutory requirements affecting the design and construction of buildings and specific legislation relating to hotels.

Verma and Thompson (1996) illustrated how discrete choice analysis can be used to design business concepts based on the importance that customers place on different product attributes. The researchers use delivery pizza as an example, but the technique could be applied to the development or design of any concept.

New product design
Several articles looked at the development of new products. Jones (1995) applied Scheuing and Johnson's model for new service development to flight catering. His research found that airlines lack many of the systematic procedures suggested by Scheuing and Johnson. Shoemaker (1996) looked at how customers develop a series of actions regarded as necessary or appropriate for a service transaction. Variations from the script can be a source of dissatisfaction. Thus, when developing new service delivery systems, companies must assist customers in developing a new script. Miner (1996) presented a customer focused approach to developing new products in a restaurant. The six stage process includes product ideas, initial evaluation, consumer reaction, sensory testing, field testing, and product introduction.

Specific products
Another set of research looked at the design of special projects. Goldman (1993) discussed the importance of concept selection for independent restaurants. He discussed the different external factors that affect concept selection. Makens and Bowen (1996) discussed merchandise opportunities for restaurants. Design consideration for restaurants wanting to implement a merchandising programme include space to merchandise the products and storage space. Bowen and Morris (1995) looked at the design of a menu to increase product sales. They found that menu design in a sit-down service restaurant may not be as effective in selling products as previously thought. Monteson and Singer (1992) explained how spas can add value as an amenity in a destination hotel or resort. They gave advice on how to manage and market a spa properly, so it creates maximum value for the guests and adds to the bottom line of the hotel.

Conner (1991) focused on how renovations could capture the original glitz and glamour of the hotel, while making the hotel operationally efficient. Conner provides specific examples from design renovations in New York City. Knapp (1991) provides a case study of the renovation of the Sheraton Palace in San Francisco.

Theme 5: internal marketing
The hospitality industry is unique in that employees are part of the product. When

Table V
Internal marketing

Authors	Focus	Sub-theme
Ross (1994)	Explores how they work	Culture
Meudall and Gadd (1994)	Culture in short life organizations	Culture
King and Garey (1997)	Environment's influence on employee attitudes	Culture
Shimko (1994)	Barriers to service orientation	Service orientation
Dienhart *et al.* (1992)	Factors that influence service orientation	Service orientation
Dienhart *et al.* (1991)	Factors that influence service orientation	Service orientation
Barsky (1992)	World class service	Service orientation
Samenfink (1991)	Predicting service orientation	Service orientation
Francese (1993)	Organizational structures and customer satisfaction	Service orientation
Brownell (1994)	Management-employee communication	Listening
Sparks (1994)	Communication and customer satisfaction	Listening
Lashley (1997)	Framework for employee empowerment	Empowerment
Lashley (1995)	Benefits of empowerment	Empowerment
Sparrowe (1994)	Psychological empowerment	Empowerment
Brymer (1991)	Framework for employee empowerment	Empowerment
Hales and Mecrate-Butcher (1994)	Use of internal marketing in British Hotels which are part of consortia	Internal marketing – overview

people think of marketing, they usually think of efforts directed externally towards the marketplace; but a hotel or restaurant's first marketing efforts should be directed internally to employees. Managers must make sure that employees know their products and believe that they are good value. The employees must be excited about the company they work for and the products they sell; otherwise, it will be impossible for the guests to become excited. External marketing brings customers into the hotel but does little good if the employees do not perform to the guest's expectations. The sub-themes identified in the research relating internal marketing include culture, service orientation, empowerment and listening.

Culture

An internal marketing programme flows out of a service culture. A service marketing programme is doomed to failure if its organizational culture does not support serving the customer. It is difficult to establish an effective culture in a permanent organization and even harder to establish a culture in a temporary organization. Meudell and Gadd (1994) looked at the establishment of a culture in short-life organizations. The authors used an organizational beliefs questionnaire to investigate the National Garden Festival Wales' organizational culture. This article built on

earlier work by the authors on short-life organizations.

Service orientation

If management expects employees' attitudes to be positive towards the customer, management must have a positive attitude towards the customer and the employees. Too often organizations hire trainers to come in for one day to get their customer-contact employees excited about providing quality customer service. The effect of these sessions is usually short-lived because the organizations do little to support the customer-contact employees. A company must develop policies and an organizational structure to support its service orientation.

Barsky (1996) described how to build a system to deliver world-class service. In the article he provided numerous examples from hospitality firms, including a sample of a guest survey. Barsky also provided examples of how to map the customer cycle. At the heart of this process is a step that redesigns exiting processes based on both customer and employee input. The second part of this step is to develop employee programmes that support the new processes.

Shimko (1994) explained how existing decision-making polices, coupled with the manner in which organizations reward conforming behaviour, may result in polices that

John T. Bowen
A market-driven approach to business development and service improvement in the hospitality industry

prevent employees from providing optimal customer service. King and Garey (1997) looked at how the organizational context in which a service encounter takes place affects employee interactions with customers, and resulting guest satisfaction. They found that stress-related factors including a bureaucratic climate were negatively related to guest satisfaction ratings. Dienhart *et al.*(1991) and Dienhart *et al.* (1992) investigated factors that might influence restaurant employees' degree of service orientation. The authors developed a questionnaire that was administered to supervisory and non-supervisory employees. The results of the research suggest that increasing employee's job involvement, job satisfaction, and job security could assist in improving their overall service orientation.

Listening

Perhaps one of the most important research areas of internal marketing is the management of listening. Employees have the potential for collecting information directly from the guests. Through proper training and information collection systems employees can provide more information than market research costing tens of thousands of dollars. However, for these systems to work, employees must trust the organization. Good communication between employees and managers not only provides good customer information, but it also supports a service culture by identifying management problems and solutions to those problems. Several researchers investigated the area of listening and communication.

Brownell(1994) focused on the importance of managers creating an environment that fosters good communication between employees and management. She stated, "The vision of strong listening environments may foster practices and attitudes that become the most important tools managers bring with them into the twenty-first century". Sparks (1994) found that customers evaluate the quality of the service, in part, on the manner in which information is communicated by employees. Thus, part of customer satisfaction is dependent on the ability of employees to listen to customers and communicate with them.

Empowerment

Empowerment has been associated with a number of benefits including increased employee and customer satisfaction. The increased customer satisfaction comes through better complaint resolution, ability to customize products, and more responsive service. One problem in the implementation of empowerment can be lack of management

support. Most of the research on empowerment dealt with the process of empowering employees.

Brymer (1991) presented a framework for implementing employee empowerment and also provided some guides which will help measure the results of empowerment. Lashley (1995) provided an overview of the benefits of empowerment and illustrated how different hospitality companies have implemented empowerment. Lashley (1997) later provided frameworks for employee empowerment and called for research to investigate the tradeoffs between employee empowerment and improved organizational performance. Sparrowe (1994) proposed that investments in psychological empowerment among hospitality employees seem worthwhile, as satisfaction with promotion opportunities should rise and intent to leave should decline. Thus, empowerment can not only lead to guest satisfaction, it can also result in employee satisfaction.

Thematic interrelationships

The linkage between the themes is shown in Figure 1. Through market analysis, perceptual maps are developed providing insights into attractive market segments. Much of the research in the area of market segmentation focused on the importance different market segments place on product attributes. The target market determines the design of the product. Quality management ensures that the product is being delivered at a level which will create repeat business. Quality measurement validates that the quality management system is working. The quality measurement also monitors changes in wants and expectations of the target market. Changes in market expectations or wants can be met through product redesign. Thus, the link between quality measurement and product design indicates an ongoing process of shaping the product to meet the needs of the target market.

Since employees are part of the product, they need to be included in the design of service delivery systems. Employees that deliver good service also contribute to the quality of the organization and will be included in the quality management process. Finally, quality impacts on brand image.

Customer retention is one of the objectives of most businesses. Figure 1 shows that brand image, service customization, and internal marketing all affect customer retention. At the heart of this model is the target market or customer. When a company chooses a market segment that can create value for the firm, then the firm must deliver a product that creates value to the market segment. The literature reviewed in this article will help hospitality managers gain insight into the process of choosing the right target markets and delivering value to their target markets.

Summary and conclusions

This article reviewed a broad set of research relating to business development. One common thread through the research is responsive communication. Companies need to communicate with their markets and employees. Employees need to communicate with customers. But communication alone is not enough. The communication must be responsive. The information gained through the marketing intelligence system must be used to identify desired target markets, create products for those markets, gain a desired position in the marketplace, understand the price sensitivity of markets, and to enable internal customers, the employees, to serve the customer better. If an organization can achieve these ends, its business will flourish.

Figure 1
A market-driven approach to business development and service improvement

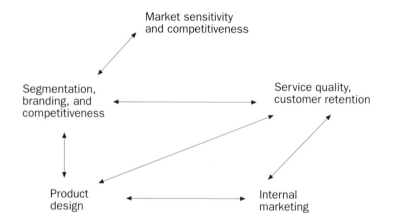

References

Almanza, B.A., Jaffe, W. and Lin, L. (1994), "Use of the service attribute matrix to measure consumer satisfaction", *Hospitality Research Journal*, Vol. 17 No. 2, pp. 63-75.

Ananth, M., DeMicco, F.J., Moreo, P.J. and Howey, R.M. (1992), "Marketplace lodging needs of mature travellers", *The Cornell Hotel and Restaurant Quarterly*, Vol. 33 No. 4, pp. 12-24.

Barsky, J.D. (1992), "Customer satisfaction in the hotel industry: meaning and measurement", *Hospitality Research Journal*, Vol. 16 No. 1, pp. 51-73.

Barsky, J.D.(1996), "Building a program for world-class service", *The Cornell Hotel and Restaurant Quarterly*, Vol. 37 No. 1, pp.17-27.

Barsky, J.D. and Laubagh, R. (1992), "A strategy for customer satisfaction", *The Cornell Hotel and Restaurant Quarterly*, Vol. 33 No. 5, pp. 32-40.

Becker-Suttle, C.B., Weaver, P. and Crawford-Welch, S. (1994), "A pilot study utilizing conjoint analysis in the comparison of age-based segmentation strategies in the full service restaurant market", *Journal of Restaurant and Food Service Marketing*, Vol. 1 No. 2, pp. 71- 91.

Bowen, J. and Morris, A. (1995), "Menu design: can menus sell?," *International Journal of Contemporary Hospitality Management*, Vol. 7 No. 4, pp. 4-9.

Brownell, J.(1994), "Creating strong listening environments: a key hospitality management task", *International Journal of Contemporary Hospitality Management,* Vol. 6 No. 3, pp. 3-10.

Brownell, J. and Jameson, D. (1996), "Getting quality out on the street-", *The Cornell Hotel and Restaurant Quarterly*, Vol. 37 No. 1, pp. 28-33.

Brymer, R.A. (1991), "Employee empowerment: a guest driven leadership strategy", *The Cornell Hotel and Restaurant Quarterly*, Vol. 32 No. 1, pp. 58-68.

Bull, A.O. (1994), "Pricing a motel's location", *International Journal of Contemporary Hospitality Management*, Vol. 6 No. 6, pp. 10-15.

Buttle, F. and Bok, B. (1996), "Hotel marketing strategy and the theory of reasoned action", *International Journal of Contemporary Hospitality Management*, Vol. 8 No. 3, pp. 5-10.

Callan, R.J. (1990), "Hotel award schemes as a measurement of service quality – an assessment by travel industry journalists as surrogate consumers", *International Journal of Hospitality Management*, Vol. 9 No. 1, pp. 45-58.

Callan, R.J. (1996), "An appraisement of UK business travellers' perceptions of important hotel attributes", *Hospitality Research Journal,* Vol. 19 No. 4, pp. 113-27.

Connell, J. (1992), "Branding hotel portfolios", *International Journal of Contemporary Hospitality Management,* Vol.4 No. 1, pp. 26-32.

Conner, F.L. (1991), "NYC hotels show the reasons why", *The Cornell Hotel and Restaurant Quarterly,* Vol. 32 No. 4, pp. 24-34.

Dev, C.S. and Ellis, B. (1991), "Guest Histories: an untapped service resource,"*The Cornell Hotel and Restaurant Quarterly*, Vol. 32 No. 2, pp. 29-37.

Dev, C.S., Morgan, M.S. and Shoemaker, S. (1995), "A positioning analysis of hotel brands", *The Cornell Hotel and Restaurant Quarterly,* Vol. 36 No. 6, pp. 48-55.

Dienhart, J.R., Gregorie, M.B. and Downey, R.G.(1991), "Service orientation of restaurant employees", *Hospitality Research Journal,* Vol. 14 No. 2, pp. 421-9.

Dienhart, J.R., Gregorie, M.B., Downey, R.G. and Knight, P. K. (1992), "Service orientation of restaurant employees", *International Journal of Hospitality Management*, Vol. 11 No. 4, pp. 331-46.

Dube, L., Renaghan, L.M. and Miller, J.M. (1994), "Measuring customer satisfaction for strategic management", *The Cornell Hotel* and Restaurant Quarterly, Vol. 35 No. 1, pp. 39-47.

Elliott, J. and Johns, N. (1993), "The influence of international tourism trends on the design of leisure resorts", *International Journal of Contemporary Hospitality Management*, Vol. 5 No. 2, pp. 6-9.

Francese, P. (1993), "Breaking the rules: delivering responsive service", *Hospitality Research Journal,* Vol. 16 No. 2, pp. 55-74.

Goldman, K. (1993), "Concept selection for independent restaurants", *The Cornell Hotel and Restaurant Quarterly*, Vol. 34 No. 6, pp. 59-72.

Griffin, R.K. (1995), "A categorization scheme for critical success factors of lodging yield management systems", *International Journal of Hospitality Management*, Vol. 14 No. 3/4, pp. 325-38.

Grönroos, C. (1982), *Strategic Management is the Service Sector*, Swedish School of Business Administration, Helsgfors, Finland.

Hales, C. and Mercrate-Butcher, J. (1994), "'Internal marketing' and human resource management in hotel consortia", *International Journal of Hospitality Management,* Vol. 13 No. 4, pp. 313-26.

Hallam, G. and Baum, T. (1996), "Contracting out food and beverage service in hotels: a comparative study of practice in North America and the United Kingdom", *International Journal of Hospitality Management,* Vol. 15 No. 1, pp. 41-50.

Heymann, K. (1992), "Quality management: a ten-point model", *The Cornell Hotel and Restaurant Quarterly*, Vol. 33 No. 5, pp. 51-60.

Hu, C. and Hiemstra, S. (1996), "Hybrid conjoint analysis as a research technique to measure meeting planners' preferences in hotel selection", *Journal of Travel Research*, Vol. 35 No. 2, pp. 62-9.

Jeffrey, D. and Hubbard, N.J. (1994), "A model of hotel occupancy performance for monitoring and marketing in the hotel industry", *International Journal of Hospitality Management*, Vol. 13 No. 1, pp. 57-71.

Johns, N. (1992a), "Quality management in the hospitality industry: Part 1. Definition and specification", *International Journal of Contemporary Hospitality Management,* Vol. 4 No. 3, pp. 14-20.

Johns, N. (1992b), "Quality management in the hospitality industry: Part 2. Applications, systems, and techniques", *International Journal of Contemporary Hospitality Management,* Vol. 4 No. 4, pp. 3-7.

Johns, N. (1993), "Quality management in the hospitality industry: Part 3. Recent developments", *International Journal of Contemporary Hospitality Management,* Vol. 5 No. 1, pp. 10-15.

Jones, P. (1995), "Developing new products and services in flight catering", *International Journal of Contemporary Hospitality Management*, Vol. 7 No. 2/3, pp 24-8.

Kim, H. (1996), "Perceptual mapping of attributes and preferences: an empirical examination of hotel F&B products in Korea", *International Journal of Hospitality Management*, Vol. 15 No. 4, pp. 373-91.

King, C.A. and Garey, J.G. (1997), "Relational quality in service encounters", *International Journal of Hospitality Management*, Vol. 16 No. 1, pp. 39-63.

Knapp, F. (1991), "The Sheraton Palace: preserving the past, positioning for the future", *The Cornell Hotel and Restaurant Quarterly,* Vol. 32 No. 4, pp. 13-21.

Knutson, B., Malk, M. and Schmidgall, R. (1995), "When it's smart to turn away business", *The Cornell Hotel and Restaurant Quarterly*, Vol. 36 No. 6, pp. 56-61.

Knutson, B., Stevens, P., Wullaert, C., Patton, M. and Yokoyama, F. (1991), "LODGSERV: A service quality index for the lodging industry," *Hospitality Research Journal,* Vol. 14 No. 2, pp. 277-84.

Lashley, C. (1995), "Towards an understanding of employee empowerment in hospitality services", *International Journal of Contemporary Hospitality Management*, Vol. 7 No. 1, pp 27-32.

Lashley, C. (1997), "Research issues for employee empowerment in hospitality organisations", *International Journal of Hospitality Management*, Vol. 15 No. 4, pp. 333-46.

Lee, Y.L. and Hing, N. (1995), "Measuring quality in restaurant operations: an application of SERVQUAL instrument", *International Journal of Hospitality Management*, Vol. 14, No. 3/4, pp. 293-310.

Lewis, R.C. (1990), "Advertising your hotel's position", *The Cornell Hotel and Restaurant Quarterly,* Vol. 31 No. 2, pp. 84-91.

Luchars, J.Y. and Hinkin, T.R. (1996), "The service quality audit", *The Cornell Hotel and Restaurant Quarterly,* Vol. 37 No. 1, pp. 34-41.

Makens, J.C. (1992), "Children at resorts: customer service at its best", *The Cornell Hotel and Restaurant Quarterly*, Vol. 33 No. 4, pp. 25-35.

Makens, J.C. and Bowen, J. (1996), "Increasing restaurant profits with product merchandising", *The Cornell Hotel and Restaurant Quarterly*, Vol. 37 No. 1, pp. 72-9.

Manzanec, J. (1992), "Classifying tourists into market segments: a neural network approach", *Journal of Travel and Tourism Marketing*, Vol. 1 No. 1. pp. 39-59.

Mazanec, J.A. (1995), "Positioning analysis with self-organizing maps", *The Cornell Hotel and Restaurant Quarterly,* Vol. 36 No. 6, pp. 80-95.

Meudell, K. and Gadd, K. (1994), "Culture and climate in short life organizations: sunny spells or thunderstorms?", *International Journal of Contemporary Hospitality Management,* Vol. 6 No. 5, pp. 27-32.

Miner, T. (1996), "Customer-focused menu marketing", *The Cornell Hotel and Restaurant Quarterly,* Vol. 37 No. 3, pp. 36-41.

Monteson, P.A. and Singer, J. (1992), "Turn your spa into a winner", *The Cornell Hotel and Restaurant Quarterly*, Vol. 33 No. 3, pp. 37-49.

Oh, H. and Jeong, M.(1996), "Improving marketers' predictive power of customer satisfaction on expectation-based target market levels", *Hospitality Research Journal,* Vol. 19 No. 4, pp. 65-85.

Page, C. (1994), "Sutcliffe catering's approach to continuous improvement", *International*

Journal of Contemporary Hospitality Management, Vol.6 No. pp. 19-24.

Pannell Kerr Forster Associates (1993), "Factors influencing the design of hotels", *International Journal of Contemporary Hospitality Management*, Vol. 5 No. 2, pp. 17-19.

Partlow, C.G. (1993), "How the Ritz-Carlton applies 'TQM'", *The Cornell Hotel and Restaurant Quarterly*, Vol. 34 No. 4, pp. 16-24.

Partlow, C.G. (1996), "Human-resources practices of TQM hotels", *The Cornell Hotel and Restaurant Quarterly*, Vol. 37 No. 5, pp. 67-77.

Quain, W.J. (1992), "Analysing sales-mix profitability", *The Cornell Hotel and Restaurant Quarterly*, Vol. 33 No. 2, pp. 57-62

Reid, L.J. and Reid, S.D. (1993), " Communicating tourism supplier services: building repeat visitor relationships", *Journal of Travel and Tourism Marketing*, Vol. 2 No. 2/3, pp. 3-19.

Ross, L.E. (1994), "Exploring the influence of work-related attitudes and behaviors in the hospitality work environment", *International Journal of Hospitality Management*, Vol. 13 No. 2, pp. 155-71.

Samenfink, W.H. (1991), "Identifying the service potential of an employee through the use of the self-monitoring scale", *Hospitality Research Journal*, Vol. 15 No. 2, pp. 1-10.

Shaw, M. (1992), "Positioning and price: merging theory, strategy, and tactics", *Hospitality Research Journal*, Vol. 15 No. 2, pp. 31-9.

Shaw, M., Lewis, R.C. and Khorey, A. (1991), "Measuring meeting planner satisfaction with hotel convention services: a multivariate approach", *International Journal of Hospitality Management*, Vol. 10 No. 2, pp. 137-46.

Shimko, B. W. (1994), "Breaking the rules for better service", *The Cornell Hotel and Restaurant Quarterly*, Vol. 35 No. 4, pp.18-22.

Shoemaker, S. (1996), "Scripts: precursor of consumer expectations", *The Cornell Hotel and Restaurant Quarterly*, Vol. 37 No. 1, pp. 42-53.

Sparks, B. (1993), "Guest history: is it being utilized", *International Journal of Contemporary Hospitality Management*, Vol.5 No. 1, pp. 22-7.

Sparks, B.(1994), "Communicative aspects of the service encounter", *Hospitality Reserach Journal*, Vol. 17 No. 2, pp. 39-50.

Sparrowe, R.T. (1994), "Empowerment in the hospitality industry: an exploration of antecedents and outcomes", *Hospitality Reserach Journal*, Vol. 17 No. 3, pp. 51-73.

Stevens, P., Knutson, B. and Patton, M. (1995), "DINESERV: A tool for measuring service quality in restaurants", *The Cornell Hotel and Restaurant Quarterly*, Vol. 36 No. 2, pp. 56-60.

Toh, R.S., Rivers, M. and Withiam, G. (1991), "Frequent-guest programs; Do they fly?", *The Cornell Hotel and Restaurant Quarterly*, Vol. 32 No. 1, pp. 46-52.

Verma, R. and Thompson, G.M. (1996), "Basing service management on customer determinants", *The Cornell Hotel and Restaurant Quarterly*, Vol. 37 No. 3, pp. 18-23.

Watson, H. E., McKenna, M. A. and McLean, G. M. (1992), "TQM and services: implementing Change in the NHS", *International Journal of Contemporary Hospitality Management*, Vol. 4 No. 2, pp. 17-20.

Weatherford, L.R. (1995), "Length of stay heuristics, do they really make a difference", *The Cornell Hotel and Restaurant Quarterly*, Vol. 36 No. 6, pp. 70-9.

Weaver, P.A. and Oh, H.C. (1993), "Do American travellers have different hotel service requirements?", *International Journal of Contemporary Hospitality Management*, Vol. 5 No. 3, pp. 16-21.

West, A. and Purvis, E. (1992), "Hotel design: the need to develop a strategic approach", *International Journal of Contemporary Hospitality Management*, Vol. 4 No. 1, pp. 15-22.

Wight, P. (1996), "North American ecotourists: market profile and trip characteristics", *Journal of Travel Research*, Vol. 34 No. 4, pp. 2-10.

Wuest, B.E.S., Tas, R.F. and Emenheiser, D.A. (1996), "What do mature travellers perceive as important hotel/motel customer services?", *Hospitality Research Journal*, Vol. 20 No. 2, pp. 77-93.

Yousin, M.M. and Zimmerer T.W. (1995), "The role of benchmarking in achieving continuous service quality", *International Journal of Contemporary Hospitality Management*, Vol. 7 No. 4, pp. 27-33.

Responsive communication: the key to business development and service improvement

John T. Bowen

Research Director (North America) Worldwide Hospitality and Tourism Trends

In conducting marketing analysis, planning, implementation and control, managers need information at almost every point in the cycle. One marketing executive put it this way: "...to manage a business well is to manage its future and to manage the future is to manage information". Discusses the communication flows needed to manage business development activities effectively and relates them to practical illustrations and examples.

Introduction

In carrying out marketing analysis, planning, implementation, and control, managers need information at almost every turn. They need information about customers, competitors, suppliers, and other forces in the marketplace. One marketing executive put it this way: "To manage a business well is to manage its future; and to manage the future is to manage information". An important source of information is communication with customers and employees.

In an article in this issue titled, "A market-driven approach to business development and service improvement", the author reviewed research in the areas of: market sensitivity and competitiveness; segmentation, branding, and service customization; customer retention and service quality; product design, and internal marketing. This article will be referred to as "Business development". Figure 1 evolved during the process of doing the review to show the linkages between the areas reviewed in "Business development". One of the observations about Figure 1 is that it diagrams the flow of communication for a business, both externally and internally. These communication flows are important sources for information for business development and service improvement. This article will discuss the communication flows in Figure 1.

During the past century, most hotels and restaurants were independently owned or a part of a small regional chain. Managers obtained information by being around their customers, observing them, and asking questions. During this century, many factors have increased the need for more and better information. As companies become national or international in scope, they need information on larger, more distant markets. As companies become more selective, they need better information about how buyers respond to different products and appeals. As companies use more complex marketing approaches and face intensified competition, they need information on the effectiveness of their marketing tools. Finally, in today's rapidly changing environments, managers need up-to-date information to make timely decisions. It does

no good to receive information if the information is not acted upon or responded to within the organization. The sections of the article that follow discuss the information provided by the communication flows represented in Figure 1.

Figure 2 relates to marketing intelligence. Marketing intelligence includes everyday information about developments in the marketing environment that help managers prepare and adjust marketing plans and short-run tactics. Marketing intelligence systems determine information sources, collect information, deliver it in a useful format to marketing managers, and provide feedback to managers and employees.

Hotel owners and managers are essential parts of a marketing intelligence system. John F. Power, the general manager of the New York Hilton and Towers, served in this role on a trip to Japan. "I realized how different a Japanese breakfast is from our own", said Power, "and while most people like to sample the cuisine of the country they are visiting, everyone prefers to eat familiar food for breakfast". As a result of marketing intelligence gathered on Power's trip, the New York Hilton now serves *miso* soup, *nori* (dried seaweed), *yakizanaka* (grilled fish), raw eggs, *natto* (fermented beans), *oshiako* (pickled vegetables), and rice as an authentic Japanese breakfast buffet (Anonymous, 1989).

In Figure 2 the arrow going to market segmentation represents information the firm is receiving from the marketplace. This includes information on the business environment that affects a firm's target market. Marketing intelligence can also be used to identify emerging markets as well as declining markets, allowing company's to adjust their marketing strategy. Another use of communication with the marketplace is to determine how customers perceive a company's brand and products.

There are three major steps in target marketing (Kolter *et al.*, 1996). The first is market segmentation, dividing a market into distinct groups of buyers who might require separate products and/or marketing mixes. The company identifies different ways to segment the market and develops profiles of the resulting market segments. The second step is market

John T. Bowen
Responsive communication:
the key to business
development and service
improvement

targeting, evaluating each segment's attractiveness and selecting one or more of the market segments. The third step is market positioning, developing a competitive positioning for the product and an appropriate marketing mix.

A product's position is the way the product is defined by consumers on important attributes – the place the product occupies in consumers' minds relative to competing products.

Figure 1

A market-driven approach to business development and service improvement

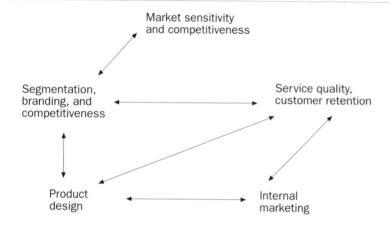

Figure 2

Flow of external communication positioning decisions

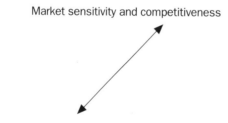

Consumers are overloaded with information about products and services. They cannot re-evaluate products every time they make a buying decision. To simplify buying decision making, consumers organize products into categories. They "position" products and companies in their minds. To gain an effective position, managers need information to identify a set of competitive advantages on which to build a position, selecting the right competitive advantages from this set and effectively communicating and delivering the chosen position to a carefully selected target.

Dev *et al.* (1995) present a case study on the positioning of business class hotels

(Inter-Continental, Hilton, Hyatt, Marriott, Meriden, Radisson, Sheraton, Stouffer, and Westin). The authors explains the process of understanding a brand's position. They explain how to collect information from the market and develop perceptual maps showing how a company's brand is positioned in the consumer's mind *vis-à-vis* its competition. This study covers a three-year period. It is possible to see clearly the movement of each brand's position over this relatively short period. This is good news for companies that have a poor position – it is possible to improve your position in a relatively short time. Likewise, brands that do nothing to manage their position can see their position deteriorate fairly quickly. One of the important aspects of managing a brand's position is regular communication with the marketplace to see how the market is positioning the brand *vis-à-vis* the competition.

Responsive communication and product design

Given the rapid changes in tastes, technology, and competition, a company cannot afford to rely on its existing products. Customers want and expect new and improved products. Customers and employees can provide the firm with information that helps develop market oriented products.

Communicating with customers: Informal sessions and focus groups

One of the easiest ways to communicate with customers is by creating informal situations, which customers will enjoy attending. For example, some hotel managers often invite a group of hotel guests from a particular market segment to have a free breakfast with them. During the breakfast the manager gets a chance to meet the guests and discuss what they like about the hotel and what the hotel could do to make their stay more enjoyable and comfortable. The guests appreciate this recognition, and the manager gains valuable information. Restaurant managers use the same approach by holding discussion meetings with guests at lunch.

A more formal way of gaining communication is through focus groups. This type of interviewing is usually conducted by inviting six to ten people to gather for a few hours with a trained moderator to talk about a product, service, or organization. The moderator needs objectivity, knowledge of the subject and industry, and some understanding of group and consumer behaviour. Participants normally receive a small sum or gift certificate for attending. The meeting is held in a

John T. Bowen
*Responsive communication:
the key to business
development and service
improvement*

pleasant place, and refreshments are served to create a relaxed environment. The moderator starts with broad questions before moving to more specific issues, encouraging open and easy discussion to foster group dynamics that will bring out true feelings and thoughts. At the same time, the interviewer "focuses" the discussion, hence the name focus group interviewing.

Figure 3
Flows of communication used in product design

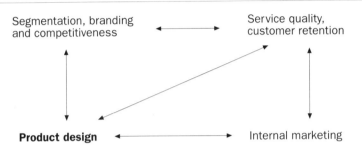

Here is an example of how a restaurant used focus group interviews to revive its business successfully. A steak house suffering from declining sales went to its customers to gain insight into the causes of its problem. Two focus groups were conducted, one composed of customers who indicated they would return and another composed of those who said they would not. From these sessions the owners learned that patrons considered the restaurant a fun place but thought the food was boring. The problem was solved by expanding and upgrading the menu (Welch, 1985).

Communicating with customers: surveys
One of the popular ways of communicating to customers is through questionnaires. These questionnaires can be designed specifically to give insights into new product development. Surveys are also conducted to provide information for segmentation strategies.

One of the problems with survey data is often the analysis does not give information on the importance of the attributes. It simply provides customer ratings. Shaw *et al.* (1991) illustrated how to get more information out of survey data by using a multivariate approach. They were able to show that responsiveness of the convention service manager was the number one variable influencing the overall satisfaction of the meeting planner with the hotel and that although billing received poor ratings, it had a low impact on overall satisfaction. In the article, the authors gave these and other examples of how to get more out of your data by using

multivariate analysis. To design a product effectively, managers need to know how important different features are to the target market.

Conjoint analysis is another approach that can be used to gain insight into the utility values the customers place on different levels of attributes. A typical conjoint study involves a client being shown product bundles containing different levels of attributes. The consumer is asked to rank these product bundles. For example, if a hotel was looking at the corporate business customer and wanted an idea of the value they placed on the following attributes; health club (three levels – full service, room with exercise bikes and a workout machine, no health club), breakfast (three levels – full breakfast, continental breakfast, no breakfast), business centre (three levels – 24 hour business centre, 8 a.m. to 5 p. m. business centre, no business centre) and price (three levels – $125, 150, 175). Cards are developed with different combinations of the attribute levels. A computer program develops the optimum number of cards to give statistically valid results. While ranking the product bundles, the customer must make trade-offs between the attributes. The levels for each attribute will be mixed on the various cards, thus forcing the customer to trade off the optimum level of one attribute for a secondary level of another attribute. The way the customer ranks the various cards provides information on which attributes and which level of those attributes, have the highest utility value for the customer. For example, in a study conducted by the author, it was found that business travellers placed a low utility value on breakfast, but a high utility value on a full service health club. This study also found the business travellers had a negative utility value for a workout room with exercise bikes and a workout machine. It appears the customer wanted either a full service health club or no health club. Thus, implications to management would be free access to a health club would create value, but only if it was a full service club and a breakfast creates little value for the business traveller.

For more information on the use of conjoint analysis one is encouraged to read about applications of conjoint analysis to the hospitality industry. Becker-Suttle *et al.* (1994) used conjoint analysis to compare seniors versus non-seniors on their preferences for various restaurant attributes. Among other things, the study found that nutrition was very important to seniors, having a large number of menu items was not important seniors, while it was important to the non-senior group. A sample of all the product choices,

John T. Bowen
*Responsive communication:
the key to business
development and service
improvement*

with the different levels of attributes is included in the appendix of the article. The study also provided easy-to-follow explanations of conjoint analysis and how to use it in the hospitality industry.

There has been much research done on specific segments. Reviewing these studies provides managers with two benefits. First, it can provide them with insights into overlooked segments. For example, Makens (1992) provides an overview of the family market at resorts. He focuses on children's programmes that will encourage parents to select a resort based on its children's programme. Examples of children's programmes from three resorts are provided as part of the study. Research can also provide useful insights into newly selected target markets. For example, a manager targeting ecotourists would be advised to read Wight's (1996) study on ecotourists. The study includes a comprehensive market profile including demographics, trip expenditures, times of the year the ecotourists travel, favourite activities and length of stay.

The published research on segmentation is a great resource for managers, providing background information on different segments and information on different methodologies that can be used in segmentation studies. For a list of segmentation studies, see "Business development." It should be noted that previous segmentation studies provide valuable information but they are not a substitute for communicating with one's own customers. Regional and cultural differences make it important for companies to communicate with their customers when they do segmentation studies. Secondary information alone is not enough.

Responsive communication and total quality management

Gummesson (1993) created a model that depicts total quality management as the bridge between an organization's internal and external orientations. The internal component is technical or production oriented quality management. The external component is market orientation and the linkage between the two is a systems approach which brings them together. One part of a total quality management system is to collect information continually from guests. An objective of these surveys is to find the satisfaction level of current guests and what could be done to increase their satisfaction levels. Product development or enhancement is often the outcome of these surveys.

For example, Christopher Page, the group quality director for Sutcliffe Catering in the UK, provides an example of how information from their quality management system

changed their service system. He stated, "Through a quality perception study some feedback from our market surveys showed that clients would like to deal with more mature people who understood business better. As a result, we are now working toward placing older, more mature people at the general manager level. We believe this has given us a competitive advantage" (Page, 1994).

Responsive communication and internal marketing

Juran (1988) stated that internal marketing was an important part of quality management. Listening posts and empowerment are two vehicles used to develop responsive communication between the employee and the customer.

Communicating with customers: listening posts

One of the most important marketing concepts for hospitality firms is "listening posts". Listening posts are points at which the organization can listen to the guest. In a hotel or a restaurant every customer contact employee has a chance to listen to the customer. Each employee can be like a little microphone collecting and recording customer information. For listening posts to be effective they have to be systematic. Employees have to be trained how to listen and how to feed back the information to management. Management has to feed back the information to the employees so they know the system is working. For companies that are able to set up an effective system of listening to the customer the rewards can be great. One of the benefits of listening posts is they provide information on products; how well guests like current products, what additional product attributes they desire and how they perceive the competitors' products.

One of the world's greatest listening organizations is the Ritz-Carlton chain of luxury hotels. At Ritz Carlton the staff is trained to listen for guest preferences, not always stated in the form of direct enquiries. A preference can be as incidental as a certain brand of bottled water with a meal. When a guest preference becomes known it is noted on a guest preference form by any frontline service person. This information is then downloaded into the chain's database and each morning guest preference histories are queried for the day's reservations (Heskett *et al.* 1997). The benefits of this listening posts system are increased satisfaction and word of mouth advertising by satisfied guests.

John T. Bowen
Responsive communication: the key to business development and service improvement

Employee empowerment

Hospitality products are simultaneously produced and consumed. A hotel is producing the services and products that will impact on a guest's stay while the guest is staying in the hotel. A manufacturer of durable goods is able to put the product through a series of quality control measures before the product is put on the shelf. The hospitality industry does not enjoy the time required to put products through rigorous quality checks. Employees often receive feedback from customers that allows them to fix the product while it is being produced or to customize a product to meet the needs of a customer better. In order to make these product adjustments employees must be empowered. Lashley (1995) wrote that empowerment results in more responsive service, higher customer satisfaction and higher quality. For a step-by-step guide of how to integrate employees into the product design process, see Barsky (1996).

Indirect links

Two indirect communication links flow out of service quality. First, there is a link between service quality and the target market. The original objective of communicating with the target market may not be for product design. However, in this communication often results information on product design concerns. Through communication channels that develop with employees as a result of total quality management ideas for product design will emerge as employees feed back information received from the guest. For example, Accor Group, Hilton, and McDonald's use quality circles to gain ideas from employees. These ideas often result in product changes.

Summary

The purpose of this article is to discuss some of the important flows of responsive communication. In "Business development" the author provided an overview of recent research that relates to business development. This article focused on the flows of communication that are a requisite of business development. In today's rapidly changing business environment managers must keep in touch with their customers and respond to their changing wants. Horst Schulze, President of Ritz Carlton stated it this way, "…Keep on listening to your customers because they change… And if you have 100 per cent (satisfied customers) then you have to make sure that you listen and change – just in case they change their expectations, that you change with them" (Harvard, 1994). In this article communication flows which enable businesses to respond effectively to changing customer are presented. Each communication flow is accompanied by examples and research references. Companies that want to develop and improve their service must develop responsive communication.

References

Anonymous (1989), "Making them feel at home", *The Cornell Hotel & Restaurant Administration Quarterly*, Vol. 30 No. 3, p. 4.

Barsky, J.D. (1996), "Building a program for world-class service", *The Cornell Hotel and Restaurant Quarterly*, Vol. 37 No. 1, pp. 17-27.

Becker-Suttle, C.B., Weaver, P., and Crawford-Welch, S. (1994), "A pilot study utilizing conjoint analysis in the comparison of age-based segmentation strategies in the full service restaurant market", *Journal of Restaurant and Food Service Marketing*, Vol. 1 No. 2, pp. 71-91.

Dev, C.S., Morgan, M.S. and Shoemaker, S. (1995), "A positioning analysis of hotel brands", *The Cornell Hotel and Restaurant Quarterly*, Vol. 36 No. 6, pp. 48-55.

Gummesson, E. (1993), *Quality Management in Service Organizations*, International Service Quality Association, New York, NY.

Harper Jr M. (1961), "A new profession to aid management", *Journal of Marketing,* Vol. 25 No. 1, p. 1.

Harvard (1994), Quoted from *Listening to Customers* (Video), Harvard Business School Publishing Management Production, Cambridge, MA.

Heskett, J.L., Sasser, W.E. and Schlesinger, L.A. (1997), *The Service Profit Chain*, Free Press, New York, NY, pp. 66-8.

Juran, J.M. (1988), *Juran on Planning for Quality,* Free Press, New York, NY.

Kolter, P., Bowen, J. and Makens, J. (1996), *Marketing for Hospitality and Tourism,* Prentice Hall, Englewood Cliffs, NJ..

Lashley, C. (1995), "Towards an understanding of employee empowerment in hospitality services", *International Journal of Contemporary Hospitality Management*, Vol. 7 No. 1, pp 27-32.

Makens, J.C. (1992), "Children at resorts: customer service at its best", *The Cornell Hotel and Restaurant Quarterly,* Vol. 33 No. 4, pp. 25-35.

Page, C. (1994), "Sutcliffe catering's approach to continuous improvement", *International Journal of Contemporary Hospitality Management,* Vol. 6 No. 1/2, pp. 19-24.

Shaw, M., Lewis, R.C. and Khorey, A. (1991), "Measuring meeting planner satisfaction with hotel convention services: a multivariate approach", *International Journal of Hospitality Management,* Vol. 10 No. 2, pp. 137-46.

Welch, J.L. (1985) "Focus groups for restaurant research", *Cornell Hotel and Restaurant Administration Quarterly*, pp. 78-85.

Wight, P. (1996), "North American ecotourists: market profile and trip characteristics", *Journal of Travel Research*, Vol. 34 No. 4, pp. 2-10.

Current concerns: a thematic analysis of recent hospitality industry issues

Shane C. Blum
Research Manager (North America) Worldwide Hospitality and Tourism Trends

Reviews articles published during 1996 in the *Hospitality Research Journal, Cornell Hotel and Restaurant Administration Quarterly* and *Florida International University Review.* Identifies recent contributions to the literature in these North American-based journals with reference to: people and organizations; service quality and customers; strategy and operations; food service; education; and eco-tourism and legal issues.

Introduction

The purpose of this review is to examine 109 articles published during 1996 in the *Hospitality Research Journal (HRJ), Cornell Hotel and Restaurant Administration Quarterly,* and *Florida International University (FIU) Review.* A review of articles published from 1989 through 1995 in these journals was published in the *International Journal of Contemporary Hospitality Management* (Vol. 8 No. 7). The current review is designed to update those reviews and identify similarities and differences between the themes addressed during these periods.

The articles published in the above mentioned journals during 1996 were divided into the following seven main themes:
1   people and organizations;
2   service quality and customers;
3   strategies and operations;
4   food service;
5   education;
6   eco-tourism; and
7   legal considerations.

Each theme is subsequently divided into sub-themes, and the overall focus of the articles published in these journals during 1996 can be quickly ascertained by viewing the accompanying tables associated with each main theme.

During 1996, the *Cornell Hotel and Restaurant Administration Quarterly* had six publications, the *Hospitality Research Journal* three, and the *Florida International University Review* two. Subsequently, this review comprises 63 articles from the *Cornell Quarterly,* 28 articles from the *HRJ* and 18 from the *FIU Review.* Some journals focus on certain aspects of the hospitality industry which others may not. Where certain articles were published will be identified in an effort to allow readers to better select journals which address topics of interest to them.

Theme 1: people and organizations

As in the previous review, a number of articles published in 1996 addressed issues regarding human resource management in the hospitality industry. Eleven articles from the *Cornell Quarterly* examined ways in which people interact within organizations.

Some may argue that the leadership of an organization has a profound impact on how others in the organization interact. Cichy and Schmidgall (1996) surveyed 181 lodging financial executives who identified four keys to their leadership style as:
1   trusting subordinates;
2   developing vision;
3   simplifying; and
4   remaining under control.

Many articles in this review addressed the characteristics of effective leaders found in diverse areas of the hospitality industry. The attributes of successful bed-and-breakfast operators were identified by Kaufman *et al.* (1996) as: prior experience in the lodging industry; knowledge of financial data and accounting; and family support. Results from research conducted by Graves (1996) indicated that hospitality management recruits perceived that energy was the most important trait for success; while human resource executives reported trustworthiness as the greatest trait for success. Surveys conducted by Tas *et al.* (1996) found that interacting smoothly with a wide variety of people and operating effectively under pressure were the most important competences for property-management trainees.

Once the leadership of an organization is in place, it is their responsibility to make strategic decisions which may affect the organization's culture. Executives from 78 hotel-operating companies reported that debate, trust, and collaboration all enhanced decision quality, while avoiding confrontation impeded it (Simons, 1996). Strategic decisions regarding total quality management (TQM) are often topics of concern to hospitality executives. Partlow (1996) identifies some key TQM human resource practices such as employee involvement in operating decisions, appropriate measurements and rewards for accomplishment, proper training, and a secure, safe work environment. Additionally, Donnellan (1996) catalogues five core principles for developing a culture of service excellence. Among those principles were developing employees

Table I
People and organizations

Authors	Focus	Sub-theme
Cichy and Schmidgall (1996)	Identifies four keys to leadership for financial executives as: trusting subordinates, developing vision, simplifying and remaining under control	Leadership qualities
Clay and Stephens (1996a)	In some cases, giving a negative reference could open a manager to the threat of a defamation suit	Employee references
Tas *et al.* (1996)	Interacting smoothly with a wide variety of people and operating effectively under pressure were identified as the most important competences for property-management trainees	Management competences
Young and Lundberg (1996)	Management can help alleviate uncertainty and anxiety in new employees by focusing on job aspects that are most critical to the newcomers	Employee orientation
Simons (1996)	Identifies debate as the single most important factor for high-quality strategic decisions among hotel executives	Conflict management
Donnellan (1996)	Establishes five core principals for developing a company-wide culture of service excellence	Staff development
Graves (1996)	Survey respondents identify energy and trustworthiness as the most important traits for successful hospitality managers	Personality traits
Tracey and Cardenas (1996)	Examines the impact of the work environment on pre-training motivation and its corresponding effect on knowledge acquisition and training reactions	Training
Roush *et al.* (1996)	More than 100 hospitality management programmes require Internship from their students. Discusses the internship developed and programmes implemented by Walt Disney World Co.	Internships programme
Kent and Cannon (1996)	Suggests that teamwork is no longer an option for an organization, it is a vital key to its survival. Identifies team management practices of selected organizations	Teamwork

for long-term careers and involving leaders in employees' development.

Proper employee development and a positive organizational culture may both begin at the same time – the employee's first day on the job. Young and Lundberg (1996) found that a sample of hospitality-industry newcomers remembered mostly negative aspects of their first day. The authors suggested that management attempt to make newcomers feel welcome and provide emotional support in order to alleviate anxiety. Proper socialization into the organization can affect a newcomer's performance, satisfaction, and commitment to the organization.

Once newcomers are oriented into the organization's culture, further indoctrination occurs during their training period. Tracey and Cardenas (1996) discovered that employees' perceptions regarding managerial support and the availability of training equipment directly influenced their pre-training motivation.

In today's hospitality organization, once the leadership has been established, decisions have been made and implemented to enhance the organization's culture, and employees have been selected, oriented and trained, employees are often placed in teams to perform the functions of the organization. Kent and Cannon (1996) state that, "teaming is not really an option for most organizations; it is a vital key to their survival and ultimate success". The authors provide examples of organizations effectively utilizing teamwork, and they suggest that in order for teams to work properly a transformation of the entire organization's culture may be needed.

Theme 2: service quality and customers

The main function which a hospitality organization's members must perform is the delivery of quality services to its customers. Eight articles from the *Hospitality Research Journal* discuss how employees can best deliver quality service to the organization's customers.

Barsky (1996) suggests that customers may be excellent sources of information for management on how the organization can provide quality service. Through surveys and focus

Table II

Service quality and customers

Authors	Focus	Sub-theme
Barsky (1996)	Suggests that through surveys and focus groups, customers can suggest not only service problems, but their potential solutions	Customer service
Luchars and Hinkin (1996)	By using a service-quality audit, hotel managers can identify errors, assign costs to fixing them, and establish steps to prevent them	Service quality
Cho et al. (1996)	Discusses how concierge service can be augmented through the use of expert systems	Technology
Gundersen et al. (1996)	Defines customer satisfaction and assesses business travellers' perceptions of the tangible and intangible aspects of certain hotel departments	Customer satisfaction
Oh and Jeong (1996)	Expectation-based market segmentation is used to predict customer satisfaction in fast-food restaurants	Market segmentation
Greathouse et al. (1996)	Travellers who stopped at visitor information centres rated cleanliness of room, value for price, friendliness of staff, and security of property as most important in hotel accommodation	Customer preferences
Lynn and Graves (1996)	Discusses other motives for tipping which may undermine its role as an incentive/reward to the service provider	Tipping
Berkley (1996)	Uses function analysis to specify and objectify service design concepts in order to enhance service delivery systems	Service functions

groups, customers can help management determine which service areas are most in need of improvement.

Management may also choose to create an internal service-quality audit which can identify errors and determine their frequency, assign costs of fixing (or not fixing) the error, and identify the steps to prevent them. Luchars and Hinkin (1996) described an example of such an audit conducted at a full-service hotel to determine the cost of errors in transactions at the front desk. The most common error was failure to post late charges to the guest's folio, which cost the hotel an estimated $250,000 per year.

This internally and externally derived information can assist management in its endeavours to satisfy customers. Gunderson *et al.* (1996) defined customer satisfaction as, "a guest's post-consumption judgment of a product or service that can, in turn, be measured by assessing guest's evaluation of a performance on specific attributes". The authors' research revealed that business travellers were most concerned with the tangible aspects of housekeeping (e.g. room amenities) and the intangible aspects of the front desk (e.g. receptionists' willingness to provide service).

Being able to provide services which customers prefer is obviously a starting point for providing customer satisfaction. A relatively easy way to determine what services customers prefer is simply to ask them. Travellers who Greathouse stopped at visitor information centres rated cleanliness of room, value for price, friendliness of staff, and security of property as some of the most important attributes of a hotel .

Theme 3: strategies and operations

Customer satisfaction can best be obtained through the development of strategies, policies and procedures geared towards quality service. Of the seven main themes addressed in this review, the strategies and operations theme had the most articles published with 28. One third of the articles published in the *FIU Review* during 1996 were categorized under this theme.

Technological advancements in the hospitality industry is not a main theme in this review, although it certainly could be. Instead, how technological improvements are affecting the industry in each main theme is addressed. This was done, in part, to illustrate specifically how pervasive technological change is throughout all areas of the hospitality industry.

Numerous articles addressing strategic management decisions discuss how technology can be used to enhance the decision-making process. Smith and Lesure (1996) realized that lodging operators disliked forecasts because they worry that optimistic predictions will attract competitors and negative outlooks will chase away financing. The

Shane C. Blum
*Current concerns: a thematic
analysis of recent hospitality
industry issues*

Table III
Strategies and operations

Authors	Focus	Sub-theme
Smith and Lesure (1996)	Discusses how a statistically reliable database can be used to create short-term forecasts for the lodging industry	Forecasting
Thompson (1996)	Newly devised mathematical models can be used to reduce a manager's scheduling burden when fluctuations in consumer demand arise	Scheduling
Parsa (1996)	The changes in the balance of power between franchisees and franchisors is examined	Franchising
deRoos and Corgel (1996)	Attempts to develop the best possible index of lodging-property returns formed from publicly available data	Performance
Umbreit (1996)	Examines Fairmont Hotels' top-line strategy of boosting occupancy and market share at the expense of average rate	Target markets
Poorani (1996)	Six activities were identified as contributing to trade show success. The key objectives of hospitality exhibitors were generating and qualifying sales leads	Trade shows
Sangree and Hathaway (1996)	Survey results reveal a continuing trend towards shorter hotel management contracts and more incentive fees. During the past decade, the average duration of a contract fell from 17 years to six years	Management contracts
Van Hoof *et al.* (1996)	Compares technology perceptions among lodging managers from the UK, the USA and Canada	Information technology
Griffin and Olsen (1996)	Electronic database support systems which provide information regarding the organization's internal and external environments can be used for strategic planning activities	Database support systems
Kasavana (1996)	Describes the technology behind computer-controlled slot machines and exposes some of the popular operating myths	Gaming technology
Bach and Pizam (1996)	Identifies security devices that were associated with impacting on crime levels in Central Florida hotels	Security
Baum and Mudambi (1996)	Discusses how government agencies are increasing their involvement in providing investment support to attract foreign direct investment in the hotel industry	Investments

authors suggest that operators create a statistically reliable database which can be used to develop short-term forecasts for the lodging industry.

David *et al.* (1996) state that despite massive investment by hotel operators in information technology, evidence of improved employee productivity is scant. They suggest, however, that productivity may not always be the reason for installing new technology. Instead, hoteliers are installing technology to improve the guest experience.

Other authors examined how technology can be utilized to assist hotel operators with marketing on the Internet (Murphy *et al.*, 1996b); scheduling of employees using newly devised mathematical models (Thompson, 1996); and developing strategic plans using electronic database support systems (Griffin and Olsen, 1996). Kasavana (1996) even researches the technological advances which have recently been made in slot machine construction. Apparently technological

advancements have been introduced into all arenas of the hospitality industry and this trend is sure to continue at an astonishing rate.

Other non-technological, strategic decisions were also discussed in articles published during 1996. Umbreit (1996), for example, examines how a small hotel chain was able to increase profitability by focusing on a top-line strategy of boosting occupancy and market share at the expense of average rate. The chain's president set rates and policies to meet the needs of corporate customers while simultaneously providing price promotions for leisure travellers. The result was a steady increase in occupancy with no substantial loss in revenue per available room.

A number of articles also examined some longer term strategic decisions. Sangree and Hathaway (1996) discovered a trend in the length of hotel management contracts. They determined that the average duration of a management contract fell from 17 years in the

1980s to six years in 1990s' contracts. Baum and Mudambi (1996) investigated long-term investments in hotels, and discovered that government agencies are becoming involved in providing investment support to attract foreign direct investments.

Theme 4: food service

Much of the material reviewed to this point has dealt specifically with issues related to the hotel industry. Naturally, these three journals address food service related topics as well. In all, 17 articles were identified as being geared directly to the food service industry, with 13 of those published in the *Cornell Quarterly.*

The controversial topic of smoke-free dining was tackled by Corsun *et al.* (1996). Their research was conducted four months after the 1995 Smoke-Free-Air Act was passed in New York City. They found that while smokers dined out less often, any lost revenue was made up by non-smokers who dined out more often. Their article states that a strategy of total smoke-free dining may accommodate as much as 83.5 per cent of the population.

Smith (1996) presents 13 principles for operating a successful restaurants – smoke-free or not. He defines the basic rule for success as putting customers first – making them welcome and exceeding their expectations. One means of putting customers first is by simply giving them what they want.

Miner (1996) identifies a trend in food service chains towards customer-focused menus. Some chains are broadening their definition of possible menu items, and even chains that base their success on menu standardization have diversified their menus to accommodate regional preferences.

Success can also be achieved by reducing food costs as Shuldiner and Norkus (1996) recommend. They suggest that restaurateurs trade in the commodity-futures market as a means of gaining some assurance of what price they will pay for the commodities they need. They explain how food service operators can cross-hedge and direct-hedge to take best advantage of the commodities market.

Another ingredient for a successful restaurant is quality, well-prepared food. The test for food product liability has been redefined in many states. Sherry (1996a) states that California has adopted a "reasonable-expectations" test that allows customers to argue that there is a reasonable expectation that even naturally occurring objects should be removed during preparation of a food item.

How genetically altered foods may affect food service operations was examined by Nelson and Poorani (1996). This issue is highly controversial since it involves the creation of new life forms. The authors agreed that management is attracted by the potential benefits of genetically altered food products,

Table IV
Food service operations

Authors	Focus	Sub-theme
Corsun *et al.* (1996)	Examines the effect of New York City's Smoke-Free-Air Act on restaurant-consumers' behaviour	Smoke-free environment
Cotter and Snyder (1996)	Investigates whether changes in the Mobile Travel Guide ratings affected price changes in restaurants in four areas	Menu pricing
Shuldiner and Norkus (1996)	Examines how food service operators can trade in the future prices of commodities in order to gain some assurance of what price they will pay for their necessities	Food costs
Miner (1996)	Explores how some food service chains are broadening their definition of what types of foods they offer. Identifies chains that diversify their menus to accommodate regional preferences	Menu marketing
Sherry (1996a)	Identifies a recent adaptation of the food-product liability test that now allows customers to argue that there is a "reasonable expectation" that even naturally occurring objects be removed during preparation of the food	Food preparation
Pickert and Miller (1996)	Determines current food production forecasting techniques used by commercial food service operations	Forecasting
Nelson and Poorani (1996)	Discusses that food service managers are often attracted by the potential benefits of genetically altered foods, but are also apprehensive of possible negative consumer perceptions	Genetically altered foods

Shane C. Blum
*Current concerns: a thematic
analysis of recent hospitality
industry issues*

but they are also leery about possible negative consumer perceptions.

Theme 5: education

Much that is written in these journals is designed to meet the needs of industry practitioners, however, all three journals also gear certain articles to hospitality academicians. The *Hospitality Research Journal* appears to concentrate on the educational aspects of the hospitality industry more than the other two journals. Of the nine articles identified in this main theme, six were published in the *Hospitality Research Journal*.

The importance of technology has already been examined as it applies to industry. Kluge (1996), on the other hand, conducts a literature review of information technology in the hospitality curriculum. Through this review, he attempts to answer questions regarding what should be included in the curriculum, how should it be delivered, and what is the future direction of technology in the hospitality classroom?

One example of the use of technology in the classroom is the trend towards distance education courses. Iverson (1996) studied hospitality students' interest in distance education and determined that students most likely to pursue distance education were those with the highest GPA, the highest degree of external constraint, and full-time employment. All students were most interested in pursuing computer-mediated instruction, which emphasized the importance of more technologically sophisticated delivery modes in distance education.

Technological capabilities is one criterion students may use when determining which hospitality programme they wish to attend. Diaz and Krauss (1996) examined other criteria Asian hospitality students used when choosing an American university. They discovered that the services most desired were tutors, scholarships, matched peer advisors,

home newspapers, and helpful faculty advisors. A similar study was conducted by Huang and Brown (1996), who focused on international graduate students' school choice, career expectations, and academic adjustments. The study revealed that obtaining practical work experience created the major problem for students.

Graduate students' perceptions were also examined in a survey done by Ramakrishna and Nebel (1996). They also surveyed corporate hotel executives and discovered a gap between the perceptions of the two groups. The students appeared to have unrealistic expectations of securing a corporate-level position immediately on graduation, while most of the executives started their careers at the operations level.

Theme 6: eco-tourism

Regardless of whether students begin their careers at the corporate or operations level, they will most assuredly need to contend with environmental issues which are affecting the hospitality industry. This topic is so critical that the publishers of the *Cornell Quarterly* saw fit to dedicate half of an entire issue of their journal to "Eco" management.

A historical view of the US lodging industry and the environment is presented by Stipanuk (1996) in the above mentioned issue of the *Cornell Quarterly*. Historical records show that from the early part of the twentieth century hoteliers have been concerned with environmental-management initiatives. Although the industry may have lapsed in its environmental responsibilities during the rush to expand in the 1980s, as a whole, the lodging industry has posted many positive environmental accomplishments.

In fact, the term "ecoresort" has been coined for lodging properties that have become efficient in preserving their surrounding environment. Ayala published two articles addressing the challenges facing

Table V
Education

Authors	Focus	Sub-theme
Kluge (1996)	Summarizes literature which has helped define the role of information technology in hospitality management curricula	Information technology
Iverson (1996)	Examines students' interest in pursuing distance education with regard to their demographic factors and other attributes	Distance education
Ramakrishna and Nebel (1996)	Reveals a gap between the expectations of master's level hospitality students and the actual career paths of corporate hotel executives	Master's programmes
Diaz and Krauss (1996)	Identifies services desired by Asian hospitality students attending American universities as tutors, scholarships, peer advisors, home newspapers, and helpful faculty advisors	International students

Table VI
Eco-tourism

Authors	Focus	Sub-theme
Ayala (1996a; 1996b)	Suggests that resorts should strive to become "ecoresorts" which can enhance tourism in the area while sustaining the character of the natural resources	"Ecoresorts"
Khatri (1996)	Identifies how resorts have been able to create environmental-improvement programmes based on four "Rs": reduce; reuse; recycle; and rethink	Environmental improvements
DeFranco and Weatherspoon (1996)	Provides a self-inspection inventory comprising checklists which concentrate on energy, solid waste, and water conservation	Environmental checklist
Farmer (1996)	Examines historical data on job creation, export growth, and return on investment credited to tourism in the USA	US Tourism
Remington and Escoffier (1996)	Discusses tourism's positive versus negative socio-economic effects, and how tourism will change as we approach the next century	Socio-economics of tourism

"ecoresorts" in the twenty-first century. She states that the main challenge is, "to enhance the tourism value of the natural and cultural resources in a way that will produce a ripple effect through local and national economies and also sustain the character of those resources" (Ayala, 1996b).

In order to meet this and other challenges, hospitality managers must establish programmes and procedures designed to preserve the environment. Khatri (1996) identifies an environmental-improvement programme based on four "Rs": reduce, reuse, recycle, and rethink. For example, the island resorts which enacted this programme dealt with a shortage of potable water by altering their system to use seawater, and they solved their soil erosion problem by mulching the ground with coconut husks.

A more structured programme was offered by DeFranco and Weatherspoon (1996) who presented a two-page environmental-procedures inventory for hotel operators. This self-inspection inventory comprised checklists which concentrate on energy, solid waste, and water conservation. The importance of environmental programmes such as these can not be overlooked, and managers at all levels must be concerned with how their operation can potentially effect the environment.

Theme 7: legal considerations

If managers fail to be proactive in dealing with environmental issues, they had better be prepared for the legal repercussions which are sure to follow. Today's hospitality managers must keep abreast of myriad legal concerns regarding the environment, sexual harassment, taxes, and other labour-related laws. This being the case, it is no surprise that all three journals in this review address issues regarding the legal aspects of the hospitality industry.

Perhaps no legal issue has received more attention recently then that of sexual harassment. Aalberts and Seidman (1996) state that judges are unlikely to dismiss charges against an employer unless the firm has implemented a proper workplace sexual harassment policy. Their article identifies eight components of an appropriate policy which includes training that teaches supervisors to recognize sexual harassment. It is imperative that employees at all levels know what the organization's policy is regarding harassment in the workplace.

Child-labour laws, on the other hand, do not receive much attention, and subsequently many hospitality-industry operators are unfamiliar with them. Clay and Stephens (1996b) remind operators that children aged 14 and 15 may not work more than 18 hours per week during the school year and may not work past 7 p.m. on school nights. In addition, no one under the age of 18 may be hired for work that involves the operation of machinery, including motor vehicles. Restaurant operators, in particular, should be more aware of these laws since they frequently hire teenage employees.

The above legal concerns primarily occur at the operations level, however, there are numerous legal issues which appear at the strategic level. For example, Turkel and Stewart (1996) explain how the Stouffer Hotel Company was found guilty of breach of contract and gross negligence primarily because their upper-management tried to impose a four-star market position on a three-star hotel property.

Tarras identifies other strategic legal concerns in two separate articles. He states that one of the best ways for hotel developers to save money is to minimize construction costs by rehabilitating an existing structure. Developers can take advantage of tax credits they receive for all qualified expenditures incurred

Table VII
Legal considerations

Authors	Focus	Sub-theme
Aalberts and Seidman (1996)	Addresses the eight components of an appropriate sexual-harassment policy	Sexual harassment policies
Sherry (1996b)	Examines how chain-restaurant franchisors who require franchisees to make certain purchases may be in violation of antitrust laws	Antitrust suits
Clay and Stephens (1996)	Suggests that many hospitality operators are unfamiliar with child-labour laws. Reminds operators that children aged 14 and 15 may not work more than 18 hours per week during the school year	Child-labour laws
Turkel and Stewart (1996)	Discusses testimony from the trial of a hotel management company found guilty of tortious breach of contract, gross negligence, misrepresentation, and breach of fiduciary duty	Management negligence
Tarras (1996a)	Identifies one of the best ways to save money, and benefit from tax credits, is to rehabilitate an existing property	Tax incentives

Figure 1
Review of 1996: summary of main themes and sub-themes

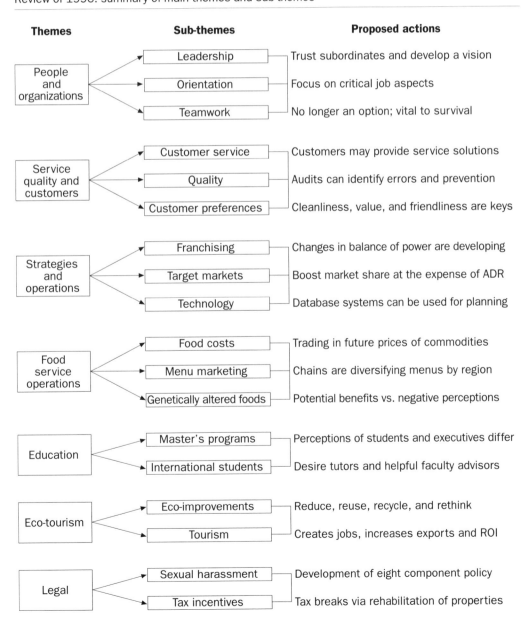

Shane C. Blum
*Current concerns: a thematic
analysis of recent hospitality
industry issues*

in the rehabilitation (1996a). In addition, developers and entrepreneurs can also receive significant tax savings by exchanging their hotel property for another (Tarras, 1996b).

Conclusion

This review of articles published during 1996 in the *Hospitality Research Journal, Cornell Hotel and Restaurant Administration Quarterly*, and *Florida International University Review* addressed many of the same themes as the initial review of these journals. Although the sub-themes of technology and the environment were examined in the previous review, these two issues were much more prevalent in articles published during 1996. Academicians should continue to conduct research in these areas in an effort to provide industry practitioners with cutting-edge information which can be utilized in the operation of their organizations.

Figure 1 provides a summary of the main themes and sub-themes examined in this review. The significant themes which researchers have identified are linked with proposed actions which may prove useful to managers in the hospitality industry. Hopefully, this summary can serve as a quick reference for readers to identify actions which can be taken to address concerns they may have regarding each theme.

References

Aalberts, R.J. and Seidman, L.H. (1996), "Sexual-harassment policies for the workplace – a tale of two companies", *Cornell Hotel and Restaurant Administration Quarterly*, Vol. 37 No. 5, pp. 78-85.

Ayala, H. (1996a), "Resort ecotourism: a paradigm for the 21st century", *Cornell Hotel and Restaurant Administration Quarterly*, Vol. 37 No. 5, pp. 46-53.

Ayala, H. (1996b), "Resort ecotourism: a master plan for experience management", *Cornell Hotel and Restaurant Administration Quarterly*, Vol. 37 No. 5, pp. 54-61.

Bach, S. and Pizam, A. (1996), "Crimes in hotels", *Hospitality Research Journal,* Vol. 20 No.2, pp. 59-76.

Barsky, J.D. (1996), "Building a program for world-class service", *Cornell Hotel and Restaurant Administration Quarterly*, Vol. 37 No. 1, pp. 17-27.

Baum, T. and Mudambi, R. (1996), "Attracting hotel investment: insights from principal-agent theory", *Hospitality Research Journal,* Vol. 20 No.2, pp. 15-30.

Berkley, B.J. (1996), "Designing services with function analysis", *Hospitality Research Journal,* Vol. 20 No.1, pp. 73-100.

Cho, W., Sumichrast, R.T. and Olsen, M.D. (1996), "Expert-system technology for hotels: concierge application", *Cornell Hotel and Restaurant Administration Quarterly,* Vol. 37 No. 1, pp. 54-60.

Cichy, R.F. and Schmidgall, R.S. (1996), "Leadership qualities of financial executivies in the US lodging industry", *Cornell Hotel and Restaurant Administration Quarterly*, Vol. 37 No. 2, pp. 56-62.

Clay, J.M. and Stephens, E.C. (1996a),"The defamation trap in employee references", *Cornell Hotel and Restaurant Administration Quarterly,* Vol. 37 No. 2, pp. 18-24.

Clay, J.M. and Stephens, E.C. (1996b), "Child-labor laws and the hospitality industry", *Cornell Hotel and Restaurant Administration Quarterly*, Vol. 37 No. 6, pp. 20-5.

Corsun, D.L, Young, C.A. and Enz, C.A. (1996), "Should NYC's restaurateurs lighten up? Effects of the city's smoke-free-air act", *Cornell Hotel and Restaurant Administration Quarterly*, Vol. 37 No. 2, pp. 25-33.

Cotter, M.J. and Snyder, W.W. (1996), "How mobil stars affect restaurant-pricing behavior", *Cornell Hotel and Restaurant Administration Quarterly*, Vol. 37 No. 2, pp. 34-41.

DeFranco, A.L. and Weatherspoon, K.E. (1996), "Go green: an environmental checklist for the lodging industry", *Cornell Hotel and Restaurant Administration Quarterly*, Vol. 37 No. 6, pp. 84-5.

deRoos, J.A. and Corgel, J.B. (1996), "Measuring lodging-property performance: a difficult task with imperfect results", *Cornell Hotel and Restaurant Administration Quarterly,* Vol. 37 No. 4, pp. 20-7.

David, J.S., Grabski, S. and Kasavana, M. (1996), "The productivity paradox of hotel-industry technology", *Cornell Hotel and Restaurant Administration Quarterly*, Vol. 37 No. 2, pp. 64-70.

Diaz, P.E. and Krauss, J.L. (1996), "A needs analysis of an expanding hospitality market – Asian students", *Hospitality Research Journal*, Vol. 20 No.1, pp. 15-26.

Donnellan, L. (1996), "Lessons in staff development", *Cornell Hotel and Restaurant Administration Quarterly*, Vol. 37 No. 6, pp. 42-5.

Farmer, G. (1996), "A new vision: US travel and tourism industry", *FIU Hospitality Review,* Vol. 14 No.1, pp. 1-6.

Graves, N.S. (1996), "Personality traits in successful managers as perceived by food and beverage human resources executives and recruiters", *Hospitality Research Journal,* Vol. 20 No.2, pp. 95-112.

Greathouse, K.R., Gergoire, M.B., Shanklin, C.W. and Tripp, C. (1996), "Factors considered important in hotel accommodations by travelers stopping at visitor information centers", *Hospitality Research Journal*, Vol. 19 No.4, pp. 129-40.

Griffin, R.K. and Olsen, M.D. (1996), "Electronic database support systems for strategic planning activities in the hospitality industry", *FIU Hospitality Review,* Vol. 14 No.1, pp. 59-78.

Gunderson, M.G., Heide, M. and Olsson, U.H. (1996), "Hotel guest satisfaction among business travelers", *Cornell Hotel and Restaurant Administration Quarterly,* Vol. 37 No. 2, pp. 72-81.

Huang, S.E. and Brown, N.E. (1996), "First-Choice international graduate students in hospitality programs: school choice, career expectations, and academic adjustment", *Hospitality Research Journal*, Vol. 20 No.1, pp. 109-18.

Iverson, K. (1996), "Exploring student interest in hospitality distance education", *Hospitality Research Journal*, Vol. 20 No.2, pp. 31-44.

Kasavana, M.L. (1996), "Slot machines: methodologies and myths", *FIU Hospitality Review*, Vol. 14 No.2, pp. 37-44.

Kaufman, T.J., Weaver, P.A. and Poynter, J. (1996), "Success attributes of B&B operators", *Cornell Hotel and Restaurant Administration Quarterly,* Vol. 37 No. 4, pp. 29-33.

Kent, W.E. and Cannon, D.F.(1996), "Teams: vehicle of choice for transporting the organizational future", *FIU Hospitality Review*, Vol. 14 No.2, pp. 65-76.

Khatri, N. (1996), "A '4R' environmental model for Andaman and Nicobar", *Cornell Hotel and Restaurant Administration Quarterly*, Vol. 37 No. 5, pp. 62-6.

Kluge, E.A. (1996), "A literature review of information technology in the hospitality curriculum", *Hospitality Research Journal,* Vol. 19 No.4, pp. 45-64.

Luchars, J.Y. and Hinkin T.R. (1996), "The service-quality audit: a hotel case study", *Cornell Hotel and Restaurant Administration Quarterly*, Vol. 37 No. 1, pp. 34-41.

Lynn, M. and Graves, J. (1996), "Tipping: an incentive/reward for service?", *Hospitality Research Journal,* Vol. 20 No.1, pp. 1-14.

Miner, T. (1996), "Customer-focused menu marketing", *Cornell Hotel and Restaurant Administration Quarterly*, Vol. 37 No. 3, pp. 36-41.

Murphy, J., Forrest, E.J., Wotring, C.E. and Brymer, R. (1996b), "Hotel management and marketing on the internet: an analysis of sites and features", *Cornell Hotel and Restaurant Administration Quarterly*, Vol. 37 No. 3, pp. 70-82.

Nelson, R.R. and Poorani, A.A. (1996), "Genetically altered foods: a policy issue for multi-unit food service operators", *FIU Hospitality Review,* Vol. 14 No.1, p. 79.

Oh, H. and Jeong, M. (1996), "Improving marketers' predictive power of customer satisfaction on expectation-based target market levels", *Hospitality Research Journal*, Vol. 19 No.4, pp. 65-86.

Parsa, H.G. (1996), "Franchisor-franchisee relationships in quick-service-restaurant systems", *Cornell Hotel and Restaurant Administration Quarterly*, Vol. 37 No. 3, pp. 42-9.

Partlow, C.G. (1996), "Human-resources practices of TQM hotels", *Cornell Hotel and Restaurant Administration Quarterly*, Vol. 37 No. 5, pp. 67-77.

Pickert, M.J. and Miller, J. (1996), "Food production forecasting in six commercial foodservice operations: a pilot study", *Hospitality Research Journal,* Vol. 20 No.2, pp. 137-44.

Poorani, A.A. (1996), "Trade-show management: budgeting and planning or a successful event", *Cornell Hotel and Restaurant Administration Quarterly*, Vol. 37 No. 4, pp. 77-84.

Ramakrishna, J. and Nebel, E.C. III (1996), "An empirical study of the challenges facing hospitality master's programs: a hotel industry perspective", *Hospitality Research Journal,* Vol. 20 No.2, pp. 45-58.

Remington, J. and Escoffier, M. (1996), "Tourism: who needs it?", *FIU Hospitality Review*, Vol. 14 No.1, pp. 19-26.

Roush, P., Dickson, D.R. and LeBruto, S.M. (1996), "Disney's internship program: more than hands-on experience", *FIU Hospitality Review*, Vol. 14 No.1, pp. 27-36.

Sangree, D.J. and Hathaway, P.P. (1996), "Trends in hotel management contracts: shorter lengths and changing fee structures", *Cornell Hotel and Restaurant Administration Quarterly*, Vol. 37 No. 5, pp. 26-37.

Sherry, J.E.H. (1996a), "Food-servers' product-liability law revisited: the traditional foreign-natural test is being replaced by a reasonable-expectations test", *Cornell Hotel and Restaurant Administration Quarterly,* Vol. 37 No. 6, pp. 18-19.

Sherry, J.E.H. (1996b), "Antitrust implications of food-service franchising agreements: regulation of franchisors' marketing practices", *Cornell Hotel and Restaurant Administration Quarterly*, Vol. 37 No. 4, pp. 18-19.

Shuldiner, A. and Norkus, G.X. (1996), "'Buying prices' on the commodity futures market", *Cornell Hotel and Restaurant Administration Quarterly*, Vol. 37 No. 3, pp. 30-5.

Simons, T. (1996), "Executive conflict management: keys to excellent decisions and smooth implementation", *Cornell Hotel and Restaurant Administration Quarterly*, Vol. 37 No. 6, pp. 34-41.

Smith, D. (1996), "A baker's dozen — thirteen principles for a successful restaurant", *Cornell Hotel and Restaurant Administration Quarterly*, Vol. 37 No. 2, pp. 42-6.

Smith, R.A. and Lesure, L.D. (1996), "Don't shoot the messenger: forecasting lodging performance", *Cornell Hotel and Restaurant Administration Quarterly*, Vol. 37 No. 1, pp. 80-8.

Stipanuk, D.M. (1996), "The US lodging industry and the environment—an historical view", *Cornell Hotel and Restaurant Administration Quarterly,* Vol. 37 No. 5, pp. 39-45.

Stipanuk, D.M. and Ninemeier, J.D. (1996), "The future of the US lodging industry and the environment", *Cornell Hotel and Restaurant*

Shane C. Blum
*Current concerns: a thematic
analysis of recent hospitality
industry issues*

Administration Quarterly, Vol. 37 No. 6,
pp. 74-83.

Tarras, J.M. (1996a), "Using tax incentives reduces construction costs", *FIU Hospitality Review*, Vol. 14 No.1, pp. 55-8.

Tarras, J.M. (1996b), "Property exchange rules offer tax opportunities for hotel owners", *FIU Hospitality Review*, Vol. 14 No.2, pp. 27-36.

Tas, R.F., LaBrecque, S.V. and Clayton, H.R. (1996), "Property-management competences for management trainees", *Cornell Hotel and Restaurant Administration Quarterly*, Vol. 37 No. 4, pp. 90-6.

Thompson, G.M. (1996), "Controlling action times in daily workforce schedules", *Cornell Hotel and Restaurant Administration Quarterly*, Vol. 37 No. 2, pp. 82-96.

Tracey, J.B. and Cardenas, C.G. (1996), "Training effectiveness: an empirical examination of factors outside the training context", *Hospitality Research Journal*, Vol. 20 No.2, pp. 113-24.

Turkel, S. and Stewart, R.O. (1996), "A landmark decision: the Stouffer Valley Forge Hotel", *FIU Hospitality Review*, Vol. 14 No.1, pp. 37-48.

Umbreit, W.T. (1996), "Fairmont Hotels' turnaround strategy", *Cornell Hotel and Restaurant Administration Quarterly*, Vol. 37 No. 4, pp. 50-7.

Van Hoof, H.B., Verbeeten, M.J., and Combrink, T.E. (1996), "Information technology revisited—international lodging industry technology needs and perceptions: a comparative study", *Cornell Hotel and Restaurant Administration Quarterly*, Vol. 37 No. 6, pp. 66-91.

Young, C.A. and Lundberg, C.C. (1996), "Creating a good first day on the job – allaying newcomers' anxiety with positive messages", *Cornell Hotel and Restaurant Administration Quarterly*, Vol. 37 No. 6, pp. 26-33.

Further reading

Allam, Y.H. and McGrath, M. (1996), "Assessing the readiness of Atlanta hotels to host international visitors during the '96 Summer Olympics", *FIU Hospitality Review*, Vol. 14 No.1, pp. 49-54.

Brownell, J. and Jameson, D. (1996), "Getting quality out on the street: a case of show and tell", *Cornell Hotel and Restaurant Administration Quarterly*, Vol. 37 No. 1, pp. 28-33.

Bartholomew, P.S. and Garey, J.G. (1996), "An analysis of determinants of career success for elite female executive chefs", *Hospitality Research Journal*, Vol. 20 No.2, pp. 125-36.

Bojanic, D.C. (1996), "The smoking debate: a look at the issues surrounding smoking bans in restaurants", *Hospitality Research Journal*, Vol. 20 No.1, pp. 27-38.

Borchgrevink, C.P. and Susskind, A.M. (1996), "The validity of the Hinkin and Schriesheim power scales and superior-subordinate power relationships within hospitality", *Hospitality Research Journal*, Vol. 20 No.1, pp. 39-56.

Bosselman, R.H. (1996), "Current perceptions of hospitality accreditation", *FIU Hospitality Review*, Vol. 14 No.2, p. 77.

Callan, R.J. (1996), "An appraisement of UK business travelers' perceptions of important hotel attributes", *Hospitality Research Journal*, Vol. 19 No.4, pp. 113-28.

Canina, L. (1996), "Underpricing and overperformance: initial public offerings in the hospitality industry", *Cornell Hotel and Restaurant Administration Quarterly*, Vol. 37 No. 5, pp. 18-25.

Clark, J.D., Price, C.H. and Murrmann, S.K. (1996), "Buying centers: who chooses convention sites?", *Cornell Hotel and Restaurant Administration Quarterly*, Vol. 37 No. 4, pp. 72-6.

Conroy, P.A., Lefever, M.M., and Witham, G. (1996), "The value of college advisory boards", *Cornell Hotel and Restaurant Administration Quarterly*, Vol. 37 No. 4, pp. 85-9.

deRoos, J.A. and Rushmore, S. (1996), "Investment values of lodging property: proof of value for selected models", *Cornell Hotel and Restaurant Administration Quarterly*, Vol. 37 No. 1, pp. 89-95.

Enghagen, L.K. (1996), "Recent developments in sexual harassment law: implications for the hospitality/tourism industry", *Hospitality Research Journal*, Vol. 19 No.4, pp. 31-44.

Evans, M.R., Clark, J.D. and Knutson, B.J. (1996), "The 100-percent, unconditional, money-back guarantee", *Cornell Hotel and Restaurant Administration Quarterly*, Vol. 37 No. 6, pp. 56-61.

Fenich, G.G. (1996), "The uses and abuses of multipliers: a current case", *Hospitality Research Journal*, Vol. 20 No.1, pp. 101-8.

Ghiselli, R. and Ismail, J. (1996), "Characterizing poor performance in for-profit and not-for-profit food service operations", *FIU Hospitality Review*, Vol. 14 No.2, pp. 53-64.

Go, F., Choi, T. and Chan, C. (1996), "Four Seasons-Regent: building a global presence in the luxury market", *Cornell Hotel and Restaurant Administration Quarterly*, Vol. 37 No. 4, pp. 58-65.

Grant, Y.N.J. and Weaver, P.A. (1996), "The meeting selection process: a demographic profile of attendees clustered by criteria utilized in selecting meetings", *Hospitality Research Journal*, Vol. 20 No.1, pp. 57-72.

Griffin, R.K. (1996), "Factors of successful lodging yield management systems", *Hospitality Research Journal*, Vol. 19 No.4, pp. 17-30.

Gustin, M.E. and Weaver, P.A. (1996), "Are hotels prepared for the environmental consumer?", *Hospitality Research Journal*, Vol. 20 No.2, pp. 1-14.

Jones, P. (1996), "Managing hospitality innovation", *Cornell Hotel and Restaurant Administration Quarterly*, Vol. 37 No. 5, pp. 86-95.

Shane C. Blum
Current concerns: a thematic analysis of recent hospitality industry issues

Jones, T. and Teeters, K. (1996),"Occupational illness in the hospitality industry: 'sick buildings' and the bottom line", *Cornell Hotel and Restaurant Administration Quarterly*, Vol. 37 No. 4, pp. 66-71.

Kelley, C.L. and Marquette, R.P. (1996), "A tax primer for bed and breakfasts", *Cornell Hotel and Restaurant Administration Quarterly*, Vol. 37 No. 4, pp. 34-42.

Kimble, D. (1996), "Barriers and opportunities in Singapore", *Cornell Hotel and Restaurant Administration Quarterly*, Vol. 37 No. 3, pp. 50-4.

Landry, D. (1996), "Franchise opportunities abound with new and established brands", *FIU Hospitality Review*, Vol. 14 No.2, pp. 1-6.

Lanier, P. and Johnson, J. (1996), "The importance of F&B in small inns", *Cornell Hotel and Restaurant Administration Quarterly,* Vol. 37 No. 4, pp. 43-9.

Lombardi, D. (1996), "Trends and directions in the chain-restaurant industry", *Cornell Hotel and Restaurant Administration Quarterly,* Vol. 37 No. 3, pp. 14-17.

Lowery, C.M. and Lambert, C.U. (1996), "Union organizing among hospitality workers", *Hospitality Research Journal*, Vol. 19 No.4, pp. 3-16.

Lynn, M. (1996), "Seven ways to increase servers' tips", *Cornell Hotel and Restaurant Administration Quarterly*, Vol. 37 No. 3, pp. 24-9.

Makens, J.C. and Bowen, J.T. (1996), "Increasing restaurant profits with product merchandising", *Cornell Hotel and Restaurant Administration Quarterly*, Vol. 37 No. 1, pp. 72-9

Meyer, R.A. (1996), "Waikiki faces major problems: does new master plan hold solutions?", *FIU Hospitality Review*, Vol. 14 No.1, pp. 7-18.

Miller, L. (1996), "Carnival's Fantasy Class cruise ship: ticket to success", *FIU Hospitality Review,* Vol. 14 No.2, pp. 45-52.

Moncarz, E.S. (1996), "Recipes for success: lessons learned from successful hospitality companies", *FIU Hospitality Review*, Vol. 14 No.2, pp. 13-26.

Muller, C. and Inman, C. (1996), "Characteristics and behavior of top chain-restaurant CEOs", *Cornell Hotel and Restaurant Administration Quarterly*, Vol. 37 No. 3, pp. 64-9.

Murphy, J., Forrest, E. and Wotring, C.E. (1996a), "Restaurant marketing on the world wide web", *Cornell Hotel and Restaurant Administration Quarterly*, Vol. 37 No. 1, pp. 61-71.

Oshins, M.L. (1996), "'Skip' Sack and Applebee's: how pub ventures went public", *Cornell Hotel and Restaurant Administration Quarterly*, Vol. 37 No. 3, pp. 55-63.

Pasumatry, K., Dolinsky, A., Stinerock, R. and Korol, T. (1996), "Consumer behavior and marketing strategy: a multinational study of children's involvement in the purchase of hospitality services", *Hospitality Research Journal*, Vol. 19 No.4, pp. 87-112.

Roberts, C. and Shea, L. (1996), "Core capabilities in the hotel industry", *Hospitality Research Journal,* Vol. 19 No.4, pp. 141-54.

Schmidgall, R.S., Woods, R.H. and Rutherford, D.G. (1996), "Journal and periodical usefulness as rated by hospitality faculty members", *Cornell Hotel and Restaurant Administration Quarterly*, Vol. 37 No. 2, pp. 47-55.

Sheel, A. and Lefever, M.M. (1996), "The implications of digital cash for hotels and restaurants", *Cornell Hotel and Restaurant Administration Quarterly*, Vol. 37 No. 6, pp. 92-6.

Sherry, J.E.H. (1996), "Land regulation and property rights: when regulation means 'taking of property'", *Cornell Hotel and Restaurant Administration Quarterly*, Vol. 37 No. 2, pp. 16-17.

Shoemaker, S. (1996),"Scripts: percursor of consumer expectations", *Cornell Hotel and Restaurant Administration Quarterly*, Vol. 37 No. 1, pp. 42-53.

Strand, C.R. (1996), "Lessons of a lifetime: the development of Hilton International", *Cornell Hotel and Restaurant Administration Quarterly,* Vol. 37 No. 3, pp. 83-95.

Tulgan, B. (1996), "Common misconceptions about Generation X", *Cornell Hotel and Restaurant Administration Quarterly,* Vol. 37 No. 6, pp. 46-54.

Urdang, B.S. (1996), "Investing in hospitality operations in the People's Republic of China: the legal framework", *FIU Hospitality Review*, Vol. 14 No.2, pp. 7-12.

Verma, R. and Thompson, G.M. (1996), "Basing service management on customer determinants: the importance of hot pizza", *Cornell Hotel and Restaurant Administration Quarterly,* Vol. 37 No. 3, pp. 18-23.

Walker, J.R. and Braunlich, C.G. (1996), "Quality leadership in the service industries", *Hospitality Research Journal*, Vol. 19 No.4, pp. 155-64.

Williams, C.E. (1996), "The british pub—an industry in transition", *Cornell Hotel and Restaurant Administration Quarterly*, Vol. 37 No. 6, pp. 62-73.

Wuest, B.E.S., Tas, R.F. and Emenheiser, D.A. (1996), "What do mature travelers perceive as important hotel/motel customer service?", *Hospitality Research Journal*, Vol. 20 No.2, pp. 77-94.